Shakespeare's Sequel
to Rumi's Teaching

Wes Jamroz

Troubadour Publications

Shakespeare's Sequel to Rumi's Teaching

Editing: *Dominique Hugon, Seth Rosenblum, Trudy Rosenblum*
Cover design: *Sandra Viscuso*

Montreal, QC, Canada

TroubadourPubs@aol.com
http://www.troubadourpublications

ISBN: 978-1-928060-01-7

Table of Contents

INTRODUCTION

Rumi and Shakespeare

Jalaluddin Rumi, who lived in the 13th century, is called one of the greatest, sometimes the very greatest of poets, philosophers and spiritual teachers of all time. Rumi's spiritual couplets entitled the "Mathnawi" remain one of the purest literary glories of Persian poetry. His teachings have an almost uncanny relevance to our lives today by stimulating a thirst for knowledge of his writings and their inner meaning. This thirst is probably as great at the present time as it has ever been.

According to Rumi's own account, his life completely changed when he met Shams of Tabriz, a wandering dervish. Rumi recognized in Shams his spiritual guide. Afterwards, Rumi was transformed from an accomplished preacher and jurist into the greatest poet of Persian literature. It was Shams who requested that Rumi should record his teaching.

Shakespeare was an English playwright and poet who lived in the second part of the 16th century and at the beginning of the 17th century. Shakespeare's plays and his Sonnets remain one of the greatest works of English literature. According to Shakespeare's own account given in his Sonnets, at the beginning of his writing career he met his spiritual guide. Like in the case of Rumi, it was his guide who completely changed his life. His guide pointed out to Shakespeare that he was wasting his time and talent on useless activities and meaningless writings. Then his guide taught him what to write, how to write, and when to write. His guide led Shakespeare through a sequence of experiences that allowed the poet to start to perceive the true value of his talent and the way in which his talent could be of use to a greater purpose.

However, there is much more in common between these two titans of poetry who lived some 350 years and 2,000 miles apart. In his Sonnets Shakespeare acknowledged that his writings were inspired by Rumi's poetry. He referred to Rumi as one of "Alien pens" whom he was asked to study. He described Rumi as "He of tall building, and of goodly pride". Shakespeare admitted that Rumi's verses were so powerful that they were stopping his thoughts before he was able to formulate them.

Rumi's and Shakespeare's writings are primarily instrumental, i.e., they are not meant for enjoyment, emotional stimulation, or display of their skills. The function of their writings was to project specific evolutionary concepts and ideas ahead of their actual realization. In this way the human mind could be prepared for their correct assimilation. In other words, Rumi's and Shakespeare's writings were based on the same inner design; they both belonged to the same school that operated in different places and at different times. Rumi explained the nature of spiritual technology, i.e., the function of various techniques and methodologies. His immediate audiences were Persian and Arabic speaking people who were mostly Muslims. This is why he widely used quotations from the Koran and the traditions of Mohamed as well as episodes and characters from Persian and Arabian literature. Shakespeare, who lived in Elizabethan and Jacobean England, used references to the Bible and previously published texts from English, Italian, French, and Spanish literature. Shakespeare's writings are an example of an unaltered illustration of the implementation of the spiritual technology that was described by Rumi. Shakespeare's plays illustrate how this technology was applied to plan, design, and form the European civilization. With this respect, Shakespeare's writings are unique within the entire corpus of Western literature.

Although Shakespeare was strongly influenced by Rumi's poetry, it should be emphasized that his function was to prepare Western society for the next phase of the evolutionary process. Therefore, his writings were not merely an adaptation of Rumi's illustrations from an Eastern environment into the Western culture. Such understanding would greatly diminish Shakespeare's role. Shakespeare was charged with the task of projecting these aspects of the spiritual technology that were needed at his time in order to keep the evolution of human mind in sync with changes of the cosmic matrix.

In this context we may look at Shakespeare's writings as a sort of magnifying glass that unveils further dimensions of Rumi's teaching. His writings allow us to discern the complexities and the intricacies of the evolutionary process that was described by Rumi. Shakespeare's magnifying glass, however, could not work if some basic concepts of Rumi's teaching had not been absorbed, at least partially, by the 16th century European society. At this point it should be mentioned that some of Rumi's quotations may be found in English literature as early as the 14th century. For example, there are several direct quotes from Rumi in Geoffrey Chaucer's poetry (Geoffrey Chaucer, a 14th century poet, is known as the Father of English literature). By analyzing Shakespeare's writings it is possible to realize that they were addressed to an audience that was exposed, directly or indirectly, to the impact of Rumi's teaching. This is why it is so important to analyze Rumi's and Shakespeare's writings together. In this way we may be able to gauge if, and to what extent, humanity made any evolutionary progress between the 13th and the 16th centuries. Shakespeare alluded to this sort of a measure in his Sonnets when he asked his guide to show him his own image from his previous appearances; because by looking at such an image he would be able to tell whether mankind made any progress, or whether men were caught up in a sort of evolutionary vicious circle.

"Shakespeare's Sequel to Rumi's Teaching" is an attempt at answering the question if and what sort of evolutionary gains were achieved between the 13th and the 16th centuries. The answer may be found by looking at the techniques and methodologies of the spiritual technology introduced in 13th century Asia Minor and how this technology was advanced and used at the end of the 16th century in Western Europe.

Evolution of Man

The evolution of the human race was directed and continues to be guided, encouraged or restrained into alignment with the universal plan. In accordance with this plan, humanity is evolving to a certain destiny. For the past ten thousand years or so, humanity has been given the possibility of conscious evolution. As the matter of fact, the future of humanity depends on this more rarefied evolution. As part of this recent phase of evolution, the human organism is producing a new complex of inner faculties. These inner faculties are concerned with transcending time and space. Sporadic and occasional bursts of telepathic or prophetic power are the initial markings of the working of these same faculties.

In accordance with the universal plan, a succession of evolutionary energies was made available on the earth at different times in the planetary history. These various energies were needed to execute the evolutionary process. Constructive, vital, sensitive, conscious, creative, unitive, and supracognitive energies were switched on in-turn. Each mode of energy was higher in its developmental potentiality than the one before. The switching-on of constructive energy led to the formation of the mineral world. This was followed by the activation of vital energy that was needed for the appearance of the vegetable world. Sensitive energy triggered the formation of the animal world. Conscious energy led to the appearance of man, with his intellect and reason. Creative energy provided man with the possibility of the activation of man's inner faculties.

Rumi explains how the evolutionary process is reproduced within the life of every man:

> First, man appeared in the class of inorganic things. Next he passed from the inorganic class into that of plants. For years he lived as one of the plants, remembering nothing of his previous inorganic state. Then he passed from the vegetable to the animal state. He had no remembrance of his state as a plant, except the inclination he felt towards plants. Especially at the time of spring, he felt an attraction to green trees and the aroma of flowers. Then again, man was led from the animal state towards humanity. In this way he did advance from one world of being to another, till he became intelligent and rational. He has no memory of his former states. During these periods man did not know where he was going but he was being taken on a long journey nonetheless.
> From his present state, man needs to continue his migration so that he may escape from his rationality and intellectuality which are driven mostly by greed and egotism. There are a hundred thousand more marvellous states ahead of him. He fell asleep and became oblivious of the past. This world is the sleeper's dream and the sleeper's fancies. Till all of a sudden there shall rise the dawn of death and he shall be delivered from ignorance.
> (Book IV, 3637-3667)

In the context of Rumi's description, these various modes of energies may be compared to different kinds of "food" that, at different times and at different places on the planet, were made available to mankind. The switching-on of each of the modes marked a new spiritual millennium. Constructive energy corresponds to the ordinary food of ordinary man. It is needed for the formation of man's physical form. The vital energy triggers the development of the self faculty that functions as the dominating faculty. Its main function is man's self-preservation. The sensitive energy triggers the formation of the manifest faculties of heart and intellect. In their ordinary form, these two faculties are under the control of the self faculty. They are used to satisfy man's greed and sensuality. The conscious energy is needed for the proper alignment (reformation) of man's manifest faculties, i.e., when the intellect and the heart are able to subdue the self faculty. The creative energy leads to the activation of the inner layers of the heart and the intellect (purification). The unitive energy of love, which is the second highest energy available in the galaxy, is needed to fuse together (unite) the inner layers of the intellect and the heart. The fused inner layers can then be transmuted into a new organ of perception. The supracognitive energy is the highest energy available in the galaxy. It acts as the catalyst that is needed for the activation of this inner organ of perception. The organ of inner perception is sometimes referred to as the angelic soul. It allows man to perceive and function in accordance with the requirements of the Realm, i.e., beyond the ordinary space-time limitations. The organ of inner perception existed already in eternity and was required to be actualized in time. Though latent since man emerged from his primate ancestry, it is an organ of experience that has only intermittently been active in certain exceptional individuals. Man is due to inherit it one day as part of his total experience.

Modern man has been faced with the very difficult challenge of accommodating these new evolutionary potentialities that were offered to him. The sequence and the effects of these 'switching-ons' suggest that each new mode of evolutionary energy is made available while man is still struggling to come to terms with the previous ones. Therefore, the developmental techniques and approaches have to be adjusted in such a way as to be compatible with these various energies as well as with the specific characteristics of the localities and people that are directly exposed to these evolutionary impacts. The custodians of the evolutionary process have been adapting and fine tuning their techniques and methodologies in order to meet these challenges.

Rumi's "Mathnawi" describes the spiritual technology, i.e., techniques, instruments and methodologies that were needed in 13th century Asia Minor to allow mankind to keep up with those evolutionary challenges. Shakespeare's plays and his Sonnets describe the spiritual technology that was applied in 16th century Western Europe. At that time the spiritual technology was adjusted in such a way as to meet the evolutionary challenges that 16th century man was faced with. These advanced approaches were implemented through several evolutionary branches that were activated in various parts of Western Europe.

Spiritual Technology

The Absolute emanates the evolutionary cosmic matrix. This matrix contains a blue-print of evolutionary plans for mankind. These plans are encoded onto rays of creation that percolate through an evolutionary transmission chain. This transmission chain links the Absolute with the level of ordinary man.

The level immediately below the Absolute is described as the Realm or the "Garden". The Realm is the top level of the evolutionary transmission chain. Below the Realm there is a multi-level structure, which consists of higher worlds, intermediate worlds, lower worlds, and the physical world.

The higher worlds are located one level below the Realm. They operate outside ordinary existence. The higher worlds are linked with the next level that corresponds to the intermediate worlds. The intermediate worlds operate outside the limitations of conventional time. The intermediate worlds are in-turn linked with the lower worlds. The lower worlds are linked with the physical world. Ordinary man belongs to the physical world.

An electricity distribution grid may be used as a simplified analogy of the evolutionary transmission chain. Electrical energy is transmitted from a power plant to distribution stations via high voltage transmission links. The high voltage is then gradually reduced by being passed through a number of intermediate substations before the electricity can be fed into houses. The main electrical panel located in a house is the lower link of the transmission grid. The panel is needed to connect a house to the source of electrical energy.

The worlds referred to above correspond to the various meditative or inspirational states of the human mind.

In this hierarchical structure man's ordinary faculties, i.e., his intellect, heart, and self, constitute an ordinary state of mind. The first step of the evolutionary ladder corresponds to the proper alignment of these manifest faculties. Proper alignment means that the intellect controls the heart and the heart rules over the self. Such an alignment is formed during the process that is known as spiritual reformation. The reformation leads to the first manifestations of inspirational states of the mind. It allows man to lift himself up from his ordinary animal-like life.

The intellect and the heart faculties are not homogenous. They consist of a multi-layered inner structure. Their inner structure may be unfolded, layer-by-layer, during the purification process. This may be compared to the splitting of atomic orbitals. In their natural form the orbitals remain degenerate; but when exposed to a strong magnetic field, they may be split into several sub-levels. In the case of human being, such a split is realized by the presence of evolutionary energies. In this way the inner or subtle faculties may be activated. The subtle faculties form the second step of the evolutionary ladder. The subtle faculties are entangled. This means that they are intertwined with each other even though each of the subtle faculties may be exposed to different experiences.

Uniting the subtle faculties leads to the formation of a new organ of supracognitive perception. The organ of supracognitive perception brings man to the Realm. In practical terms this means that man is able to retrace the various stages of the evolutionary process and access the Realm or the "Garden". In this way he may overcome the limitations of time and space and acquire permanency.

Rumi and Shakespeare describe the processes of activation, formation, and maintenance of these various inspirational states of mind. Some of these states are only partially operational; some are on the verge of becoming active; and some are still latent. This corresponds to certain experiences that are (i) somehow familiar but still not quite comprehensible; (ii) possible but not encountered yet; (iii) seemingly impossible. Such experiences may be presented as a series of events taking place in (i) somewhat familiar environment; (ii) remote locations and at other times; (iii) imaginary places. By using such settings it is possible to illustrate the nature of the spiritual process, the conditions required for the activation of higher states of mind, and the sequence of their manifestation. Such an allegorical presentation is a reflection of man's struggle towards the fulfillment of his ultimate purpose.

Rumi's and Shakespeare's writings are examples of instrumental literature, i.e., literature that depicts the various elements of spiritual technology. The spiritual technology here means the methodologies, techniques, instruments, and symbols that are used to guide and keep humankind on its evolutionary course. The instrumental literature provides allegorical descriptions of experiences that lead man from his ordinary state to the higher states. The experiences associated with the higher states are invisible to the ordinary rational person. This is why Rumi states that the texts that belong to the corpus of instrumental literature contain outer and inner meanings. The inner content is based on seven layers, i.e., an evolutionary cycle consists of seven stages that lead man from his ordinary state to the fulfilment of his evolutionary purpose. The first layer of the inner meaning is perceptible by ordinary intellect. The second and the higher layers are beyond the reach of the rational mind. Therefore, any written interpretation and explanation of Rumi's and Shakespeare's writings are limited to the first layer of their inner meaning.

Outline

The outline of "Shakespeare's Sequel to Rumi's Teaching" follows the layout of Rumi's "Mathnawi".

The "Mathnawi" is presented in 6 books. It is structured around a number of leading stories. The leading stories are interwoven with each other. Very often they are interrupted and broken up into several parts. The leading stories are accompanied by Rumi's commentary and numerous quotations from the Koran, the traditions of Moses, Jesus, and Mohamed, anecdotes from lives of the famous literary and historical characters. The commentary includes multiple and often contradictory points of view.

According to Rumi's motto, "things outwardly opposed may inwardly be working together", such opposite points of view serve the same purpose: they indicate the limitations of ordinary intellect and rationality.

"Shakespeare's Sequel to Rumi's Teaching" is arranged in such a way that the chapters correspond to Rumi's leading stories. The selection of the leading stories closely resembles that used by Whinfield in his abridged translation of "Mathnawi"[1]. The stories presented here, however, have been extracted and abridged from Nicholson's "The Mathnawi of Jalaluddin Rumi"[2]. The stories have been referenced to Nicholson's translation.

Shakespeare's writings are based on the same design as that of the "Mathnawi". This means that the same template may be used to unfold the inner meaning of Rumi's and Shakespeare's poetry. Therefore, it is possible to apply Rumi's stories and his commentary to explain Shakespeare's allegories. At the same time, Shakespeare's allegories may help the contemporary readers to recognize and understand the inner dimension of Rumi's poetry. In "Shakespeare's Sequel to Rumi's Teaching", Rumi's stories are accompanied and explained by corresponding scenes and quotes from Shakespeare's plays and his Sonnets.

It should be pointed out that the same template may also be used to reactivate ancient stories, mythological tales and legends that belonged to the corpus of the instrumental literature and which became corrupted or outdated. This was the reason that so many of Rumi's and Shakespeare's episodes were adapted from previously known storylines. A detailed analysis of the modifications introduced by Rumi and Shakespeare would show that their purpose was to realign the storylines in accordance with

---

[1] "Teaching of Rumi – The Masnavi", Abridged & Translated by E.H. Whinfield (The Octagon Press, 1979)

[2] "The Mathnawi of Jalaluddin Rumi", Books I-VI, Edited and Translated by Reynold A. Nicholson (The E.J.W. Gibb Memorial Trust, 1982)

the operating evolutionary matrix that was projected at two different times, i.e., in the 13th and the 16th centuries, respectively. In this way Rumi and Shakespeare were able to reactivate previously released narratives so they could serve their originally intended purpose.

Book 1. Spiritual King

The whole of the universe presents an integrated pattern and all created things are linked together. The universe is arranged according to a universal design that is based upon the principle of hierarchy. This hierarchy is compared to the patterns observed in nature, among plants, animals, and heavenly bodies. For example, the rose to the flowers bears the same relation as the oak to the trees, or the honeybee to the insects, or the eagle to the birds, or the lion to the beasts, or the sun to other heavenly bodies. Among men a king is above his subjects. However, the notion of "king" is used in a different context than that ordinarily applied. Namely, a spiritually developed man is superior to other men. The developed man is just as much a separate species among the various kinds of men, as man is a separate species amongst other creatures. It is in this context that the term "king" is used in instrumental literature. This is why a reigning king is often compared to a lion, an eagle, or the sun. In this symbolic language, the "king" represents a developed human being, while members of the royal court symbolize other aspects of this being. These various aspects, in turn, represent the various inner faculties of the human mind. In other words, the concept of kingdom is used to illustrate the inner structure of the human soul.

The spiritual king, or the guide, is a discernible feature of Rumi's and Shakespeare's writings. Let's make it clear though: Rumi's and Shakespeare's guide is not a guru, a preacher, or a facilitator of rituals. He is a living exemplar of human perfection. The guide's function and his actions remain invisible to ordinary men. Depending on the environment in which he has to work, the guide's appearance may vary. In Shakespeare's plays, for example, he appears as a king, a queen, a husband, a wife, a rogue, a fool, a prince, a maiden, a nobleman, a bastard, a magician, a craftsman, a general, or a clown. In the Sonnets, the guide appears as a young handsome man. Unlike Rumi, Shakespeare does not identify the guide. He leaves it up to the audience to recognize the guide by his actions and his effect on those around him. It is in this context that familiarity with Rumi's poetry may help to understand Shakespeare's plays and his Sonnets.

The initiation of a new evolutionary cycle is usually marked by the appearance of a new guide. The purpose of the guide is to reveal the main objectives of that particular stage of the cycle and its applicable spiritual technology. The applicable spiritual technology is encoded within a set of symbols used by the guide. This means that the guide reveals and explains the meaning of the symbols. He also adjusts the developmental methodology that is needed for a given time and place. The nature of the adjustments made by the guide is a reflection of the progress achieved during the previous stages of the evolutionary process. It is in this context that the following Shakespeare's lines from Sonnet 59 may be understood:

> "Oh that record could with a back-ward look,
> Even of five hundred courses of the Sun,
> Show me your image in some antique book,
> Since mind at first in character was done.
> That I might see what the old world could say,
> To this composed wonder of your frame,
> Whether we are mended, or where better they,
> Or whether revolution be the same."
> (Sonnet 59, 5-12)

Let's recall that the Sonnets are a record of the interactions between the poet and his guide. In other words, there are two voices in the Sonnets. Some Sonnets are spoken by the guide, the others by the poet. Sonnet 59 is addressed by the poet to his guide.

The poet makes a reference to an evolutionary cycle that symbolically is described as "five hundred courses of the Sun". The poet says that any progress made along the evolutionary ladder would be reflected by a change in the "image" of the guide. Therefore, he asks the guide to show his "image" from his previous appearances. By looking at it and by comparing it with the present "image", the poet would know whether mankind made any progress, or whether men regressed[3].

And here are a couple of quotes from Rumi's "Mathnawi" that further emphasise the guide's (Pir's) function:

> "The Pir is the moon, other people are like night."
> (Book I, 2939)

> "The Pir is so old, that he has no beginning; there is no rival to such a unique Pearl.
> Choose a Pir, for without a Pir this journey is exceeding full of woe and affright and danger." (Book I, 2941-3)

In Prologue to Book 1, Rumi outlines the function of the guide by comparing him to a musician. Ordinary man is like a hollow reed that is separated from its origin. The guide, with his breath, fills man with life by awakening his latent soul:

> The reed is a hollow pipe with some holes in it. On its own, the reed is just an empty shell that was cut-off from its reed-bed. But when filled with the breath of a musician, the reed becomes alive. It is then that the reed can tell its tale; a tale of sorrows caused by separations. The reed's lamentation is not mere vibrating air; its longing is like fire. It is the fire that transmutes man's inner being. This is why a man who lacks such a fire is like a dead person. The reed's tale serves as guidance for everyone, because everyone is parted from his origin and

---

3 "Shakespeare's Sonnets or How heavy do I journey on the way" (Sonnet 59)

is ever longing for the day of return. By listening to the reed's story it is possible to find a way towards fulfillment. The reed warns, however, that its story is not comprehensive to ordinary ears and eyes. A soul in a body is like the musician's breath enclosed in a hollow pipe. Ordinary senses cannot see or hear the soul's complains; inner senses are needed to hear and comprehend the meaning of the tale. The reed tells that preoccupations, doubts, and anxieties separate man from true reality and cause all sorts of sufferings. They undermine man's existence. One is wasting his life by allowing suffering to invade and dominate one's self. As long as man allows himself to be dominated by sufferings, he remains at a lower state of being. Yet, the sufferings may help him to weaken his worldly attachments. Only then sufferings can be mastered and eliminated. By making the right efforts man may be propelled towards a superior goal. The ultimate goal of man is to return to his origin. Man should live until he reaches his higher aim. (Book I, 1-35)

The tale of the reed tale is about the very essence of man's inner state. The reed indicates that a skilful musician is needed to awaken man's soul. Shakespeare used this analogy in "Hamlet" to indicate that, for example, Guildenstern, Hamlet's foolish friend, was incapable of making such music or of grasping the concept. Here is Hamlet's comment about it:

> "Why, look you now, how unworthy a thing you make of
> me! You would play upon me; you would seem to know
> my stops; you would pluck out the heart of my
> mystery; you would sound me from my lowest note to
> the top of my compass: and there is much music,
> excellent voice, in this little organ; yet cannot
> you make it speak."
> (Hamlet, III.2)

A rather surprising or even shocking function of the guide is his role in sustaining humanity. Both Rumi and Shakespeare are very clear on this point:

> "If the Guide would vanish, destiny would come upon us and the entire world would collapse." (Book I, 97-99)

The same description of the guide's role is given by Shakespeare in Sonnet 18:

> "So long as men can breathe or eyes can see,
> So long lives this, and this gives life to thee."
> (Sonnet 18, 13-14)

In the Sonnet Shakespeare points out that the guide is a link to the evolutionary transmission chain and in this way preserves humanity[4]. As long as the guide is recognised by men, humanity will be provided with the means for evolutionary growth ("so long as men can breathe or eyes can see, so long lives this"). The guide will be present as long as there are people who are able to recognize his function ("and this gives life to thee").

Rumi illustrates the guide's role and his function in sixteen stories included in Book 1.

1.1 The King and the Slave-girl

The spiritual guide is often compared to a cosmic physician. His role is to diagnose the state of the human soul and prescribe a remedy. Afterwards, the guide monitors the patient's recovery and brings it back to a fully healthy state. The guide has access to a

---

[4] "Shakespeare's Sonnets or How heavy do I journey on the way" (Sonnet 18)

whole repertoire of techniques, instruments, and medicines. So he is in the position to treat his patient effectively.

The commanding self, i.e., the corrupted self faculty is man's main disease. The "corrupted" self means the self faculty in its ordinary state in which it dominates the other faculties. Such a disease may be cured by killing man's overriding attachments to worldly pleasures and desires. "To die before dying" is a technical term used to describe this particular phase of the spiritual therapy. In instrumental literature, these attachments are illustrated by various characters who personalize specific attachments or desires. In this symbolic presentation, therefore, killing such a character or getting rid of him or her represents a gradual freeing oneself from the influence of that specific attachment. Rumi illustrates such a process in his first story:

> A king, while engaged on a hunting expedition, espied a fair maiden. He bought her and brought her to his palace to satisfy his desires. After a time she fell sick, and the King had her tended by his physicians. Because of lack of understanding, their treatment was of no avail. So the King prayed for help. During his prayer he fell asleep. In his dream he was told that a skilful physician will arrive at his court. And indeed, a stranger arrived at the court on the following day. The King recognized that the stranger was the physician foretold in his dream. By a very skilful diagnosis, the physician discovered that the real cause of the maiden's illness was her love for a certain goldsmith of Samarkand, a worthless and a shallow character. In accordance with the physician's advice, the King sent to Samarkand and fetched the goldsmith. Then he married the goldsmith to the lovesick maiden. During six months the pair lived together satisfying their desire, till the girl was wholly restored to health. At the end of that period, the physician gave the goldsmith a poisonous potion,

which caused his strength and beauty to decay. He then
lost favour with the maiden. She did not even notice
when he died. When the goldsmith died, the maiden was
cured from her illness. (Book I, 36-246)

The king represents a man on the path. His hunting expeditions are
a symbolic reference to his spiritual exercises. The slave-girl
illustrates his inner heart. During his "exercises" the king awakened
his inner heart, i.e., he discovered the girl. The girl is the object of
his current desires. But the girl is sick. She is sick, because the king
is still driven by his ordinary sensual desires. This is symbolically
indicated by the girl's attraction to the goldsmith, a shallow and
worthless character. The ordinary attractions act as a veil that
separates the king from his true desire. No ordinary physician is
able to cure the king's sore heart. A specialist is needed. When the
king asks sincerely for help, help is granted. A physician is sent to
help him. The physician represents the spiritual guide.

The guide is able to diagnose the situation and is able to prescribe
the remedy. The goldsmith is brought and is allowed to satisfy the
girl's sensual desire. In parallel, this particular aspect is gradually
destroyed. This is illustrated as the guide giving him a poisonous
potion, which gradually kills him. Rumi explains the killing of the
goldsmith in the following way:

> The slaying of the goldsmith by the hand of the physician
> was not driven by hope or fear. Neither had he killed to
> satisfy the king. Such killing purifies the inner heart and
> opens the door to a new life. This is why true lovers
> experience joy at the moment when the wise slays them
> with his own hand. Such act is not committed because of
> lust, covetousness, or passion. Its purpose is spiritual
> purification, similar to the separation of the dross from
> the silver. One who is slain in such manner ends up in a
> higher state. (Book I, 222-42)

The theme of this story is used by Shakespeare in "Othello". Shakespeare describes such a purifying act as Othello killing Desdemona. Othello is the cosmic physician who arrives from Mauritania in Venice to cure the city. Desdemona, like the king's heart, has to be cured from her attachment to the earthly form of Othello. Such attachment to the earthly appearance of the guide is a kind of idolatry. Her attachment to Othello has to die before Desdemona may enter onto the final step of her journey. In other words, she has to "to die before dying". This is emphasized in the exchange between Desdemona and Othello. Desdemona says that her only sins:

> "They are loves I bear to you."

And Othello answers:

> "Ay, and for that thou diest." (Othello, V.2)

Othello killing Desdemona is an allegorical illustration of her dying to her earthly attachments. Only when she dies, is she able to continue her journey which takes her to Mauritania, i.e., the higher state and Othello's place of origin[5].

Such function of a spiritual guide is beyond the perception of ordinary men. This is why Rumi warns the readers against using their inferior faculties to judge the actions of a guide:

> The guide takes half a life and gives a hundred lives in exchange. He gives that which is beyond your imagination. So, if judging his actions by your inferior faculties, you have fallen far away from the truth. Keep this advice firmly in your mind. (Book I, 245-6)

The next story illustrates the challenges related to the recognition of the guide.

---

[5] "Transition" (Shakespeare for the Seeker, Volume 3, Chapter 6.2)

1.2 The Greengrocer and the Parrot

The guide follows the arc of ascent towards the Absolute to learn. And when he has completed the arc of ascent, he descends to be among ordinary men. He is now transmuted. Only then he may guide and teach others. He teaches from a position which is at times "in the world" because he has to maintain contact with his environment. This means that although his outward form and even a part of his essence may be visible, his whole depth only unfolds to those who are developed enough to understand and perceive it. This mode of operation is illustrated in the story about a greengrocer and his parrot:

> A greengrocer possessed a parrot which used to amuse him with its agreeable prattle, and to watch his shop when he went out. One day, the parrot sprang from the bench and spilled some bottles of rose-oil. When the greengrocer returned home he thought that the parrot had purposely done this mischief. In his anger he smote the parrot such a blow on the head as made all its feathers drop off. The parrot lost its speech. The greengrocer, in repentance, heaved deep sights. For many days he was showing the bird every sort of marvel in the hope that it would begin to speak. He was offering gifts to any man, who might get back the speech of his bird. One day a bald-headed dervish in a patched robe was passing by the shop. When the parrot saw him, it recovered its speech and cried out, 'Hey, fellow! Did you, then, spill oil from the bottle?' The bystanders laughed at the parrot's mistake, because it deemed the wearer of the patched robe to be like itself. (Book I, 247-323)

The parrot represents the greengrocer's inner being. By relying on his ordinary perception, the greengrocer made the mistake by accusing the parrot of mischief. As the result, the greengrocer lost his link to his inner being. No ordinary men were able to awaken the greengrocer's inner being. A guide was needed. The bald-headed dervish was such a guide. The story illustrates how the guide may affect the environment in which he is in. His presence was sufficient enough for the parrot to recover its speech. The bystanders are the ordinary men. They did not understand the guide's action. Instead, they amused themselves by laughing at the parrot. Rumi advises them:

> Do not measure the actions of the guides by yourself. On this account the whole world is gone astray; scarcely any one is aware of their existence and their role. There is an infinite difference between the guide and ordinary men. The guides are like bees among flying insects. Yet, there is a great difference between a honey making bee and a hornet; or between an ordinary deer and a musk deer. Both deer ate grass and drink water. Yet, from one comes dung, and pure musk from the other. Only the guide knows the difference. If you want to learn that art – you have to find him. (Book I, 263-76)

Ordinary man uses worldly or ordinary senses. The Guide has fully developed his spiritual or inner senses. This is why he is able to perceive the true meaning of every situation:

> Worldly senses are the ladder of earth; spiritual senses are the ladder of heaven. The health of the former is sought of the leech, the health of the latter of the Guide. (Book I, 303-4)

The entire corpus of Shakespeare's plays is based on the concept of such a "ladder of heaven". The ladder leads to the Realm. The steps of the ladder correspond to the stages within the invisible worlds. For example, the higher world that operates outside of existence is presented in the plays as imaginary places (Pentapolis in "Pericles, Prince of Tyre", Mauritania in "Othello", Messaline in

"Twelfth Night"). The intermediate world, which operates outside of the limitations of time, is presented as islands (Mytilene in "Pericles, Prince of Tyre"; Cyprus in "Othello"; Sicily in "The Comedy of Errors", "The Winter's Tale", and "Much Ado About Nothing"). In "The Merchant of Venice", Shakespeare inserted a brief episode from the Book of Genesis to illustrate how the ladder functions. This episode is quoted by Shylock, one of the characters of the play:

> "When Laban and himself were compromised
> That all the eanlings which were streak'd and pied
> Should fall as Jacob's hire, the ewes, being rank,
> In the end of autumn turned to the rams,
> And, when the work of generation was
> Between these woolly breeders in the act,
> The skilful shepherd peel'd me certain wands,
> And, in the doing of the deed of kind,
> He stuck them up before the fulsome ewes,
> Who then conceiving did in eaning time
> Fall parti-colour'd lambs, and those were Jacob's."
> (The Merchant of Venice, I.3)

In this story, Jacob, who was inspired by an Angel, outsmarted Laban by employing a trick with partially peeled sticks. Jacob placed the sticks in front of breeding ewes ("peel'd me certain wands"). As a result, the ewes gave births to partly-coloured eanlings ("fall parti-colour'd lambs"). According to his contract with Laban, all partly coloured eanlings became Jacob's property ("and those were Jacob's").

Shakespeare selected this particular story because it is an allegorical illustration of how an instruction is projected down the ladder onto the world of ordinary man[6]. Namely, we may recognize that the Angel, Jacob, the conceiving ewes, and the eanlings symbolically

---

6 "Villains" (Shakespeare for the Seeker, Volume 3, Chapter 6.4)

represent the Realm and the three steps of the evolutionary ladder. The peeled sticks represent the instruction, which is projected from the Realm. The instruction, in the form of a partly-coloured pattern, percolates from the Realm (the Angel) through the higher world (Jacob) and the intermediate world (the conceiving ewes) till it reaches ordinary man (the eanlings). By retracing these steps of the ladder, man may "profit" by reaching towards the Realm.

1.3 The King and the Vizier

Before the evolutionary ladder may be used, man has to first recognize his greatest enemy. It is his corrupted self faculty, which is often illustrated as an old villain. In the following story, Rumi compares such a corrupted self faculty to a villainous vizier. The story emphasizes the fact that man has to be capable of recognizing and following a spiritual scent. This will allow him to recognize the time of change, i.e., the activation of a new phase of an evolutionary cycle. Such a change is usually marked by the appearance of a new guide. The king in the story represents a man who is attached to the previous phase of the teaching. His Vizier is his corrupted inner self that opposes any changes that may limit its influence.

> There was a king who used to persecute a community
> which followed a different doctrine than his own. This
> was at the time when a new evolutionary cycle was
> activated. The king was attached to the previous phase of
> teaching. The prosecuted community was following the
> updated form of the evolutionary projection. The King's
> Vizier persuaded the King to try a stratagem. Namely, he
> suggested that he should mutilate the Vizier himself, and
> expel him from his court. Then the Vizier might take

refuge with the persecuted community and stir up mutual dissensions amongst them. The King adopted the Vizier's suggestion. He mutilated the Vizier's nose and ears. The Vizier fled to the persecuted community. He found no difficulty in persuading them that he had been treated in that barbarous way on account of his attachment to their faith. He soon gained complete influence over them, and was accepted as a saintly martyr and a Divine teacher. Only a few discerning men divined his treachery; the majority were all deluded by him. Members of the community were divided into twelve tribes, and at the head of each was a leader. To each of these leaders the Vizier gave secretly a volume of spiritual directions, taking care to make the directions in each volume different from and contradictory to those in the others. One volume enjoined asceticism and fasting, another generosity and enjoyment of worldly pleasures, another meditations and renunciation of the world, another hard work and observance of prohibitions, and so on. Afterwards the Vizier withdrew into a cave. In spite of all their entreaties, he refused to come out to instruct his disciples. Then he called the leaders and gave secret instructions to each to set himself up as his successor. Each leader was to follow the instructions secretly confided to him and to slay all other claimants of the apostolic office. Having given these directions, the Vizier withdrew completely from the community by slaying himself. In the event each leader set himself up as the Vizier's successor. The community was split up into many sects at enmity with one another, even as the Vizier had intended. But the malicious scheme did not altogether succeed, as the ones who from the beginning intuitively discerned the Vizier's treachery, were thus saved from the devastation. (Book I, 324-738)

The Vizier was driven by envy, a mark of a corrupted self. Anyone who is driven by envy is like a man without inner senses; he is not able to apprehend spiritual matters. This is symbolically indicated in the story by the Vizier's mutilated nose and ears: he was incapable of perceiving the inner truth. Rumi explains that before the inner being may be unveiled, the corrupted self should be reformed. Otherwise, the human evolutionary growth is like storing corn in a barn with a deceitful mouse:

> We are putting corn in this barn, and then we are losing
> the corn that has been garnered since the mouse has
> made a hole in our barn, and our barn has been ravaged
> by its guile. Therefore, one must avert the mischief of the
> mouse, and then focus his effort on garnering the corn.
> Otherwise, how can we explain the fact that forty years of
> efforts did not bring any progress? (Book I, 378-87)

The guide's spiritual state is such that he is fully awakened to the other world. This means that he is asleep day and night to the affairs of the ordinary world. In other words, he has died to the ordinary world and lives in the higher world:

> How should any one not die to self, unless he be a vile
> wretch? (Book I, 530)

The two states of being awakened and asleep to the higher world are referred to as "to be" and "not to be", respectively. Shakespeare delegated Hamlet to deliver a meditation on these two states. In Hamlet's famous soliloquy, these two states of being awake and sleeping correspond to "to be or not to be":

> "To be, or not to be: that is the question:
> Whether 'tis nobler in the mind to suffer
> The slings and arrows of outrageous fortune,
> Or to take arms against a sea of troubles
> And by opposing end them?" (Hamlet, III.1)

The state "not to be" is developmentally sterile. It corresponds to ordinary life with all its suffering of "slings and arrows of outrageous fortune". This suffering is due to the dominant role of the corrupted self faculty. On the other hand, the state "to be" corresponds to a spiritually developed man. The state of "to be" is arrived at by following a path leading to the activation of the inner faculties. This approach requires an extraordinary personal effort. The soliloquy refers to such an effort as "to take arms against a sea of troubles, and by opposing end them". This means a personal struggle against the corrupted self and freeing oneself from worldly attachments. This part of the developmental process has previously been referred to as "to die before dying".

In the soliloquy Hamlet makes a direct reference to the guide:

> "The undiscover'd country from whose bourn no
> traveller returns." (Hamlet, III.1)

The term "the undiscover'd country" refers to the state "to be". The guide is a "traveler" who has returned from "the undiscovered country". Hamlet is still ignorant of the possibilities of returning from "the undiscover'd country". At this point Hamlet does not realize that travel to "the undiscover'd country" is the solution to his problems. But first, he would have to recognize his guide[7].

1.4 The Tyrannical King

This story illustrates how those, who managed to avoid the Vizier's treachery in the previous story, were able to escape from another tyrannical king.

---

[7] "To be or not to be" (Shakespeare for the Seeker, Volume 4, Chapter 7.3)

A brief explanation of the meaning of earth, water, air, and fire may help to grasp the meaning of the story. Earth, water, air, and fire are used to indicate symbolically the stages of the development of higher states of mind. These terms are chosen partly because they consecutively represent items in increasing degree of refinement. They correspond to exposure to the specific modes of the spectrum of evolutionary energies. The higher the stage, the more refined the energy is to which a disciple is exposed to. These various modes of the evolutionary spectrum were activated on the planet at different times. Therefore, the techniques of the spiritual technology were adjusted accordingly. Rumi uses the term "fire" to indicate the most refined energy, i.e., the unitive energy of love. But "love" here refers to objective love, and not its precognitive echo in emotional attachments and sensual attractions. The unitive energy of love is needed to bring the inner being onto the highest state. It is in this sense that the unitive energy of love is the principle of all motion towards universal perfection and completion.

When a new phase of evolutionary projection is initiated, the previously prescribed techniques and methodology become obsolete.

> A certain idolatrous king made a fire and set up a huge
> idol beside it. He announced that whoever bowed down
> to this idol should escape the fire. But all those who
> refused to worship it would be cast into the fire.
> Thereupon his officers seized a woman with her child
> because she refused to worship it. They cast the child into
> the fire. The woman was about to bow down before the
> idol, but the child started to cry out to his mother that she
> should not be afraid, because the fire had no power to
> burn him. The child explained that when he was born, he
> thought that he had escaped from the narrow prison of
> the womb into the world. Now he deemed the earthly

world to be a prison like the womb, since in this fire he has seen an apparently non-existent, but in reality permanent world. The king reproached the fire for failing to do its office, but the fire replied that its consuming properties were to be used for constructive purposes and not for someone's egotistic desires. It then blazed up and consumed the king. (Book I, 739-899)

The King in the story illustrates that aspect of the human mind that was fossilized around outdated techniques. The child, on the other hand, represents a new aspect of the human mind that was activated through the implementation of a new phase of the evolutionary process. We may recognize that the activity referred to as worship of fire was needed at the time when mankind was not ready yet for exposure to "fire", i.e., the unitive energy of love. At that time "fire" was beyond the reach of ordinary men. Fire was to be worshipped but not to be experimented with. However, when mankind was correctly prepared for exposure to the unitive energy of love, then that previous prescription became invalid. This is why those who were correctly prepared for "fire" were able to benefit from it. And those who remained ignorant were destroyed.

Here it is how Shakespeare described his own experiences with air and fire[8]:

> "The other two, slight air, and purging fire,
> Are both with thee, wherever I abide,
> The first my thought, the other my desire,
> These present absent with swift motion slide."
> (Sonnet 45, 1-4)

Shakespeare says that the reforming "air" and purifying "fire" are always at his guide's disposal ("the other two, slight air, and purging fire, are both with thee, wherever I abide"). When the guide

---

[8] "Shakespeare's Sonnets or How heavy do I journey on the way" (Sonnet 45)

exposes him to "air", the poet becomes free from the limitations of ordinary intellect; at the moments of his exposure to "fire", he is able to break away from his emotional desires ("the first my thought, the other my desire"). Because of the poet's worldly attachments, however, these states are not constant yet; he slides back and forth between his ordinary and higher states ("these present absent with swift motion slide").

1.5 The Lion and the Beasts

Recognizing one's spiritual guide is the first step on the evolutionary ladder. But it is the guide who chooses his disciple. Before the guide allows himself to be recognized, the disciple has to meet certain criteria. One such criterion is to be able to overcome some of the limitations of the corrupted self faculty. The corrupted self faculty forms the artificial personality, which seeks to protect the existing ways of thought of the person. It is this artificial personality that inhibits progress, since it is dedicated to maintaining what it takes to be in equilibrium. One of the most powerful tools that are at the disposal of the corrupted self is stimulation through emotions. In the terminology of the spiritual technology, such a situation occurs when the self is in control of the heart faculty. Rumi illustrates this in the following story.

> A lion held all the beasts of the neighbourhood in subjection, and was in the habit of making constant raids upon them. He was killing them to provide himself with daily food. At last the beasts took counsel together. They agreed to deliver up one of their company every day to satisfy the lion's hunger, if he, on his part, would cease to annoy them with his disorderly raids. At first, the lion was unwilling to trust their promise, remarking that he always

preferred to rely upon his own efforts. The beasts, however, succeeded in persuading him that he would do well with relying on heavenly providence and trusting their word. Having convinced the lion, the beasts continued for some time to perform their engagement. One day it was the turn of the hare to be delivered up as a victim to the lion. But the hare requested that the others let him practice a stratagem. They scoffed at him, asking how such a silly beast as he could pretend to outwit the lion. The hare assured them that wisdom was of God, and God might choose weak things to confound the strong. At last they consented to let him try his luck. He took his way slowly to the lion, and found him sorely enraged. In excuse for his late arrival he told that he and another hare had set out together to appear before the lion, but another lion had seized the second hare; he carried it off in spite of his protests. On hearing this, the lion was exceeding angry and commanded the hare to show him the foe that had trespassed on his territory. Pretending to be afraid, the hare got the lion to take him upon his back, and directed him to a well. On looking down the well, the lion saw in the water the reflection of himself and of the hare on his back. Thinking that he saw his foe with the stolen hare, he plunged in to attack him. The lion was drowned, while the hare sprang off his back and escaped. The beasts welcomed the hare as their saviour. (Book I, 900-1389)

The lion in the story represents an aspect of the corrupted heart faculty. This particular aspect is entirely driven by egotistic needs. It took control over the entire being. In order to regain inner balance, an aspect of the intellect was needed. The hare represents such an aspect of the intellect faculty.

In his commentary Rumi says that "the lion of this world" may be overcome by reason and intellect. But to free oneself from this world "the lion of the Lord" is needed:

> The lion of this world seeks a prey and provision; the lion
> of the Lord seeks freedom and death. (Book I, 3965)

One has to seek such a lion and then let the lion do the killing. But first, man has to recognize the lion of the higher world, i.e., the guide. Otherwise the guide will not be able to help him.

Shakespeare inserted in "As You Like It" an episode in which he illustrates symbolically the stage of overcoming the influences of the "the lion of this world". In this episode Orlando encounters a lioness preying upon a "sleeping man", i.e., his hateful brother:

> "Under which bush's shade
> A lioness, with udders all drawn dry,
> Lay couching, head on ground, with catlike watch,
> When that the sleeping man should stir; for 'tis
> The royal disposition of that beast
> To prey on nothing that doth seem as dead:
> This seen, Orlando did approach the man
> And found it was his brother, his elder brother."
>
> ...
>
> "Twice did he turn his back and purposed so;
> But kindness, nobler ever than revenge,
> And nature, stronger than his just occasion,
> Made him give battle to the lioness,
> Who quickly fell before him."
> (As You Like It, IV.3)

A "hungry lioness" indicates uncontrolled emotions. Thus the message encoded in this scene may be interpreted as "a man may be awakened in the right way if he is able to overcome and control his emotions". Orlando's killing of the lioness is a sign that he was able to subdue his emotional reflexes. Afterwards, he was able to recognize his guide[9].

1.6 Omar and the Ambassador

The hare, having delivered his companions from the tyranny of the lion, urged them to engage in a greater challenge, i.e., struggle against their inward enemy. But the fight against this enemy is not the work of reason and intelligence. Only by recognizing one's guide, the seeker may become a finder. The story "Omar and the Ambassador" illustrates how one may find the spiritual guide.

> An ambassador was sent by the Emperor of Rum to the Caliph Omar. On approaching Medina this ambassador inquired for Omar's palace, and was told that Omar dwelt in no material palace, but in an inner shrine, only visible to purified hearts. The ambassador fixed his eye on seeking Omar. He abandoned his baggage and horse; he was running in every directions inquiring madly for Omar. At last a woman showed him where Omar was. When the ambassador saw him, Omar was deeply in meditation under a palm-tree. At the sight of the meditating man, awe came upon the ambassador. He drew near to him in fear. Although he previously met many kings and sultans, he never before experienced such feelings: the sight of Omar robbed him of his wits. Omar received him kindly. The ambassador asked two questions. Firstly, how can souls descend from heaven to earth? Secondly, what was the reason of imprisoning souls in the bonds of flesh and blood? Omar told him that a soul's descent into a body is like a transition from non-existence into existence. At this

---

[9] "The process" (Shakespeare for the Seeker, Volume 2, Chapter 5.2)

point a soul becomes confined in a body like a bird in a cage. A body is driven by physical senses and intellect. But a soul is directed by inner senses, which remain latent in ordinary man. The purpose of life is to activate these inner senses, free the soul, and then return to non-existence. Upon hearing this, the ambassador became overpowered by some inner force.

Rumi explains, 'When the seed reached corn-land, it became a crop of corn'. (Book I, 1390-1546)

The story underlines the conditions required for finding one's guide. In the context of the story, the ambassador's luggage symbolically represents his attachments to material goods; the horse is an indication of his emotional reflexes. The ambassador was able to find Omar only after he abandoned his luggage and the horse. It was then that Omar, while in his meditation, sent a woman who gave him directions. According to Rumi, the woman is a ray of God:

> She is a ray of God, she is not that earthly beloved: she is creative, you might say she is not created. (Book 1, 2437)

Omar accepted the ambassador as his disciple. He explained to the ambassador that the ultimate purpose of human life was to free one's soul from the ordinary world.

The story of the Ambassador is an illustration of the implementation of the "rapid technique". This technique allows to activate inner cognition by a glance or in some indirect way merely by coming into contact with a great teacher. In other words, an individual, or a group of people, may arrive at the higher state without experiencing the intermediate states. This method may be used by a guide who has access to the full spectrum of evolutionary energies. Therefore, he is able to expose his disciple to several impulses of energies at the same time. In this way, the lack of initial preparation may be overcome, for example, by coupling the disciple's sincerity with his single-mindedness. In Rumi's story, the ambassador's single-mindedness was manifested by his preoccupation with questions about the human soul. His sincerity allowed for overcoming the lack of lengthy training.

Shakespeare indicates that the rapid technique was implemented in Europe during the recent phases of the evolutionary process. In accordance with Shakespeare's presentation, modern European civilization was formed through simultaneous exposure to several impulses of evolutionary energies. These impulses were released during the Middle Ages in four different parts of Europe, i.e., England, France, Italy, and Central Europe. Consequently, these impulses provided seeds for the four evolutionary branches that are illustrated in Shakespeare's History, French, Italian, and Bohemian plays. Shakespeare describes the details of the rapid technique in his Bohemian plays. Namely, its implementation is illustrated in "Twelfth Night". "Twelfth Nights" is set-up in Illyria, i.e., on the western cost of the Balkan Peninsula.

Feste, the Fool, is the guide who directs the process implemented in Illyria. Illyria symbolically represents an ordinary state within the Bohemian evolutionary branch. At the time of Feste's arrival, a quite sophisticated evolutionary impulse was sent directly to Illyria. The impulse was symbolically represented by the twins Viola and Sebastian. They were swept onto the Illyrian shore during a terrible sea storm. Like the woman in the story of the Ambassador, Viola and Sebastian were representing a ray of creation. Sebastian alluded to the nature of his spiritual "essence" in the following comment:

> "A spirit I am indeed;
> But am in that dimension grossly clad
> Which from the womb I did participate".
> (Twelfth Night, V.1)

Viola's and Sebastian's arrival in Illyria is like light passing through a prism. In the same way as light is refracted into various colours, so they were split into two modes of spiritual energies:

> "How have you made division of yourself?
> An apple, cleft in two, is not more twin
> Than these two creatures."

> "One face, one voice, one habit, and two persons,
> A natural perspective, that is and is not!"
> (Twelfth Night, V.1)

Sebastian and Viola were separated because each of them was directed at a different target. Viola was designated for Duke Orsino; Sebastian was targeted for Lady Olivia. In accordance with Shakespeare's allegorical presentation, the Illyrian union was symbolically illustrated by two married couples. This is why at the end of the play Viola was married to Orsino and Olivia to Sebastian. It was then and there that a spiritual union ("a solemn combination ... of our dear souls") was rapidly activated:

> "When that is known and golden time convents,
> A solemn combination shall be made
> Of our dear souls."
> (Twelfth Night, V.1)

Because of the lack of preparatory training, the implementation of the rapid technique usually leads to a temporary union. Such a temporary union is difficult to sustain because it is not very stable. This means that the process implemented within the Bohemian branch involved a certain risk. It would indicate an urgency that required the acceleration of the process in this particular geographical region. It may be presumed that the accelerated formation of the union was dictated by the situation in Central Europe. It was at that time that certain destructive trends were starting to negatively affect the implementation of the evolutionary process. Therefore, it was necessary to accelerate this process, and this required the rapid activation of the Illyrian union[10].

1.7 The Merchant and his Parrot

Developing one's inner being is realized through the technique known as to die before dying. The following story illustrates how the experience of dying before dying may be transmitted indirectly to those who are ready to follow it.

> A merchant kept a sweet-voiced parrot in a cage. He was going to India, the land from which the bird came. He asked her whether he could bring anything back. The bird asked the merchant to visit a jungle in India and announce her captivity to the free birds that were there. And to tell them that she desires to learn from them the means and way of being guided to her freedom. The merchant did so, and no sooner had he spoken when a wild bird, just like his own, fell senseless out of a tree on to the ground. The merchant thought that this must be a relative of his own bird. He felt sad that he should have caused his death. When he got home, the bird asked him whether he had brought good news from India. 'No', said the merchant, 'I fear that my news is bad. One of your relatives collapsed and fell at my feet when I mentioned your captivity'. As soon as these words were spoken the bird collapsed and fell to the bottom of the cage. 'The news of her kinsman's death has killed her too', thought the merchant. Sorrowfully he picked up the bird and put it on the window-sill. At once the bird revived and flew to a near-by tree. 'Now you know', the bird said, 'that what

---

[10] "Evolutionary impulse" (Shakespeare for the Seeker, Volume 4, Chapter 7.1)

you thought was disaster was in fact good news for me;
and how the teaching of how to free myself was
transmitted to me through you, my captor'. And the bird
flew away, free at last. The merchant said to himself, 'This
is a counsel for me; I will follow her teaching, for this
teaching is shining with light'. (Book I, 1547-1912)

Similarly, Friar Francis in Shakespeare's play "Much Ado About
Nothing" prescribed to Hero the recipe of "die to live":

"For to strange sores strangely they strain the cure.
Come, lady, die to live."
(Much Ado About Nothing, IV.1)

In this way, Claudio, Hero's beloved, was cured from his
blindness[11].

In his Sonnets Shakespeare used the process of distillation of
flowers to illustrate such dying before dying:

"For never resting time leads Summer on,
To hideous winter and confounds him there,
Sap checked with frost, and lusty leaves quite gone.
Beauty o'er-snowed and bareness every where,
Then were not summer's distillation left
A liquid prisoner pent in walls of glass,
Beauty's effect with beauty were bereft,
Nor it, nor no remembrance what it was."
(Sonnet V, 5-12)

Through distillation flowers may survive the frost and snow of the
winter. In this way, the beauty of summer is preserved. Like the
perfume of the distilled flowers, the inner being is immune to
death.

---

[11] "Invisible assistant" (Shakespeare for the Seeker, Volume 3, Chapter 6.3)

1.8 The Harper

In the following story, Rumi illustrates how a guide chooses his disciples.

> In the time of the Caliph Omar there lived a harper, whose voice was so sweet that he was in great request at all feasts. But he grew old, and his voice broke, and no one would employ him any longer. When he became indebted for a single loaf of bread, he said to himself: 'For seventy years I have been playing to earn my living; today I can earn nothing. Therefore I will play the harp for God, who has bestowed many favours on me'. He took his harp and went to the graveyard of Medina. Having finished his songs at the graveyard, he fell asleep and dreamed he was in heaven. At that very time such drowsiness came upon Omar that he could not keep himself from slumber. In his sleep a Divine voice told him to go to the graveyard of Medina and relieve an old man whom he should find there. Omar proceeded to the place and found the harper. When the harper saw Omar, he started to tremble with fear. Omar calmed him down and gave him money, saying 'fear me not, I bring you good news'. The harper started to weep and despair, realizing that his preoccupation with music and songs diverted him from the straight path. He dashed the harp on the ground and broke it into pieces. Omar bade him turn away from weeping and turn into wakefulness. Omar explained that remorse of the past is like a veil separating him from Reality. Past and future hold man away from truth; to be present leads to happiness. Omar revealed to the harper the mysteries of the path. It was then that the harper's inner heart was awakened. His ordinary soul departed and his angelic soul came to life. (Book I, 1913-2243)

In "Hamlet" Shakespeare also used a scene at a graveyard to illustrate an encounter with a guide. The encounter took the form of an interview, a period of questions and answers. The gravedigger, like Omar in the story, gave Hamlet several clues that should have helped him recognize who he really was. In other words, by recognizing the guide Hamlet would demonstrate that he was worthy to be guided. Unlike the harper, however, Hamlet appeared to be clueless, even gullible. He sarcastically commented on the gravedigger as being a witty peasant who became so clever that he could even outdo the courtiers:

> "How absolute the knave is! we must speak by the
> card, or equivocation will undo us. By the Lord,
> Horatio, these three years I have taken a note of
> it; the age is grown so picked that the toe of the
> peasant comes so near the heel of the courtier, he
> gaffs his kibe." (Hamlet, V.1)

Hamlet failed to recognize his guide and, because of that, he could not save Elsinore from its evolutionary fiasco[12].

1.9 The Bedouin and his Wife

An ignorant man is driven by destructive emotions such as anger and lust. Such a man uses his fierceness to achieve his crude desires. Therefore, he will never have the chance to experience more subtle impacts. On the other hand, a kind and affectionate man does not have such crude reactions. In such a case, the self faculty switches to more subtle means to exercise its control. As a result, such a man is exposed to qualitatively different experiences,

---

[12] "Encounter at the graveyard" (Shakespeare for the Seeker, Volume 4, Chapter 7.3)

which may bring him closer to the guide. This is illustrated in the story of the Bedouin and his wife.

> A Bedouin lived with his wife in the desert in extreme poverty. The wife at last lost patience and began to abuse her husband. She urged him to improve their condition. The Bedouin rebuked her for her covetousness, reminding her that poverty was a better preparation for death than riches. He threatened to divorce her if she was to continue her complaining. At this point, she changed her strategy and started to cry and apologize for her lack of respect for her husband. Seeing her tears, the Bedouin felt sorry and asked her what she wanted him to do. The covetous wife asked him to take a jug with rain-water and go to the Caliph of Baghdad and offer him the water as a gift. Accordingly, the Bedouin travelled to Baghdad. When he arrived there he became overwhelmed by the city's splendour and its beauty. He realized that he came there looking for gold, but what he found was beyond his expectation. He laid his gift at the feet of the Caliph. The Caliph received the gift graciously, and in return filled the jug with pieces of gold. Then he sent the Bedouin back to his home by boat up the River Tigris. The Bedouin was lost in wonder at the benignity of the Caliph who, having so much water in the Tigris, had recompensed him so bountifully for his gift of dirty water. (Book I, 2244-2933)

The Bedouin in this story represents the ordinary intellect; his wife personalizes his unsatisfied inner self. This pair is engaged in endless quarrel. The intellect is concerned with the Realm. However, the intellect's prime focus is overshadowed by the influence of his selfish desires. The main point of the conflict between these two tendencies resides in the fact that the intellect faculty consists of latent subtle layers. The evolutionary potential of man is determined by his ability to activate these subtle layers. The challenge is how to overcome the distractive influence of the self, whose desires cannot ever be satisfied. Because of his natural kindness, the Bedouin did not use force to subdue his wife. Therefore, she had to change her approach and appeal to his gentleness. In this way she was able to convince her husband to travel to Baghdad. But she did not know to what sort of experiences her husband would be exposed in Baghdad:

> I brought water as a gift for the sake of getting bread:
> hope of bread led me to the highest place in Paradise.
> (Book I, 2797)

While in Baghdad, the Bedouin got his first taste of the greatness that was not available at his dwelling.

The story illustrates the limitations of moralistic approaches that offer a formula of what is bad and what is good. Such a moralistic approach is too simplistic to be effective. What matters is to arrange situations that may lead to constructive experiences. Certain actions, which from a moral point of view seem to be improper, may in reality lead to evolutionary constructive outcomes. Spiritual progress is achieved by creating these situations which allow to bring into operation the more gentle aspects of the inner being. By allowing himself to be driven by his wife's greed, the Bedouin arrived at a stage where he could experience the greatness and the generosity of the Caliph:

> That jug of water is an emblem of our ordinary sorts of
> knowledge, and the Caliph is the River Tigris of Divine
> wisdom. We are preoccupied with carrying jugs of dirty
> water to the Tigris. If we do not know ourselves to be
> asses, asses we are. (Book I, 2848-9)

Man may advance his inner state by getting in contact with a spiritual guide. In the story this is described symbolically as the Bedouin coming to the Caliph by way of land; but he returned by way of water. It means that he passed from the state of "earth" to the state of "water". Yet, he did not stay with the Caliph; he was not ready for it yet. Otherwise, he would have smashed his jug and remained in Baghdad with the Caliph.

Very often the guide will have to "woo" a potential disciple in order to get his attention. Many instances of such "wooing" are illustrated by Shakespeare in his plays. For example, Othello had to woo Desdemona for nine months, before she was able to recognise him as her guide[13]:

> "I saw Othello's visage in his mind,
> And to his honour and his valiant parts
> Did I my soul and fortunes consecrate."
> (Othello, I.3)

Man has to be ready for an encounter with the guide. Otherwise, he will not be able to benefit fully from the guide's presence.

1.10 The Man who was tattooed

When one recognizes the guide, one should be fully committed to his guidance. Such commitment requires effort and the ability to do whatever is indicated. One cannot be driven by what is pleasant and avoid that which is unpleasant. This is illustrated in the story of the man who wanted to be tattooed.

> It was the custom of the men of Qazwin to have various images tattooed upon their bodies. A certain coward went to the artist to have an image of lion tattooed on his back. But when he felt the first few pricks of the needles he

---

[13] "Desdemona" (Shakespeare for the Seeker, Volume 3, Chapter 6.2)

roared with pain. He asked the artist, 'What part of the lion are you now painting?' The artist replied, 'I am doing the tail'. The patient cried, 'Never mind the tail; go on with another part'. The artist accordingly began another part, but the patient could not stand the pricks. 'What part of the lion is it this time?' he cried, 'for I cannot stand the pain'. 'This time', said the tattooist, 'it is the lion's ear'. 'Let us have a lion without an ear', grasped the patient. So the tattooist tried again. No sooner had the needle entered his skin than the patient squirmed again, 'What part of the lion is it this time?' 'This is the lion's stomach', said the artist. 'I don't want a lion with a stomach', said the man. Exasperated, the tattoo artist stood awhile. Then he threw his needles and pigments on the ground and cried: 'A lion without a head, with no tail, without a stomach? Who could draw such a thing? Even God did not!' (Book I, 2934-3012)

One has to endure some pain to free oneself from the influence of his corrupted self. Those who are not able to endure such pain and make efforts are often referred to as spiritual tourists. As soon as they are required to endure pain and make efforts, they quit and look for something else.

Shakespeare described such a group of spiritual tourists in "The Merchant of Venice". They arrived in Belmont to see Portia, "this mortal-breathing saint". The group included a number of European aristocrats, i.e., a Neapolitan prince, a County Palatine, a French lord, a young baron of England, a Scottish lord, and a young German. They all were pretenders to higher learning. In order to enter onto the path, they were required to take a test. However, prior to the test they had to make the following commitment: to not disclose details of the test; never attempt to enter onto another path; and if they fail the test - to leave Belmont immediately. In other words, only those who were able to commit themselves entirely to the chosen path could be allowed to follow it.

Those Western European princes who gathered in Belmont were like the tattooed man. They were not ready for such a commitment. After all they were just "tourists" and their main preoccupation was to drink, boast about their wealth, and talk about horses, fashion, and philosophy. Here is Nerissa, Portia's servant lady, announcing the departure of the tourists[14]:

> "You need not fear, lady, the having any of these
> lords: they have acquainted me with their
> determinations; which is, indeed, to return to their
> home and to trouble you with no more suit."
> (The Merchant of Venice, I.2)

For these Western European princes the choice was simple: they skipped the test and quickly returned to their ordinary daily routines.

1.11 The Lion who hunted in Company

The higher state of being means arriving at the state of the unity of multiplicities. The meaning of unity is to consume oneself in the presence of the One. This is further illustrated in the following story.

> A lion took a wolf and a fox with him on a hunting
> excursion. He succeeded in catching a wild ox, a goat, and
> a hare. He then asked the wolf to divide the prey. The
> wolf proposed to award the ox to the lion, the goat to

---

14 "Pilgrimage" (Shakespeare for the Seeker, Volume 3, Chapter 6.4)

himself, and the hare to the fox. The lion was enraged
with the wolf because he had presumed to talk of "My
share" and "Thy share" when it all belonged of right to
the lion. So, the lion slew the wolf with one blow of his
paw. Then, turning to the fox, he ordered him to make
the division. The fox, rendered wary by the fate of the
wolf, replied that the whole should be the portion of the
lion. The lion asked the fox from whom did he learn to
divide in such a manner. The fox answered that he learnt
from the fate of the wolf. Then the lion told him that he
is no longer a fox but a lion; therefore he may take and
keep all three animals. The fox thanks the lion for having
called him up after the wolf. (Book I, 3013-3149)

All men are in the same situation as the fox in this story. They
would better try to learn by considering the fate of the past
generations. According to Shakespeare's plays, the modern cycle of
the evolutionary process in Western Europe was implemented
based on a lesson learnt from the Roman evolutionary fiasco. At
the time when the unitive energy of love was released on the
planet, Rome was not ready for such an experience. Therefore, this
particular experience had to be delayed. Afterwards, the technique
of modulation of "beauty" was used to avoid the previously
encountered difficulty. The modulation of "beauty" allows for a
gradual exposure to evolutionary energy. Shakespeare uses young
women disguised as boys to represent such modulated elements of
evolutionary energy or "beauty". This is why, for example, when
Viola in "Twelfth Night" approached Count Orsino, she was
disguised as a young boy named Cesario[15]:

> "I'll serve this duke:
> Thou shall present me as an eunuch to him:
> It may be worth thy pains; for I can sing
> And speak to him in many sorts of music

---

[15] "Evolutionary impulse" (Shakespeare for the Seeker, Volume 4, Chapter 7.1)

That will allow me very worth his service."
(Twelfth Night, I.2)

In this way, Orsino was gradually exposed to Viola's inner beauty.

1.12 Joseph and the Mirror

There is no worse malady in man's soul than conceit of perfection. Rumi indicates that one may arrive at the state of perfection by realizing that perfection means selflessness. This is why purifying oneself from selfishness is the best and only gift that one may offer:

> An old friend came to pay his respects to Joseph. Joseph asked him what gift he had brought to show his respect. The friend replied that he had long considered what gift would be most suitable to offer. Finally he decided to bring a mirror, which he presented to Joseph. He said that he brought the mirror so that when Joseph sees his perfection in it, he may think about him. (Book I, 3150-3227)

By the same token, looking at one's own reflection in a mirror shows one's corrupted self. Shakespeare illustrated this in an episode with Jaques and Orlando in "As You Like It":

Jaques:

"By my troth, I was seeking for a fool when I found you."

Orlando:

"He is drowned in the brook: look but in, and you shall see him."

Jaques:

"There I shall see mine own figure."

Orlando:

"Which I take to be either a fool or a cipher."
(As You Like It, III.2)

Orlando indicates that Jaques is a fool[16]. He tells Jaques that he may find out for himself if he looks at his own reflection in the brook.

1.13 Mohamed's Scribe

Self-importance and pride act as a veil preventing one from recognizing the guide. The irony of this situation is that the veil may be removed but only with the help of the guide. The guide is the source of wisdom; a disciple receives wisdom as a loan.

> Mohamed had a scribe to whom he dictated the revealed verses. At last this scribe became so conceited that he imagined that all this wisdom proceeded from his own wit, and not from Mohamed. Puffed up with self-importance, he fancied himself inspired and he turned against his master. He abandoned his work as a scribe and became the malignant foe of Mohamed. (Book I, 3228-3466)

At one point in his spiritual journey Shakespeare was in a similar situation. He did not know the reason for love, because the flame of love was still burning his imperfections. Therefore, he was accusing his guide of wrongdoing. In Sonnet 34 he implied that he

---

[16] "Jaques" (Shakespeare for the Seeker, Volume 2, Chapter 5.2)

was expecting to meet his guide. It seems that because his approach was not correct, the meeting did not take place[17]:

> "Why didst thou promise such a beauteous day,
> And make me travel forth without my cloak,
> To let base clouds o'ertake me in my way,
> Hiding thy bravery in their rotten smoke.
> 'Tis not enough that through the cloud thou break,
> To dry the rain on my storm-beaten face,
> For no man well of such a salve can speak,
> That heals the wound, and cures not the disgrace:
> Nor can thy shame give physic to my grief,
> Though thou repent, yet I have still the loss,
> The offender's sorrow lends but weak relief
> To him that bears the strong offence's cross."
> (Sonnet 34, 1-12)

Instead of reflecting on the event, Shakespeare started to complain and blame his guide. He felt wounded and disgraced. According to his understanding, neither the guide's embarrassment nor repentance would be enough to heal his grief and repair his losses. If something was lost, being sorry did not help much. At this point he was like the scribe in Rumi's story; he completely misunderstood the situation.

1.14 The Chinese and the Greek Artists

There are many stations along the path towards the source of light. They are like multiple caravanserais. If a caravanserai is full of light, it is because there is a window allowing the sun to shine through.

---

[17] "Shakespeare's Sonnets or How heavy do I journey on the way" (Sonnet 34)

There are many caravanserais that must be left behind so man may reach his destination, i.e., the source of light. Such a journey is like traveling from multicolours to colourlessness. Colour is like the clouds, colourlessness is the sun, i.e., the source of light. Whatever radiance and splendour is seen in the clouds, for sure it comes from the stars, the moon and the sun. This is why those who have burnished their hearts have escaped from colour; every moment they behold light. This is further illustrated in the story of the Greeks and the Chinese artists.

> The Chinese and the Greeks disputed before the king, which of them were the better artists. In order to settle the dispute, the king allotted to each a room to be decorated. The two rooms faced each other, door to door. The Chinese procured all kinds of paints, and coloured their room in the most elaborate way. The Greeks, on the other hand, used no colours at all. They closed the door and went on burnishing the walls from the rust. The walls became clear and pure like mirrors. When the Chinese had finished their work of painting and decorating, they began drumming for joy. The king came in and saw the pictures there. The moment he encountered that sight, it stole away his wits. Then he advanced towards the Greeks, who thereupon removed the intervening curtain so that the reflection of the Chinese masterpieces struck upon the walls they had made clean of rust. All that the king had seen in the Chinese room showed lovelier here, as all the colours of the other room were reflected on its walls with an endless variety of shades and hues. (Book I, 3467-3499)

Without repetitions, books, and intellectuality the Greeks had cleansed their hearts clear of greed, covetousness, avarice, and malice. The pure heart is like a polished mirror, which receives innumerable images. The reflection of every image shines forth forever from the heart alone, and forever every new image that enters upon the heart shows forth within it free of all imperfection.

The guide is a carrier of the full spectrum of evolutionary energy or "colours". In Sonnet 53 Shakespeare says that his guide unites within himself multiple combinations of colours[18]. Ordinary man, on the other hand, carries within himself a potentiality, which corresponds to his dominating "colour":

> "What is your substance, whereof are you made,
> That millions of strange shadows on you tend?
> Since every one, hath every one, one shade,
> And you but one, can every shadow lend."
> (Sonnet 53, 1-4)

Man's potentiality may be fulfilled through the presence of the guide. This is why it is said that the guide is the reality that sustains humanity.

1.15 Mohamed and Zaid

Expert knowledge is needed to handle correctly any experience related to the appearance of the colours of true beauty. Such knowledge includes, but is not limited to, an understanding of what, how, when and to whom administer specific procedures. The following story helps to understand how to use such experiences during which some of the colours of true beauty are revealed.

> Mohamed asked Zaid, one of his disciples, to tell him
> about his latest experiences. Zaid answered that during
> the previous night he experienced that which was beyond

---

[18] "Shakespeare's Sonnets or How heavy do I journey on the way" (Sonnet 53)

the limitations of space and time. Mohamed urged Zaid to be more specific. Zaid replied that he had travelled through the eight high states and the seven low states. So now he is able to know what the destinies of men are. The body, he said, is as a mother; the inner being is like her infant; and death is the time of delivery. At the time of death, the destiny of the inner being becomes known. Because of his previous night experience, he may see whether a soul will progress or regress. Then he asked Mohamed whether he should tell this secret knowledge to other men. Mohamed told him to conceal the truth. Mohamed added that he himself is allowed to speak forth the truth, because his task is to guide men. But for Zaid it would be wrong to blab about his experiences. Mohamed compared his role to that of the moon; he is reflecting the radiance of the spiritual sun. Ordinary men are not able to bear the direct light of the sun. Mohamed explained that he has certain darkness in comparison with the spiritual sun, therefore he is less bright than the sun. This is why ordinary men may bear his radiance. In this way his light is able to illuminate the darkness of human souls. Zaid replied that it was very difficult to keep secret his visionary experiences. But Mohamed in reply instructed him that all men are masters of their own wills, and it is up to them to find the truth. (Book I, 3500-3706)

Zaid did not understand that his own experiences were induced by the presence of Mohamed. But what he experienced was not to be foretold to him by Mohamed. Zaid had to experience it by himself. In other words, spiritual guidance does not rely on foretelling future events; the guidance prepares a disciple to his or her own experiences. By the same token, a disciple is not allowed to blab about his experiences to others. Because he does not know what would be the effect of his blabbing on the others.

Viola in "Twelfth Night" alluded to such expert knowledge in her comment about Feste, the guide who appears in that play[19]:

> "This fellow is wise enough to play the fool;
> And to do that well craves a kind of wit:
> He must observe their mood on whom he jests,
> The quality of persons, and the time,
> And, like the haggard, cheque at every feather
> That comes before his eye. This is a practise
> As full of labour as a wise man's art
> For folly that he wisely shows is fit;
> But wise men, folly-fall'n, quite taint their wit."
> (Twelfth Night, III.1)

The guide knows what, how, when and to whom to disclosure specific instructions. But Feste does not disclose what he knows and what he is doing. Shakespeare left it up to the readers to perceive the true nature of Feste's work.

1.16 Ali's Forbearance

There is a time when nothing can be done; a time when something can be done; and a time when most things are achievable. It is possible to develop an inner perception that allows one to discern the different quality of time. Such an inner sense operates in the Realm, i.e., outside the limitations of our ordinary sensory perception. From the perspective of the Realm there is no such thing as past, present and future. Past, present and future appear when the Realm is projected onto our ordinary space-time limited perception. In other words, it is possible, at the level of the Realm,

---

[19] "Feste" (Shakespeare for the Seeker, Volume 4, Chapter 7.1)

to access the future in order to fix the present.

A spiritually developed man is guided by such an inner perception. This is why a developed man does not need to use intellectual power. When something is perceived through inner senses, no intellect is needed to make constructive choices. Such a man acquires back-and-forth chronological versatility. He can see past and future, which means that he can verify a situation in a way impossible to others. Going back into the past reveals the real background of a situation. Going into the future shows how sterile or fruitful the results of an action would be. A developed man doesn't attempt what he cannot do: all others depend on trial-and-error.

The operation of such an inner organ of perception is illustrated by Rumi in the following story:

> Ali, called the Lion of God, was once engaged in conflict
> with a certain knight. Ali overcame his opponent and
> raised his sword to slay him. At this moment the knight
> spat in Ali's face. Instead of taking vengeance on him, Ali
> dropped his sword. On the knight's inquiring the reason
> of such forbearance, Ali told him that he could not kill
> him while he was driven by anger. On hearing Ali's
> explanation, the knight was so much affected that he
> decided to join Ali's forces. (Book I, 3707-3974)

A developed man is able to act in accordance with the requirements of the evolutionary matrix. However, when he allows himself to be driven by emotions such as anger, vengeance, or greed, his inner sense becomes veiled. At such moments he is no longer acting in accordance with the Divine design, i.e., he is prone to making errors. Ali was able to recognize such a moment of disconnection when he realized that he was about to act in anger.

Shakespeare used an episode in "Henry V" to illustrate a similar situation[20]. The episode took place during the famous Battle of Agincourt when Henry V's troops fought the French army. The English troops were outnumbered by the French five to one. Prior to the battle, the English soldiers all believed that they would die the next morning and they waited patiently for their fate. During the battle Henry V was composed, calm, and entirely focused on his task. At one point, however, he lost his temper. He became visibly angry when he was told that the French attacked the English tents and slaughtered the young pages, who were mere children. Here is Henry V's outburst, which illustrates the moment when he was just about to make a grave error by allowing himself to be driven by anger:

> "I was not angry since I came to France
> Until this instant. Take a trumpet, herald;
> Ride thou unto the horsemen on yon hill:
> If they will fight with us, bid them come down,
> Or void the field; they do offend our sight:
> If they'll do neither, we will come to them,
> And make them skirr away, as swift as stones
> Enforced from the old Assyrian slings:
> Besides, we'll cut the throats of those we have,
> And not a man of them that we shall take
> Shall taste our mercy. Go and tell them so."
> (Henry V, IV.7)

It was at that very moment that the French herald arrived and announced the capitulation of the French army. It was then that Henry V, like Omar, regained his posture and proclaimed:

> "Praised be God, and not our strength, for it!"
> (Henry V, IV.7)

Rumi adds an episode from Ali's life which may help the readers to

---

[20] "Dawn of perfection" (Shakespeare for the Seeker, Volume 1, Chapter 1)

grasp another aspect of acting in accordance with the evolutionary matrix:

> Ali's servant was told by Mohamed that one day he was
> going to kill his master. The frightened servant asked Ali
> to kill him instead, so he might be saved from committing
> such a horrible crime. But Ali answered that because there
> is no hatred in his servant's soul, he does not consider
> this act would be coming from him. Therefore, Ali would
> not interfere with the divine design. (Book I, 3844-3947)

Ali recognized that Mohamed disclosed an event that belonged to the evolutionary matrix. Therefore he knew that he could not interfere with it. He realized that any attempt at interference would be entirely fruitless and would lead to further complications. His servant, on the other hand, was incapable of acting in the same manner. His seemingly altruistic request to Ali to kill him was a sign that he lacked inner sense.

A similar situation in described by Shakespeare in "Julius Caesar". Julius Caesar symbolically represents a spiritual guide. Although some Romans were inclined to make him a king, he refused the crown in a dramatic public display. Julius Caesar clearly indicated that he was a mortal creature. At the same time he said things that pointed out that he was special and superior to other mortals. In his own words he referred to being as unique among humans as the northern star is among other stars[21]:

> "But I am constant as the northern star,
> Of whose true-fix'd and resting quality
> There is no fellow in the firmament.
> The skies are painted with unnumber'd sparks,
> They are all fire and every one doth shine,
> But there's but one in all doth hold his place:

---

[21] "Spiritual king" (Shakespeare for the Seeker, Volume 1, Chapter 2.2)

So in the world; 'tis furnish'd well with men,
And men are flesh and blood, and apprehensive;
Yet in the number I do know but one
That unassailable holds on his rank,
Unshaked of motion: and that I am he,
Let me a little show it, even in this."
(Julius Caesar, III.1)

Caesar was aware of the coming assassination. He knew that his assassination was an unavoidable event that was part of the evolutionary matrix. Here is how he explained it:

"What can be avoided
Whose end is purposed by the mighty gods?
Yet Caesar shall go forth; for these predictions
Are to the world in general as to Caesar."
(Julius Caesar, II.2)

Caesar also alerted all those around him about the coming assassination. He made sure that everybody heard the soothsayer's warning about his assassination on the day of the Ides of March:

Caesar:

"Who is it in the press that calls on me?
I hear a tongue, shriller than all the music,
Cry 'Caesar!' Speak; Caesar is turn'd to hear."

Soothsayer:

"Beware the ides of March."
(Julius Caesar, I.2)

Caesar also knew that Brutus was one of the assassins. When he saw the assassins coming to his house he welcomed them sarcastically:

"Welcome, Publius.

> What, Brutus, are you stirr'd so early too?"
> (Julius Caesar, II.2)

Caesar's welcoming words addressed to Brutus ("What, Brutus, are you ... too?") on that morning were nearly the same as his very last and now very famous phrase that is widely used in Western literature as an epitome of betrayal:

> "Et tu, Brute!" (Julius Caesar, III.1)

Like Ali in Rumi's story, Caesar would not interfere with the Divine design. In this way Shakespeare helps the readers recognize that he uses the character of Caesar to describe a fully developed man.

Book 2. Deceiving Self

A cycle of the evolutionary process is usually described as consisting of seven stages. However, there is no linear progression from stage to stage within a cycle. There will be some "intervals" or "gaps". These intervals are the most challenging stages of the process. The musical octave with two intervals of irregular increase of frequency is a symbolic illustration of such developmental non-linearity[22]. The overall arrangement of the "Mathnawi" is based on the same principle. In prologue to Book 2 Rumi indicates the first such a gap. He refers to the gap as a delay in the release of Book 2:

> "Book 2 has been delayed for a while: an interval was
> needed in order that the blood might turn to milk. Blood
> does not become sweet milk until thy fortune gives birth
> to a new babe. Consider well these words." (Book II, 1-2)

The delay was needed so the readers had time to absorb the content presented in Book 1. Because it is necessary not only to read but also to digest the previously disclosed information before one may be exposed to the next portion of the teaching. Otherwise, the reader would be overwhelmed by the impact and would not benefit from it.

Shakespeare used a similar design in his plays, i.e., the evolutionary cycles illustrated in the plays are based on the seven stages. For example, the History Plays illustrate the English evolutionary branch of the modern evolutionary cycle. Each stage corresponds to one of the seven English kings, i.e., King John, Richard II,

---

[22] However, it would be naive and too simplistic to assume that the position of the intervals or the numerical proportions of the musical octave are fixed features of the actual evolutionary cycles.

Henry IV, Henry V, Henry VI, Richard III, and Henry VIII. The non-linearity within this branch is marked by "Henry IV" being presented in two- and "Henry VI" in three-parts.

In Shakespeare's Italian and Bohemian plays, the gaps are indicated by the "tragedies", e.g., "Romeo and Juliet" and "Hamlet", respectively. The tragedies are inserted within a sequel of comedies.

* * *

The spiritual development requires the disciple to pass through seven stages of preparation, before his inner being is ready for its full function. These stages, sometimes called "men", are degrees in the transmutation of the consciousness. In accordance with the natural capacities and character of a disciple, a guide may optimize the sequence of required experiences. Therefore, certain stages will be induced in some disciples, while others may require a different sequence, or even may be prevented from certain experiences. These various stages may be overlapped; some stages may be phased out, and later on may be phased in again. Two or more stages may appear at the same time. The time period required for the completion of each of the stages is not fixed either, it may vary from one stage to the next. The guide may compress time, if required, and he may load a few stages into a single event. Rumi explains the nature of the guide's skills in the following comment:

> The guides are they whose essence, before this world
> existed, was part of the Realm. They have received a soul
> before the creation of the form. Before their bodies were
> created they passed through many lifetimes. While
> consultation was going on as to bringing mankind into
> existence, i.e., before the soul of the universe became
> fettered by materiality, the guides were acquainted with
> the material form of every existent being. This is why
> when you see two guides meeting together, they are one,
> and at the same time they are six hundred thousand.

> Plurality is in the animal soul; the human soul is singular.
> (Book II, 168-188)

The initial stage is often referred to as the deceiving self. The deceiving self corresponds to an ordinary state, which is a mixture of hopes, fears, conditioning, imagination, and emotion. It is the state of most people who have not undergone the refinement process. The formula that allows one to overcome the deceiving self is called initiation into "proper conduct". The proper conduct, however, has nothing to do with artificial and socially acceptable rules of etiquette. A socially acceptable etiquette is of an automatic and reactive manner. It needs the constant stimulus of threat or promise. It may lead only to inferior gains, emotional or intellectual short-lived satisfaction. By acting in such a manner, a person may be able to give the impression that he or she is worthwhile or knowledgeable. However it is insufficient in the developmental process.

Proper conduct may be correctly learned only from the presence of a guide. The stories included in Book 2 illustrate how the deceiving self is manifested and how the presence of the guide may help to identify it.

2.1 The Traveller and his Beast

Ordinary man is entirely absorbed in satisfying his deceiving self. The deceiving self is often compared to a beast needed to deliver man to a certain point along the journey. Afterwards, this beast would prevent him from moving forward. At some point, therefore, the beast has to be dismounted. The more refined means of travelling requires the five spiritual senses, i.e., the subtle faculties:

"The way of physical sense-perception is the way of asses.
... Besides these five physical senses there are five
spiritual senses. Those latter are like gold, while these
physical senses are like copper." (Book II, 48-9)

It is in this context that the story of the traveller and his ass is set-up:

After a long day's journey a traveller arrived at a
monastery, where he decided to stay for the night. He
ordered a servant to take care of his ass and give it plenty
of food and water. The servant told him that he did not
need any further instructions and assured him that he
knew what to do. He promised to attend to the ass most
carefully. The traveller left his ass in the hands of the
servant and went to meet the inhabitants of the
monastery. But when the owner of the ass left, the
servant went to spent time with his friends; he completely
neglected the animal. In the meantime, the traveller
engaged himself in spiritual discussions with the monks.
When the traveller went to sleep he dreamt that his ass
was caught by a wolf. He woke up and thought it would
be improper to think that the servant would not take
good care of the ass. So he spent all night trying to purify
his thoughts by saying prayers. At that time the poor ass
was starving being left without water and food.
Consequently it became weak and unfit to travel the next
morning. In spite of the blows and kicks that were
showered on him, the ass could not carry his master. The
other travellers thought that the animal was very weak
and therefore useless. But the owner of the ass realized
that any ass fed by prayers instead of barley and water
would end up exactly like this one. (Book II, 156- 513)

During the initial phase of the journey, a beast is needed to deliver the traveller to a specific destination or an intermediate state. At that time the traveller's prime responsibility is to take good care of his carrier. As illustrated in the story, it would be sheer negligence to abandon one's beast too early or to delegate the responsibility of one's well-being to an ignorant person. The traveller has to learn how to keep the balance between taking care of the beast and other activities. There is time for the beast and there is time for prayers.

By inserting an episode with Jesus and an ignorant disciple, Rumi's draws the reader's attention to the importance of right timing:

> A disciple of Jesus saw some bones in a deep-dug hole.
> He turned to Jesus and asked him to be taught how he
> could bring these bones back to life. Jesus told him that
> he was not ready for such a task. Jesus further explained
> that many lifetimes were needed before one could
> exercise such a skill. 'In such a case', continued the
> foolish disciple, 'if I cannot, then you bring these bones
> to life'. Jesus asked him why he tried to engage himself in
> such fruitless activity. Why instead of taking care of his
> dead soul does he seek to mend the dead bones of a
> stranger? But because the disciple insisted, Jesus breathed
> life into the bones. The bones took the form of a black
> lion, which sprang forth, smote the disciple with his paw
> and killed him. When the lion was asked why he killed the
> disciple, the lion answered the reason was that Jesus was
> troubled by him. Then Jesus asked the lion why he did
> not drink the killed man's blood. The lion replied that the
> killing was for the purpose of warning others and not for
> satisfying his beastly thirst. (Book II, 141-155)

This episode serves as a warning to those who engage themselves in certain activities when they are not yet correctly prepared for it. At the same time, it may be damaging to try to misuse one's time in the company of the guide. If one is in the presence of the sustainer of life, he should be ready to "die" instead of trying to satisfy his other wants.

The requirements for right timing and right circumstances are further illustrated in the story of another traveller and his beast:

> A traveller arrived at a monastery. He halted there for the night. Unlike the traveller in the previous story, he took good care of his ass. He provided it with water and barley. Then he went and joined other travellers who stayed there. The other travellers were poor and hungry. They decided that it was their right to sell their companion's ass and get some food for themselves. With the proceeds of the sale they bought delicate meats and made a feast. The owner of the ass, who was not aware of this transaction, was invited to take part in the feast. After the feast he joined the others in mystical ceremonies that consisted of dancing and chanting. In their emotional ecstasy, the other travellers were celebrating the transaction by chanting 'the ass is gone, the ass is gone'. Without attaching any attention to their recitation, the owner enthusiastically joined the chanting. Next morning he asked his servant what had become of the ass. The servant told him that the ass was sold. And he reminded him that he himself was singing "the ass is gone, the ass is gone". So the servant assumed that the traveller knew about the transaction. (Book II, 514-584)

Despite the fact that the traveller was taking good care of his beast, he ignorantly joined a spiritual activity for which he was not ready yet. Because of this he could not reach his intermediate destination. Without his beast he could not arrive there.

These stories may help to understand Shakespeare's own experiences described in his Sonnets. In Sonnet 50, for example,

Shakespeare described the challenges of his journey travelling on his own beast:

> "How heavy do I journey on the way,
> When what I seek (my weary travel's end)
> Doth teach that ease and that repose to say
> Thus far the miles are measured from thy friend.
> The beast that bears me, tired with my woe,
> Plods dully on, to bear that weight in me,
> As if by some instinct the wretch did know
> His rider lov'd not speed being made from thee:
> The bloody spur cannot provoke him on,
> That some-times anger thrusts into his hide,
> Which heavily he answers with a groan,
> More sharp to me than spurring to his side,
> >   For that same groan doth put this in my mind,
> >   My grief lies onward and my joy behind."
> (Sonnet 50)

Shakespeare contemplates the difficulties of his current stage of journey. The poet describes his situation while travelling from the ordinary state to a higher state[23]. He refers to his destination as "weary travel's end". The ordinary state is where the guide's outward form is. The guide's inner heart is the higher state, i.e., the poet's destination. The poet's journey is slowed down because he is hesitant to leave the guide's outward form behind. The poet's deceiving self is compared to a beast ("the beast that bears me").

The poet complains that travel makes him distraught as he experiences how difficult it is to separate himself from the guide's company ("how heavy do I journey on the way, when what I seek ... doth teach that ease and that repose to say thus far the miles are measured from thy friend"). The beast's behaviour is a reflection of the poet's hesitance. The poet implies that the poor beast knows

---

[23] "Shakespeare's Sonnets or How heavy do I journey on the way" (Sonnet 50)

that he does not want to move quickly away from his worldly pleasures. Even with angry blows, like the traveller in Rumi's story, the poet is not able to force his beast to move faster. The beast answers with a groan, which hurts the poet even more, because it reminds him that his challenges and difficulties are ahead of him, and all his worldly pleasures are left behind.

2.2 The Spendthrift and the Camel Owner

Although the beast is needed to arrive at the next stage of the spiritual journey, something else is needed to point out the initial direction for such an undertaking. The initial direction may be pointed out by a guide. Fragmented or simplified approaches, such as moralistic and dogmatic impositions, are not effective enough in directing a disciple in the right direction. In the following story, the prisoners and the Kurd represent ordinary men; the spendthrift is the deceiving self; the Judge illustrates a moralistic preaching.

> A certain notorious spendthrift obtained admittance to a prison. He annoyed the prisoners by eating up all their food and leaving them none. At last they made a formal complaint to the Judge, and asked him to banish the insatiable man from the prison. The Judge summoned the spendthrift and asked him why he did not go to his own house instead of living off the prisoners. The man replied that he had no house or means of livelihood except that supplied by the prison. The Judge, therefore, ordered that a proclamation be made that the man was a notorious spendthrift and that no one should be induced to lend him money or trade with him. Accordingly, the soldiers sought for a camel upon which to carry the spendthrift through the city. They took away a camel from a Kurd

who was selling firewood. The helpless Kurd made a great outcry, but his lamentation had no effect. The spendthrift was put on the camel and was carried through the city. The laud proclamation was made in Persian, Arabic, and Kurdish that the man was a notorious spendthrift and he should not be trusted. Driven by his hope for a reward, the Kurd was following the man who was carried on the camel from morning till evening. When the evening came, the Kurd demanded payment from the spendthrift for using his camel. Of course the man refused to give him anything. Instead, he told the Kurd that if he had kept his ears open he would have heard the proclamation. Thus the Kurd spent the day in useless labour. (Book II, 585-842)

In the case of the Kurd in the story, the loud identification and repeated warning against the spendthrift did not have any effect on him. As long as the Kurd was driven by greed and false hope, he remained entirely blind and deaf to such warnings.

Rumi adds a comment saying that as long as one is driven by physical senses he is incapable of recognizing his true destination:

"O lover, inquire who your beloved really is.
If the beloved is that which the senses perceive,
every one that has senses would be in love with it.
Inasmuch as constancy is increased
by that spiritual love, how is constancy altered
by the decay of material form?" (Book II, 705-9)

Bertram in Shakespeare's play "All's Well That Ends Well" remained blind to the mischievous nature of Parolles, the character personifying his deceiving self. And because of that, he ended up with many troubles. Only towards the end of the play, was Bertram able to recognize that he was under the influence of such a deceiving fool:

"But shall we have this
dialogue between the fool and the soldier? Come,
bring forth this counterfeit module, he has deceived
me, like a double-meaning prophesier."
(All's Well That Ends Well, IV.3)

By separating himself from Parolles, Bertram removed his inner veil. Only then was he able to recognize the true beauty of Helena[24].

2.3 The King and his Two Slaves

In the following story the king represents the intellect. The two slaves represent two competing tendencies of human behaviour. One tendency is under the influence of the deceiving self; it is driven by ordinary earthly attachments. The other tendency is following the supreme priority of the Realm.

> A king purchased two slaves, one extremely handsome, and the other with a stinking mouth and black teeth. The king sent the handsome slave away to the bath, and in his absence questioned the other. He told the ugly-looking man that the other slave had given a very bad account of him, saying that he was dishonest and ill-behaved. The king asked him if this was true. The slave replied that whatever the other said was true. Then the king asked him to describe the other slave's faults. The ugly slave said that the first slave's faults were affection, loyalty, and humanity; his other faults were sincerity and cordial comradeship. And his least fault was generosity; a

---

[24] "Parolles" (Shakespeare for the Seeker, Volume 2, Chapter 5.1)

generosity that would drive him to give up even his life. The king then sent away the ugly slave away and summoned the handsome one. He told him that his fellow slave had given a bad account of him, and asked what he had to say. The handsome slave replied that this fellow was a liar and a rascal. The king realized that the handsome slave's tongue had betrayed his inner vileness. He sent him away saying that the ugly slave should be the commander; and the handsome slave should be under his command. (Book II, 843-1046)

Rumi comments:

"Know that the outward form passes away, but the world of reality remains forever. How long will you play at loving the shape of the jug? Leave the shape of the jug; go and seek the water. You have seen its outward form, but you are unaware of its reality. If you are wise, pick out a pearl from the shell. These shells or bodies are in the world, though they are all living by grace of the Sea of the Soul. Yet there is not a pearl in every shell. Therefore, open your eyes and seek the pearl by looking into the hearts of those who are around you." (Book II, 1020-4)

Shakespeare used the character of King Lear to illustrate a similar situation to that presented in the story of the two slaves. King Lear requested his daughters to demonstrate their loyalty to him. The two elder daughters gave him flattering answers. King Lear, however, was spiritually blind and deaf. He was easily pleased and satisfied with the false declarations of his daughters' supposed love. Cordelia, his youngest daughter, pointed out to him the difference between ordinary and true love:

"Good my lord,
You have begot me, bred me, loved me: I
Return those duties back as are right fit,

Obey you, love you, and most honour you.
Why have my sisters husbands, if they say
They love you all? Haply, when I shall wed,
That lord whose hand must take my plight shall carry
Half my love with him, half my care and duty:
Sure, I shall never marry like my sisters,
To love my father all."
(King Lear, I.1)

King Lear was too full of himself and too greedy for his daughter's affection to understand Cordelia's proclamation of the nature of her love. He was incapable of grasping the meaning of Cordelia's words. He flew into a rage and disowned her.

Cordelia symbolically represents an evolutionary impulse that was embedded within the 10th century BC Celtic evolutionary branch. As the result of the misuse of "Cordelia", the ancient Celtic branch was deactivated[25].

2.4 The Falcon and the Owls

Rumi compares the seeker after truth to a falcon. The seeker is the falcon who returns to the forearm of the king. He who has allowed himself to be driven by his conceived self is like the owls satisfied with their foul habitation.

A certain falcon lost his way and found himself in the waste places inhabited by owls. The owls suspected that he had come to seize their nests, and all surrounded him to make an end of him. The falcon assured them that he

---

[25] "Britain: 10th century BC" (Shakespeare for the Seeker, Volume 1, Chapter 3.1)

had no such intention as they accused him of. He told
them that his abode was on the forearm of the king, and
that he did not have any desire for their foul habitation.
The owls replied that he was trying to deceive them,
because a strange bird like him could not be a favourite of
the king. The falcon repeated that he was indeed a
favourite of the king, and that the king would assuredly
destroy their houses if they injured him. The falcon
proceeded to give them some good advice on the folly of
trusting outward appearances. He said it was true he was
not of the same substance as the king, but yet the king's
light was reflected in him. He said that he was, as it were,
the dust beneath the king's feet. But if the owls became
like him in this respect, they would be dignified as he was.
He told them if they followed him, perchance they would
also become royal falcons, although right now they were
owls.

In the same way, man's inner being receives a jewel by
coming into contact with the guide. Through this his
ordinary soul becomes pregnant with the heavenly
kingdom. (Book II, 1047-1191)

Shakespeare delegated Duke Senior in "As You Like It" to
summarize such a spiritual "pregnancy" in the following way:

"Sweet are the uses of adversity,
Which, like the toad, ugly and venomous,
Wears yet a precious jewel in his head."
(As You Like It, II.1)

The toad, like an owl, is ugly and venomous[26]. Yet, it carries within
itself the potentiality that may be symbolically compared to a
precious jewel.

---

[26] "Technical background" (Shakespeare for the Seeker, Volume 2, Chapter 5.2)

2.5 The Man, the Water, and the Wall

In the following story the wall represents earthly attractions and desires. The thirstier one is, the more quickly does he tear off the bricks of the wall:

> On the bank of the stream there was a high wall. On the top of the wall was a sorrowful thirsty man. The wall hindered him from reaching the water. So he took some of the bricks off the top of the wall and threw them into the water. The sound of the water came to his ear like delighting music, which made him drunken as though it were wine. From the pleasure of hearing that sound, the man began to tear off more bricks and hurl them down. The water cried out, 'What is the advantage to you of this hurling a brick at me?' The man answered that he had two advantages that would not stop him from that work. Firstly, he could hear the sound of the water, which for him was like heavenly music. The other advantage was that with every brick he tore off the wall, he was getting closer and closer to the running water. The destruction of the wall became a means to access the water. It was the remedy for bringing about a union with the water. (Book II, 1192-1219)

Rumi tells another story about the challenges of submitting to the water:

> The water said to the defiled one, 'come into me'. The defiled one said, 'I feel shame before the water'. Said the water, 'Without me how shall this shame go? Without me how shall this defilement be removed?'
> Every defiled one who hides from the water is letting shame hinder progress. The heart is muddied by the

bricks of the body's tank; the body is cleansed by the water of the heart's tank. (Book II, 1361-1379)

Rumi adds that there is a time limit for the quenching of such inner thirst. Namely, it has to be done:

"Before the days of old age arrive;
Before the body becomes barren, crumbling, and poor;
When strength and lust is cut off,
The eyebrows fallen down and the eyes grown moist and dim,
The face, from wrinkling, like the back of a lizard;
Speech and taste and teeth gone out of use;
It is too late because the shop is ruined and the business gone out of order;
The roots of bad habit firmly set, and the power to tear them up decreased."
(Book II, 1220-1226)

Shakespeare used the character of melancholy Jaques in "As You Like It" to deliver a similar message, i.e., that there is a time limit within which a certain progress has to be made. Otherwise one may miss entirely his opportunity. In the following quote Jaques describes the seventh, i.e., the final stage or "age" of ordinary man who ignored his evolutionary potential. Instead of evolutionary growth such a man ends up in a "second childishness and mere oblivion"[27]:

"The sixth age shifts
Into the lean and slipper'd pantaloon,
With spectacles on nose and pouch on side,
His youthful hose, well saved, a world too wide
For his shrunk shank; and his big manly voice,
Turning again toward childish treble, pipes

---

[27] "Jaques" (Shakespeare for the Seeker, Volume2, Chapter 5.2)

And whistles in his sound. Last scene of all,
That ends this strange eventful history,
Is second childishness and mere oblivion,
Sans teeth, sans eyes, sans taste, sans everything."
(As You Like It, II.7)

Rumi compares such oblivious life to the planting a thorn-bush:

A man planted a thorn-bush in the middle of the road.
The travellers reproached him and oftentimes told him to
dig it up. He refused to do so. The thorn-bush was
growing bigger. The people's feet were wounded and their
clothes were damaged by the thorns. The Governor of
that country ordered the man to dig the bush up. The
man answered that he would do it the next day. Every day
he kept promising to do it. In the meantime the bush was
growing bigger and bigger. At the same time, the man was
getting weaker and weaker. (Book, II, 1227-1360)

The Governor's appeals are an example of preaching. He is a man
of rules, who has to stick to beliefs and practices because he does
not actually know anything else. Man needs to resort to more
effective techniques in order to keep up with evolutionary
opportunity.

Every bad habit is like that thorn-bush. It hurts and wounds man's
soul. At this point Rumi offers two solutions. The first solution is
to take up an axe and cut off the bush. This corresponds to the
process referred to as spiritual reformation. Such an approach is
described by Shakespeare in "Romeo and Juliet." The play takes
place in the city of Verona. Verona's inner state is seriously
disturbed by internal strife:

"Two households, both alike in dignity,
In fair Verona, where we lay our scene,
From ancient grudge break to new mutiny,

Where civil blood makes civil hands unclean."
(Romeo and Juliet, Prologue)

This infighting is like the torn-bush; it prevents the city's inner growth. The bush must be removed. Prince Escalus is the current ruler of Verona. But Prince Escalus, like the Governor in Rumi's story, is incapable of exercising control over the city. His moralistic appeals to the citizens are ineffective in preventing conflicts between the feuding families. Much more effective means are needed to bring the city of Verona on the right path. "Romeo and Juliet" illustrates the means that were implemented in order to reform the being of Verona. This is why it was necessary for Romeo and Juliet to go through very difficult and seemingly tragic experiences: they had to die. They had to die to generate a shocking and awakening rebuke to Verona. Only in this way could the evolutionary potential of Verona be sustained[28].

The other solution is to unite the thorns with a rosebush. In this way the thorns may be turned into roses. Then roses would take possession of the garden. But this requires an experienced gardener. This second approach is known as the spiritual purification. In Sonnet 15 Shakespeare compares the purification to organic engrafting[29]:

> "When I consider every thing that grows
> Holds in perfection but a little moment.
> That this huge stage presenteth nought but shows
> Whereon the Stars in secret influence comment.
> When I perceive that men as plants increase,
> Cheered and checked even by the self-same sky:
> Vaunt in their youthful sap, at height decrease,
> And wear their brave state out of memory.
> Then the conceit of this inconstant stay,

---

[28] "Verona" (Shakespeare for the Seeker, Volume 3, Chapter 6.6)
[29] "Shakespeare's Sonnets or How heavy do I journey on the way" (Sonnet 15)

Sets you most rich in youth before my sight,
Where wasteful time debateth with decay
To change your day of youth to sullied night,
 And all in war with Time for love of you
 As he takes from you, I engraft you new."
(Sonnet 15)

In this Sonnet, the guide compares humans to other living organisms, which can manifest their perfection but only for a brief period of time. The guide compares himself to a gardener who, by his skills of grafting, is able to grow new species in his garden. He is able to ennoble the poet by grafting a sample of evolutionary matrix onto his inner being. In this way he may protect the poet against the tyranny of time.

Organic grafting is a symbolic illustration of spiritual purification. At this stage an aspirant receives an impression, just like the thorn of rose is grafted. This impression allows for holding and digesting the initial evolutionary impact.

Rumi explains that the guide's inner being is like a pearl within an oyster, or the sun that is hidden in a speckle, or the sea that is concealed in a drop of water. It is invisible to ordinary eyes and mind. This is why the behaviour of the guide may be described as various forms of madness, because his actions are incomprehensible to ordinary men. Ordinary man's behaviour is controlled by his deceiving self, which is manifested by envy, hate, and greed. At every moment, one of these different tendencies drives man's thoughts and actions. The inner being of such a man may be equated to a jungle. But the guide is very well acquainted with that jungle. He is like a lion that knows the hidden path leading to the sea. Rumi illustrates this is an episode with Dhun-Nun, called the Egyptian, who lived in the 9th century.

Dhun-Nun appeared to his ignorant friends to be mad. They confined him to a madhouse. After a time they

thought that he was not really mad, but had feigned
madness for some deep purpose. So they decided to go to
the madhouse and inquire into the state of his health.
When they arrived there, Dhun-Nun asked them who
they were. They answered that they were his devoted
friends, who were now convinced that the story of his
being mad was a calumny. Dhun-Nun jumped up and
drove them away with sticks and stones. They all run
away from him. Dhun-Nun commented that true
friendship would have been manifested in sharing his
troubles, even as pure gold is tried by fire. True friends
would not run away from him. (Book II, 1380-1461)

The guide is like gold; tribulation is like fire. Pure gold is glad when
it is in the heart of purifying fire. There are many people whose
ignorance is clearly manifested by their behaviour. But for others
the light of the guide is needed to detect their true inner state.

The scene with the Poet and the Painter in Shakespeare's "Timon
of Athens" illustrates a situation similar to that of Dhun-Nun.
Timon is a guide[30]. When he realizes that the Athenians are
dishonest and corrupted, he abandons the city and goes to a forest.
In the forest he is approached by the Poet and the Painter. The
Poet and the Painter are insincere and greedy; they hope to get
some gold from Timon. But Timon tells them that they both have
but one fault. Namely, they trust a knave who deceives them:

> "There's never a one of you but trusts a knave,
> That mightily deceives you." (Timon of Athens, V.1)

Of course the "knave" is their deceiving self:

> "Ay, and you hear him cog, see him dissemble,
> Know his gross patchery, love him, feed him,

---

[30] "Targeted impact" (Shakespeare for the Seeker, Volume 2, Chapter 4.3)

Keep in your bosom: yet remain assured
That he's a made-up villain." (Timon of Athens, V.1)

This is why Timon cannot give them gold, because "gold" is of no use to those who are still driven by their deceiving self. Timon tells the Poet and the Painter that he will give them gold if they recognize their knave and get rid of him:

"Look you, I love you well; I'll give you gold,
Rid me these villains from your companies:
Hang them or stab them, drown them in a draught,
Confound them by some course, and come to me,
I'll give you gold enough." (Timon of Athens, V.1)

Gold may be constructively used only once the manifest faculties are reformed and purified. This is the recipe for the alchemical transmutation:

"You are an alchemist; make gold of that."
(Timon of Athens, V.1)

Similarly to Rumi, Shakespeare uses the concept of alchemical transmutation as a parallel of the spiritual process.

2.6 Luqman and his Master

When a guide goes to a place where he is not known, he puts his own clothes on his disciple and makes him the leader. He himself dresses up with the disciple's clothes. By love the guide is made a slave; by love the servant is made alive. This is illustrated by Rumi in the story of Luqman and his master:

Luqman the Wise, who is sometimes identified with
Esop, was a slave. Though he was slave-born, he was
master of himself and was free from earthly attachments.
His master discovered his worth. Although he outwardly
was the Master, inwardly he became Luqman's slave. The
Master would set Luqman free, but he complied with the
wish of Luqman. Luqman desired to remain a slave, so
that none would know his secret. The Master would never
receive any delicacy without giving Luqman a share of it.
One day, having received a watermelon, he gave Luqman
the best part of it. Luqman devoured it with such
apparent relish that his Master was tempted to taste it. To
his surprise he found it was very bitter. He asked Luqman
why he had not told him of this. Luqman replied that it
was not for him, who lived on his master's bounty, to
complain when he received disagreeable things at his
hands. (Book II, 1462-1719)

The meaning of Luqman's desire to remain concealed is that man
should hide his inner work from his self-satisfaction. So even in the
moments of experiencing elevated states, he would not give away
his secret. True knowledge may be recorded only by the subtle
faculties. Therefore, the subtle faculties would have to be
developed first.

Shakespeare alluded to such an experience in Sonnet 77:

"Thy glass will show thee how thy beauties wear,
Thy dial how thy precious minutes waste,
The vacant leaves thy mind's imprint will bear,
And of this book, this learning mayst thou taste.
The wrinkles which thy glass will truly show,
Of mouthed graves will give thee memory,
Thou by thy dial's shady stealth mayst know,
Time's thievish progress to eternity.

> Look what thy memory can not contain,
> Commit to these waste blanks, and thou shalt find
> Those children nursed, deliver'd from thy brain,
> To take a new acquaintance of thy mind.
>> These offices, so oft as thou wilt look,
>> Shall profit thee, and much enrich thy book."
>> (Sonnet 77)

In this Sonnet the guide tells the poet that he has to wait till he develops his inner senses[31]. Only then will he be able to record correctly the guide's teaching. In other words, the poet is not ready yet to write. As time passes and the poet gets older, his intellect faculty will be gradually purified and transmuted. In this way the poet will be better prepared to record the guide's teaching. The ordinary intellect is useful only to remember about the unstoppable passing of time. But the guide's teaching cannot be confined to such an inferior faculty. Instead, the teaching, which the poet is exposed to, may be properly recorded in the inner layers of his intellect. But these faculties are still inactive. The guide's words are like nourishment that will activate them. The guide refers to the subtle faculties as "those children nursed, deliver'd from thy brain". It is through "those children" that the poet may prolong his life and enrich his inner being.

In "Richard II" Shakespeare used the same allegorical description by comparing the activation of the subtle levels of the mind to begetting children[32]:

> "My brain I'll prove the female to my soul,
> My soul the father; and these two beget
> A generation of still-breeding thoughts,
> And these same thoughts people this little world."
> (Richard II, V.5)

---

[31] "Shakespeare's Sonnets or How heavy do I journey on the way" (Sonnet 77)
[32] "Preliminary realization" (Shakespeare for the Seeker, Volume 1, Chapter 1)

Richard's language may seem to be obscure unless the readers realize that Shakespeare describes a certain stage of the evolutionary process. Namely, Richard realized that the mind consisted of a number of inner layers. Richard's realization was a mark of the arrival of the being of England at a certain stage of the evolutionary cycle.

2.7 Moses and the Shepherd

A set of beliefs and assumptions, which ordinary man erects around himself, prevents him from the development of real understanding. Evolutionary progress is inhibited by simplistic and incomplete thinking patterns. The overall result is that ordinary man is not sufficiently equipped to judge and understand the situations in which he finds himself. He is not able to know what is developmentally constructive and what is destructive. To illustrate this situation, Rumi gives the following example:

> Moses once heard a shepherd praying 'O God, show me where Thou art, that I may become Thy servant. I will clean Thy shoes, comb Thy hair, sew Thy clothes and fetch Thee milk'. When Moses heard the shepherd praying in this senseless manner, he rebuked him, saying, 'O foolish one, though your father was a believer, you have become an infidel. God is a Spirit, and needs not such gross grooming as, in your ignorance, you suppose'. The shepherd was abashed at Moses' rebuke. He tore his clothes and fled away into the desert. Then a revelation came to Moses, 'O Moses, wherefore have you driven away my servant? Your office is to reconcile my people with me, not to drive them away from me. I have given to each race different usages and forms of praising and

adoring me. I have no need of their praises, being exalted
above all such needs. I regard not the words that are
spoken, but the heart that offers them. I do not require
fine words, but a burning heart. Men's ways of showing
devotion to me are various, but so long as the devotions
are genuine, they are accepted'. When Moses heard these
reproaches, he ran into the desert looking for the
shepherd. At last he found the shepherd and told him that
he had good news for him; that he should not follow any
fixed rules or forms of worshipping; that he should just
say what his distressed heart desired. (Book II, 1720-
1877)

At that time Moses was incapable of discerning the shepherd's
action. Only a wise man would know the effect of scolding or
approving someone's deeds. This is further explained in the story
of the sleeping man:

A wise man was riding along when he saw a snake going
into the mouth of a sleeping man. He struck the sleeper
several powerful blows with a mace. The strokes of the
hard mace drove him in flight from the rider to beneath a
tree. There were many rotten apples on the ground which
had dropped from the tree. The rider forced the man to
eat as many apples as he could. The man was protesting
and demanding to know what he was being punished for.
But the rider forced him with his mace to run. The man
was full-fed, sleepy, and tired. At one point he started to
vomit. And all things that he had eaten came up from
him. And then he saw the snake that leapt forth from him
along with what he had eaten. When he saw the snake, the
man fell on his knees in front of the rider: he recognized
in him a benefactor. And then he apologized for swearing
at the rider, saying had he known the matter he would had
never spoken a bad word against the rider. And the rider

explained that if he had uttered a hint about the snake, the man would have been too terrorized and too frightened to do anything about it. (Book II, 1878-1931)

Katharina in Shakespeare's "The Taming of the Shrew" goes through a similar experience which allows her to wake up from her "sleep". Here is Curtis' description of the treatment that Petruchio administered to her:

"In her chamber, making a sermon of continency to her;
And rails, and swears, and rates, that she, poor soul,
Knows not which way to stand, to look, to speak,
And sits as one new-risen from a dream."
(The Taming of the Shrew, IV.1)

At the end of the play, Katharina is able to recognize in Petruchio her spiritual guide and understand his actions[33]:

"Thy husband is thy lord, thy life, thy keeper,
Thy head, thy sovereign; one that cares for thee,
And for thy maintenance commits his body
To painful labour both by sea and land,
To watch the night in storms, the day in cold,
Whilst thou liest warm at home, secure and safe;
And craves no other tribute at thy hands
But love, fair looks and true obedience;
Too little payment for so great a debt.
Such duty as the subject owes the prince
Even such a woman oweth to her husband;
And when she is froward, peevish, sullen, sour,
And not obedient to his honest will,
What is she but a foul contending rebel
And graceless traitor to her loving lord?"
(The Taming of the Shrew, V.2)

---

[33] "Taming school" (Shakespeare for the Seeker, Volume 3, Chapter 6.5)

It is obvious that Katharina's speech does not apply to ordinary marriage. If we remember that in Shakespeare's vocabulary "husband" means a spiritual guide and an exemplar of a fully developed man, then Katharina's speech becomes suddenly pregnant with an entirely different meaning. She describes the guide as a disciple's life, lord, keeper, head, and sovereign. The guide is to his disciple as a King is to his subject. If a disciple proves shrewish, like the sleeping man in Rumi's story, then he is a traitor to a loving King. In return, the guide asks only for the disciple's kindness and true obedience, which represents but a tiny payment for "so great a debt".

2.8 The Man and his Pet Bear

As introduction to the story of the Man and his Pet Bear, Rumi emphasizes the importance of being able to recognize the operation of mercy:

> A dragon was pulling a bear into its jaws. A brave man
> appeared and succoured it. The guides are like that valiant
> man. They help those who are in need. Whenever they
> hear the cry for mercy, they run in that direction. They are
> like physicians for hidden maladies. They offer their
> remedy, which is a form of true love, justice, and mercy.
> (Book II, 1932-1938)

Rumi adds that exercising mercy may lead to overcoming the deceiving self:

> Wherever is pain, the remedy goes there; whenever
> lowland is, the water runs there. It you want the water of
> mercy, become low. Then drink the wine of mercy and

become drunk. Mercy upon mercy comes. Hear from above the firmament the sound of the celestial music. Put out of your ear the deafening cotton of distractive thoughts, so you may hear the heavenly music. Remove the veil from your eyes, so you may behold the invisible garden. Remove the veil from your brain so you may perceive truth. (Book II, 1939-2009)

The operation of mercy was further explained by Portia[34] in her appeal to Shylock in Shakespeare's "The Merchant of Venice":

"The quality of mercy is not strain'd,
It droppeth as the gentle rain from heaven
Upon the place beneath: it is twice blest;
It blesseth him that gives and him that takes:
'Tis mightiest in the mightiest: it becomes
The throned monarch better than his crown;
His sceptre shows the force of temporal power,
The attribute to awe and majesty,
Wherein doth sit the dread and fear of kings;
But mercy is above this sceptred sway;
It is enthroned in the hearts of kings,
It is an attribute to God himself;
And earthly power doth then show likest God's
When mercy seasons justice."
(The Merchant of Venice, IV.1)

By exercising mercy, man may be able to overcome the limitation of bodily attractions, i.e., "this muddy vesture of decay". Here is Lorenzo in "The Merchant of Venice" explaining the nature of such limitations:

"Sit, Jessica. Look how the floor of heaven
Is thick inlaid with patines of bright gold:

---

[34] "Final touches" (Shakespeare for the Seeker, Volume 3, Chapter 6.4)

> There's not the smallest orb which thou behold'st
> But in his motion like an angel sings,
> Still quiring to the young-eyed cherubins;
> Such harmony is in immortal souls;
> But whilst this muddy vesture of decay
> Doth grossly close it in, we cannot hear it."
> (The Merchant of Venice, V.1)

Only when the muddy vesture of decay is overcome, may man hear the "heavenly music" and perceive the truth. Nick Bottom in "A Midsummer Night's Dream" described such an experience during his journey into the fairyland[35]:

> "I have had a most rare
> vision. I have had a dream, past the wit of man to
> say what dream it was: man is but an ass, if he go
> about to expound this dream. Methought I was -there
> is no man can tell what. Methought I was,- and
> methought I had, -but man is but a patched fool, if
> he will offer to say what methought I had. The eye
> of man hath not heard, the ear of man hath not
> seen, man's hand is not able to taste, his tongue
> to conceive, nor his heart to report, what my dream
> was." (A Midsummer Night's Dream, IV.1)

Bottom's experience in the fairyland was not some inexplicable wonder or an accidental miracle that "no eye has heard, no ear has seen". Bottom's journey to the fairyland was precisely designed for a specific purpose. Only a highly developed man would be capable of discharging such a purpose. A highly developed man is a person with fully developed inner faculties which transcend the ordinary physical senses: one who can hear a new music, see a new colour, and smell a new fragrance. Bottom's description "the eye of man

---

[35] "The guide" (Shakespeare for the Seeker, Volume 4, Chapter 8.3)

hath not heard, the ear of man hath not seen" symbolically alludes to such experiences.

As illustrated in the story about the horseman and the sleeping man, hostility of the guide is like a medicine for a sick soul. By the same token, the friendship of a fool is poison and a source of misery. The friendship of a fool is worse than his enmity:

> A kind man, seeing a dragon overcoming a bear, went to the bear's assistance and delivered him from the dragon. The bear was so touched by the kindness the man had done him that he followed him about wherever he went. The bear became the man's faithful slave, guarding him from everything that might annoy him. A certain passer-by asked the man what was the relationship between him and the bear. The man recounted the adventure and the story of the dragon. The passer-by warned him, saying 'O fool! Do not set your heart on a bear; the bear ought to be driven away by every means you know'. The passer-by offered his hand to guide the man along his journey. But the man ignored the warning and did not accept the offer. He was more concerned about the bear. For sure, he was of the same kind as the bear. In his ignorance he suspected the sage and deemed the bear to be affectionate and just. (Book II, 2010-2166)

In Whinfield's translation, the following conclusion is included:

> One day the man was lying asleep, and the bear, according to his custom, was sitting by him and driving off the flies. The flies became so persistent in their annoyances that the bear lost patience, and seizing the largest stone he could find, dashed it at them in order to crush them utterly. But unfortunately the flies escaped. The stone landed upon the sleeper's face and crushed it.

94

Shylock in Shakespeare's "The Merchant of Venice" demonstrated a similar attitude as the friend of the bear. Instead of exercising mercy, which would put him in the hand of a guide, he put his trust into the Venetian law:

> "The pound of flesh, which I demand of him,
> Is dearly bought; 'tis mine and I will have it.
> If you deny me, fie upon your law!
> There is no force in the decrees of Venice.
> I stand for judgment: answer; shall I have it?"
> (The Merchant of Venice, IV.1)

Shylock used a canny logic to present himself as the product of lessons taught him by the cruelty of Venetian citizens. He cleverly justified his quest for vengeance and schemed to have his revenge by ruthlessly demanding a pound of Antonio's flesh. In reality, he shrewdly planned to murder Antonio, so he would be able to protect and expand his business[36]. This is why, at the end of the play, the Venetian law served him as well as the bear managed to protect the man.

2.9 The Landlord and the Three Friends

One may continue the journey only with the presence of friends. But how can a true friend be recognized? Rumi gives the following advice:

> "As long as an inner eye is not granted to you, think always that the treasure may be in everybody." (Book II, 2155)

---

[36] "Villains" (Shakespeare for the Seeker, Volume 3, Chapter 6.4)

Rumi illustrates the role of friends in the following story:

> A landlord saw three men walking in his orchard. These
> three men were a jurist, a nobleman, and a dervish. He
> thought that they were thieves. Knowing he could not
> prevail against them while they remained united, he
> contrived by tricks to separate them. So he proceeded to
> get rid of them one by one. He said to the dervish, 'Go to
> the house and bring a rug for these companions of yours'.
> When the dervish was gone, the landlord approached the
> other two men. He told them, 'One of you is a man of
> knowledge and the other is a prince; but what is this vile
> and greedy dervish doing among you? Drive him away
> when he comes back, and then take possession of my
> orchard and field for a week'. Once the dervish was
> driven away by his two companions and was alone, the
> landlord approached him and beat him badly. Afterwards,
> the landlord told the nobleman to go to the house and ask
> a servant to fetch some bread and goose for breakfast.
> When the nobleman was gone, the landlord told the jurist
> that it was obvious that he was knowledgeable and
> therefore deserved respect. 'But your friend', he
> continued, 'only pretends to be a nobleman; his mother
> probably was fooling around with many men and who
> knows who was his real father'. The jurist became
> enraged, attacked the nobleman and drove him away from
> the orchard. Now the jurist was alone, so the landlord was
> able to get rid of him as well. The jurist remarked, 'This is
> the fit penalty for him that parts from friends'. (Book II,
> 2167-2211)

It is not so easy to recognize a true friend. But man should not give
up his search, because this treasure, i.e., the Friend, exists in the
world. Therefore, he should not deem a ruin as a place empty of
treasure. Man should make friends. And when he starts to

recognize a mark of wisdom in his friend, he should become his constant companion. The jurist, the nobleman, and the dervish represent three basic aspects of a spiritual traveller. The dervish represents that aspect that propels man to seek knowledge. The jurist provides the basic rules needed to move forward. The nobleman illustrates an inner latent aspect that needs to be activated. When only one of them is predominant, man cannot find his way. But when all these three "friends" are correctly aligned and harmonized, they may lead man to his destination.

It is in this context that Shakespeare's explanation of the function of "friends" may be understood[37]. Here is a quote from "Timon of Athens":

> "O, no doubt, my good friends, but the gods
> themselves have provided that I shall have much help
> from you: how had you been my friends else? why
> have you that charitable title from thousands, did
> not you chiefly belong to my heart? I have told
> more of you to myself than you can with modesty
> speak in your own behalf; and thus far I confirm
> you. O you gods, think I, what need we have any
> friends, if we should ne'er have need of 'em? they
> were the most needless creatures living, should we
> ne'er have use for 'em, and would most resemble
> sweet instruments hung up in cases that keep their
> sounds to themselves. Why, I have often wished
> myself poorer, that I might come nearer to you. We
> are born to do benefits: and what better or
> properer can we call our own than the riches of our
> friends? O, what a precious comfort 'tis, to have
> so many, like brothers, commanding one another's
> fortunes! O joy, e'en made away ere 't can be born!"
> (Timon of Athens, I.2)

---

[37] "Friends" (Shakespeare for the Seeker, Volume 2, Chapter 4.3)

Timon says that the "friends" represent a unique group within humanity that is instrumental to the overall evolutionary progress. The process may continue only when there are "friends" who are capable of contributing to it constructively. Otherwise, any activity would be meaningless.

2.10 Bayazid and the Sage

A pilgrimage is a symbolic representation of the evolutionary process, i.e., the journey towards the source. The journey requires the traveller to pass through seven stages. In the following story, the stages are symbolically referred to as circling seven times around the guide:

> Bayazid of Bistam, a Persian sage who lived in the 9th century, was once making a pilgrimage to Mecca. In every city to which he went, he would at first search for the wise men. He desired to find the Sage of the Age. In one of the cities he spotted an old man who was sitting with his eye closed. Bayazid sat down before him. The man asked Bayazid where he was going and what provisions he took with him for the journey. Bayazid answered that he was making the pilgrimage to Mecca and that he had two hundred silver dirhams hidden in his cloak. The man told him to give him the money and to walk seven times around him. 'In this way', continued the man, 'your greater pilgrimage would be performed and your desires achieved'. Bayazid did as he was told. He arrived at the destination of his spiritual journey because of his inner readiness: he was able to recognize in the old man the Sage of the Age. (Book II, 2212-2455)

Rumi comments that if one does not have the proper understanding and knowledge, he is not able to distinguish dung from aloe-wood. This is why it is the guide who chooses his disciple and makes himself known to him.

The story points out that the guide may compress time, if required, and may "load" a few developmental stages into a single event. Shakespeare described such an event in "As You Like It". It was Oliver, a character that appears in the play, who passed through the seven stages of his journey within a single moment[38]. Here is Rosalind's account of that event:

> "There was never any thing so sudden but the fight of
> two rams
> and Caesar's thrasonical brag of 'I came, saw, and
> overcame:' for your brother and my sister no sooner
> met but they looked, no sooner looked but they
> loved, no sooner loved but they sighed, no sooner
> sighed but they asked one another the reason, no
> sooner knew the reason but they sought the remedy;
> and in these degrees have they made a pair of stairs
> to marriage which they will climb incontinent, or
> else be incontinent before marriage: they are in
> the very wrath of love and they will together; clubs
> cannot part them." (As You Like It, V.2)

Rosalind listed the seven developmental stages, i.e., they (1) met, (2) looked, (3) loved, (4) sighed, (5) asked, (6) knew, and (7) sought. And "in these degrees" Oliver and Rosaline's sister "made a pair of stairs" leading to the happy union.

---

[38] "The process" (Shakespeare for the Seeker", Volume 2, Chapter 5.2)

2.11 The Caliph and the Whisperer

After finding and recognizing one's spiritual guide, the seeker is given a number of tools needed for the continuation of his journey. Meditations and prayers are among those tools. In the following story, Rumi describes various aspects of prayer.

> One day, the Caliph was lying asleep in his palace. The palace door was locked from the inside, because the Caliph was fatigued by visitors. Suddenly, he was awakened by a strange apparition. The Caliph asked him who he was, and the apparition replied that he was the Whisperer, i.e., the Devil himself. The Caliph then enquired why he had awakened him, and the apparition replied that the hour of prayer had come, and he feared that the Caliph would be late. The Caliph answered, 'No way! It could never be your intention to direct me in the right way. How can I trust a vile creature like you to be taking good care of my soul?' The apparition whispered, 'Remember that I was bred up as an angel and that I cannot quite abandon my original occupation. You may travel to Turkey or China, but still you retain the love of your homeland. In the same way I still retain my duty to God. I revolted against Him, but that was only from jealousy of Adam. And jealousy proceeds from love, not from denial of obedience to His command. Although I was utterly ruined, in my miserable state I still discharge my duty to God'. The Caliph thought that the Whisperer's words were not credible. His words were like the decoy calls of a fowler, which resemble the voices of the birds in order to lure them to their destruction. The Whisperer caused the destruction of hundreds of mortals, such as the people of Noah, the tribe of Ad, the family of Lot, Nimrod, Pharaoh, and so on. But the Whisperer continued his whispering, 'You are mistaken if you

suppose me to be the cause of all the evil you are thinking about. I am not able to make good evil or fair foul. Mercy and vengeance are twin Divine attributes, and they generate good and evil as seen in all earthly creatures. I am, therefore, not to be blamed for the existence of evil. I am only a mirror, which reflects the good and evil existing in the objects presented to it. God has made me an informer and truth teller, so I may tell where the ugly one is and where the beautiful'. The Caliph then prayed to be guarded against the sophistries of the Whisperer. And again, he requested the Whisperer to tell him plainly the reason why he had awakened him. The Whisperer, instead of answering, continued to justify himself, saying how hard it was that men and women should blame him when they did something wrong, instead of blaming their own evil desires. The Caliph, in reply, reproached him with concealing the truth. Ultimately, the Caliph brought him to confess why he had awakened him. The true reason was that should the Caliph had overslept and so missed the hour of prayer, he would have felt deep sorrow and have heaved many sighs. And each of these sighs would have counted for as many as two hundred prayers. Driven by his envy, the Whisperer wanted to prevent the Caliph from such a gain. The Whisperer, therefore, was tempting the Caliph to do a good deed for the purpose of driving him away from a better deed. (II.2456-3026)

In "Othello", Shakespeare illustrated another example of how the Whisperer was outmanoeuvred. Othello was a guide who arrived in Venice with the purpose of advancing the process within the Italian branch of the modern evolutionary cycle. Othello used the Whisperer to help him implement his plan. The Whisperer was personalized by the character of Iago. Iago was presented as a "fallen" disciple. At the beginning of the play, Iago was the most advanced disciple of Othello. Iago was capable of seeing and understanding things that were still hidden to other disciples. His knowledge applied to events in the past, the present, and the future. Nevertheless it was Cassio, a scholar, who was promoted by Othello to be second in command. Iago could not be "promoted" because, despite his skills, he was entirely driven by his selfish tendencies. It was then that Iago decided that he was developed enough to be his own master and he was going to prove it:

> "I follow him to serve my turn upon him:
> We cannot all be masters, nor all masters
> Cannot be truly follow'd."(Othello, I.1)

Iago's ambition to be his own master was the real driving force behind his actions. His main and only objective was to disturb the developmental process that was implemented by Othello. Iago acted as a "whisperer who withdraws after his whispering". Iago's actions were constructed in such a way that they would affect a hearer according to this hearer's inner state. His means were rather limited to a marginal degree of deceptive emphasis and biased presentation. Very often his actions were simplistic, naïve, and even ridiculous. Nevertheless they seemed to be quite effective. Of course Othello was aware of Iago's objective and of his skills. Therefore, he adapted his approach in such a way that Iago's motivations became a part of Othello's plan. In this way Othello was able to discharge his function in accordance with his own objective[39].

---

[39] "Iago – the whisperer" (Shakespeare for the Seeker, Volume 3, Chapter 6.2)

2.12 The Four Men

The current evolutionary stage is the result of the previous ones. Therefore, man should try to learn from the experiences of the earlier generations. It would be a total waste of time not to learn from the previous mistakes. Rumi illustrates this in the following story:

> Four men went to the mosque to say their prayers. Each one duly performed the prescribed ritual. During their prayers a muezzin, i.e., the person appointed to call to the prayer, happened to come in. One of the men interrupted his prayers and called out, 'Have you yet called to prayer? It is time to do so'. Then the second man addressed the first one, 'By speaking to him you have spoiled your prayers'. Thereupon the third man scolded him saying, 'O simpleton, why do you rebuke him? Rather rebuke yourself'. Last of all, the fourth man said, 'Thanks to God that I have not committed the same error as my three companions'. In this way the prayers of all four men were marred. All four faultfinders went astray more than the man who made the original mistake. A mistake by another is a warning. He makes an error, so you may profit by avoiding it. (Book II, 3027-3086)

An exchange between Gratiano and Shylock in "The Merchant of Venice" is Shakespeare's version of the Four Men:

Gratiano:

"Can no prayers pierce thee?"

Shylock:

"No, none that thou hast wit enough to make."
(The Merchant of Venice, IV.1)

Shylock implied that he himself, but not Gratiano, was capable of making an effective prayer[40].

2.13 The Old Man and the Physician

By developing his inner being, man may escape from spiritual death. Ordinary life, spent pursuing worldly desires, is simply the preparation of food for worms. This is why investing into inner development should be at the expense of earthly desires. Rumi advises the readers, 'Let the body fade away while the inner being accumulates true riches. In this way, the inner being may be fed on death, while death is fed on ordinary men'. This is further explained in the following story:

> An old man complained to his physician that he suffered from headache. The physician replied, 'That is caused by old age'. The old man next complained of a defect in his sight, and the physician again told him that his malady was due to old age. The old man went on to say that he suffered from pain in his back, from indigestion, from shortness of breath, and so on. The physician replied that each of these ailments was likewise caused by old age. The old man, losing patience, said, 'O fool, know you not that God has ordained a remedy for every malady?' The physician answered, 'This passion and choler are also symptoms of old age. Since all your parts are weak, you have lost the power of self-control, therefore you fly into impatience at every word'. The physician gave the description of an ordinary man. For ordinary man, like the old man in the story, there is no cure for his illness.

---

40 "Villains" (Shakespeare for the Seeker, Volume 3, Chapter 6.4)

He cannot retain one draught of spiritual wine. He vomits
it. The developed man, on the other hand, is made wise
by drinking wine. Outwardly he may be old, but within he
is young. He is the guide. It is because of the presence of
the guides that humanity is sustained. The only true
Mecca is the hearts of the guides. The inner essence of
the guide is the place of worship of all. (Book II, 3087-
3175)

In his Sonnet 18, Shakespeare gave a similar description of the
guide and his function:

"Shall I compare thee to a Summer's day?
Thou art more lovely and more temperate:
Rough winds do shake the darling buds of May,
And Summer's lease hath all too short a date:
Sometime too hot the eye of heaven shines,
And often is his gold complexion dimm'd,
And every fair from fair some-time declines,
By chance, or nature's changing course untrimm'd:
But thy eternal Summer shall not fade,
Nor lose possession of that fair thou owest,
Nor shall death brag thou wander'st in his shade,
When in eternal lines to time thou growest"
(Sonnet 18, 1-12)

Shall the poet compare his guide to a summer day? But the guide is
much lovelier, says the poet, and much more pleasant. Rough
winds are able to shake off the pretty buds of May, and summer
doesn't last long enough. Sometimes the sun is unpleasant because
it is too hot, and often its golden face is covered by clouds. And
everything that is beautiful, at one point stops to be attractive,
either by accident or as a result of seasonal changes. But the guide's

presence is eternal and his beauty everlasting. He is able to prolong lives, therefore death does not brag that it is able to conquer him[41].

2.14 The Arab and the Scholar

There are two types of knowledge. One type is of an evolutionary nature, the other aims at different goals. The evolutionary or objective knowledge is created by developed men, who overcame their own egos and act according to the greater design. Therefore, they are able to express the essence of knowledge. Objective knowledge opens a way towards evolutionary advances. The other form of knowledge is as necessary as objective knowledge, but there is a functional difference between them. Conventional knowledge is like self-advertisement: it flourishes only when it manages to find a purchaser. On its own it is very much limited. The story of "The Arab and the Scholar" illustrates how these two types of knowledge may be recognized:

> An Arab of the desert loaded his camel with two sacks, filling one with wheat and the second with sand, in order to balance the first. As he was proceeding on his way he met a scholar, who questioned him about the content of his sacks. On learning that one contained useless sand, he pointed out that it might be much better by putting half the wheat in one sack and half in the other. In this way the overall load will be greatly lightened. On hearing this, the Arab was so struck by the scholar's cleverness that he conceived a great respect for him. And feeling sorry for the fatigued man, the Arab resolved to mount him on his camel. Then he said, 'As you possess such great wisdom, I

---

[41] "Shakespeare's Sonnets or How heavy do I journey on the way" (Sonnet 18)

presume that you are a king or a vizier'. 'I am neither of these two', replied the scholar, 'I am of the common folk. Look at my appearance and dress'. The Arab continued his interrogation, 'Tell me then how many camels do you have? Or what kind of goods do you keep in your shop?' The scholar replied, 'I have neither these nor those'. The Arab asked, 'How much money do you have? You are one of those solitary wanderers. Within you is the elixir which changes the copper of the world into gold. Your understanding and knowledge are inlaid with pearls!' Said the scholar, 'I am a very poor man; all the riches my learning has brought me are weariness and headaches. I know not where to look for a loaf of bread'. The Arab said, 'In that case get off my camel and go your way for I see your learning brings ill luck. Take far away from me your unlucky wisdom. If you go in that direction, then I will run in this direction. One sack of wheat and the other of sand is better for me than this vain contriving'. (Book II, 3176-3335)

An example of the operation of objective knowledge is given by Shakespeare in an episode with Lord Cerimon, who appears in "Pericles, Prince of Tyre". Here is Lord Cerimon's explanation of the nature of objective knowledge:

"Virtue and cunning were endowments greater
Than nobleness and riches: careless heirs
May the two latter darken and expend;
But immortality attends the former.
Making a man a god. 'Tis known, I ever
Have studied physic, through which secret art,
By turning o'er authorities, I have,
Together with my practise, made familiar
To me and to my aid the blest infusions
That dwell in vegetives, in metals, stones;

And I can speak of the disturbances
That nature works, and of her cures; which doth give me
A more content in course of true delight
Than to be thirsty after tottering honour,
Or tie my treasure up in silken bags,
To please the fool and death."
(Pericles, Prince of Tyre, III.2)

According to Lord Cerimon, virtue and inner capacity are gifts superior to titles and riches. Because through exercising virtue and innate capacity it is possible to attain immortality and become a man of God. Lord Cerimon demonstrates his understanding by knowing what is possible and what is impossible. For example, he knew that he could not do anything to help his visitor's master:

"Your master will be dead ere you return;
There's nothing can be minister'd to nature
That can recover him."
(Pericles, Prince of Tyre, III.2)

Yet, a moment later when a casket was brought to his house, he instantly knew what it contained:

"If the sea's stomach be o'ercharged with gold,
'tis a good constraint of fortune it belches upon us."
(Pericles, Prince of Tyre, III.2)

The casket contained the dead body of Thaisa. By exercising his knowledge, Lord Cerimon was able to bring Thaisa back to life[42].

---

[42] "Protection" (Shakespeare for the Seeker, Volume 2, Chapter 4.1)

2.15 The Man who boasted

True knowledge cannot be described nor can it be expressed by ordinary means. This knowledge, in its unperturbed form, can only be provoked, experienced and cultivated. Spiritual technology allows to bridge the gap between an inexpressible holistic experience and the working of the hard-and-fast linear way of ordinary thinking. Rumi explains that everything on the Earth exists because it has an origin in another dimension, where that thing is perfect and where the multiplicity of forms exists as unity. This is why a guide regards things "of the world" as being valuable only as far as they help towards experiencing their inner meaning. Interest in the phenomenal world that is separated from such framework is regarded as prone to developing into a form of idolatry. In this context, idolatry is the technical term used for fixations and conditioned reactions. This is why a guide diagnoses as fetishists those people who rigorously follow the externals form of worship. Rumi gives an example of such an attitude in the following story.

> At the time of Jethro, i.e., the father-in-law of Moses, a man was boasting that he had many faults and committed many wrong actions, yet God did not punish him for them. Jethro addressed the man saying that he was a fool. Jethro told the man that he was following the wrong way and as the result got lost and ended up in the wilderness. He continued saying that his heart became covered by layers and layers of rust and because of that he was blind to the signs of his punishment. His heart became like a blackened kettle; when the kettle had been blackened, it was impossible to perceive the effect of the smoke upon it. In response, the man asked him, 'If God punished me, what was the form of that punishment?' Jethro cried out desperately, 'O Lord! He rebuts me; he seeks the sign of that punishment'. At that moment Jethro heard a voice

saying, 'One sign of My punishing him is that he has not
made any progress along the way despite his prayers,
almsgiving, and fasting. He performs many acts and deeds
of devotion. However, he has not experienced even one
moment of spiritual delight. Spiritual delight is needed so
devotions may bear fruits. His devotions only appear to
be good in their external form, but their spiritual value is
naught'. (Book II, 3336-3505)

An indiscriminate application of outward laws manifests itself,
among other things, by the implementation of rigid, severe,
dogmatic but ineffective measures. Shakespeare's play "Measure
for Measure" illustrates the limitations of such an approach. The
character of Angelo in "Measure for Measure" is presented as an
authoritarian deputy, who immersed himself in the indiscriminate
application of the outward form of the law:

"We must not make a scarecrow of the law,
Setting it up to fear the birds of prey,
And let it keep one shape, till custom make it
Their perch and not their terror."
(Measure for Measure, II.1)

The indiscriminate application of the law does not lead to a
meaningful change of the distractive characteristics. Angelo's
himself is immune to the effects of the law, which he tries to
impose on others. Angelo's "inner shrew" manifests itself as soon
as he is provided with the means to exercise his power[43]. Angelo's
flawed modus operandi is exposed during his encounters with
Isabella. Here is Isabella's rebuke of Angelo's false claim:

"Could great men thunder
As Jove himself does, Jove would ne'er be quiet,
For every pelting, petty officer

---

[43] "Angelo" (Shakespeare for the Seeker, Volume 4, Chapter 7.2)

Would use his heaven for thunder;
Nothing but thunder! Merciful Heaven,
Thou rather with thy sharp and sulphurous bolt
Split'st the unwedgeable and gnarled oak
Than the soft myrtle: but man, proud man,
Drest in a little brief authority,
Most ignorant of what he's most assured,
His glassy essence, like an angry ape,
Plays such fantastic tricks before high heaven
As make the angels weep; who, with our spleens,
Would all themselves laugh mortal."
(Measure for Measure, II.2)

In her comment, Isabella compares Angelo's obsession with the execution of the law to tricks played by "an angry ape".

2.16 The Insatiable Dervish

As long as one's inner shrew dominates one's thinking and action, it is impossible to know what is right and what is wrong. Conventionally, some rigid and simplified rules are used as guidance. Ordinary man believes that by conforming to such rules he is advancing. It may be necessary to conform to certain kinds of expected behaviour in order to learn something. But when this conformism becomes the only driving force, evolutionary progress is inhibited. Instead of learning, man is just practising conformism. This is why a guide may deliberately court opprobrium, not for masochistic or attention-arousing purposes, but in order to show others how readily they will respond to his outward behaviour, without understanding its meaning. An example of such a teaching is illustrated in the following story.

In a certain convent there lived a dervish whose conduct
was offensive to all the brethren. They brought him
before their Sheikh and thus accused him, 'This dervish
has three very bad qualities; he babbles exceedingly like a
bell, he eats more than twenty men, and when he sleeps
he snores like a bear'. The Sheikh admonished the
dervish, insisting on the obligation of keeping a balance
between extremes. But the dervish excused himself on the
grounds that balance is relative. What is excess in one
man is moderation in another; he who is led by an
evolutionary inner voice is no longer subject to the
outward law. It is his 'inner voice' which rules his
conduct. In other words, balance is relative and depends
on the man's spiritual attainment. (Book II, 3506-3640)

In a similar manner, Petruchio in Shakespeare's "The Taming of
the Shrew" seemingly humiliated Katharina, his wife-to-be, by
arriving late for their wedding. He arrived riding on a broken-down
horse. He looked and behaved like a clown. By no means, however,
was he ignoring her or the wedding ceremony. Quite the contrary,
he was very well prepared for it. He arrived dressed in an elaborate
although ridiculous outfit:

> "Petruchio is coming in a new hat and an old
> jerkin, a pair of old breeches thrice turned, a pair
> of boots that have been candle-cases, one buckled,
> another laced, an old rusty sword ta'en out of the
> town-armory, with a broken hilt, and chapeless;
> with two broken points: his horse hipped with an
> old mothy saddle and stirrups of no kindred;
> besides, possessed with the glanders and like to mose
> in the chine; troubled with the lampass, infected
> with the fashions, full of wingdalls, sped with
> spavins, rayed with yellows, past cure of the fives,
> stark spoiled with the staggers, begnawn with the

bots, swayed in the back and shoulder-shotten;
near-legged before and with, a half-chequed bit
and a head-stall of sheeps leather which, being
restrained to keep him from stumbling, hath been
often burst and now repaired with knots; one girth
six time pieced and a woman's crupper of velure,
which hath two letters for her name fairly set down
in studs, and here and there pieced with packthread."
(The Taming of the Shrew, III.2)

Petruchio told Katharina that she was marrying him and not his clothes. He indicated that the man beneath the attire was not the same as the attire itself. When later in the play her dress was the issue, he told her:

"Our purses shall be proud, our garments poor;
For 'tis the mind that makes the body rich;
And as the sun breaks through the darkest clouds,
So honour peereth in the meanest habit.
What is the jay more precious than the lark,
Because his fathers are more beautiful?
Or is the adder better than the eel,
Because his painted skin contents the eye?
O, no, good Kate; neither art thou the worse
For this poor furniture and mean array."
(The Taming of the Shrew, IV.3)

By behaving in such a way, Petruchio was able to produce a certain constructive effect on those around him. It was an example of the shock technique, by which a disciple is exposed to a certain impact that affects his or her inner being. Petruchio did not care about himself and what others would think about him. This was not of his concern. His aim was the same as that of the insatiable dervish, i.e., to help others realize that there is another way of looking at the situation, another way of thinking, another way of evaluating themselves and those around them[44].

2.17 The Tree of Life

Reality, although single in its essence, is the source of thousands of derivative effects. Everlasting life is the least of its effects. Whoever attaches himself to names and clings to concepts without being able to see that these derivative things are only stages, sometimes barriers to understanding, stays at the stage of secondary things. He remains in a sub-culture of emotional stimulus, fantasy and dogmatic beliefs. One should abandon looking for externals and instead start to look for the essence. Rumi explains this in the following story:

> A certain wise man related that in India there was a tree of such wonderful virtue that whosoever ate of its fruit would live forever. Hearing this, a king sent one of his courtiers to go in quest of it. The courtier accordingly went to India. He traveled all over that country, inquiring of every one he met where this tree was to be found. Some of these persons professed their ignorance, others made fun of him, and others gave him false information. Years passed in this way, until the courtier lost all his hope of success, and made the decision to return to the royal court and confess his dismal failure. As a last resource, however, he stopped to see the sage who had first spoken of the tree. He begged him for further information about it. The sage laughed at him and said, 'O simpleton, this is the tree of knowledge that resides in

---

[44] "Taming school" (Shakespeare for the Seeker, Volume 3, Chapter 6.5)

the sage. Because you have taken as your aim images and forms, i.e., secondary names for things, you have not been able to find what lies beyond. It has many names: it may be called the Water of Life, the Sun, an Ocean and even a Cloud. But the emblem is not the thing itself. And the sage explained that the courtier's search was in vain because instead of looking for reality he was going after the form. This reality has hundreds of thousands of names. But the sage is one being. (Book II, 3641-3765)

The Syracusian brother in Shakespeare's "The Comedy of Errors" also embarked on a journey in his quest for the "ocean". He compared himself to a drop of water seeking another drop in the ocean[45]:

> "I to the world am like a drop of water
> That in the ocean seeks another drop,
> Who, falling there to find his fellow forth,
> Unseen, inquisitive, confounds himself."
> (The Comedy of Errors, I.2)

In his Sonnets Shakespeare also realized that his guide represented all guides from the past. The guide was a carrier and transmitter of the entire spectrum of evolutionary energy. In Sonnet 31, for example, he indicated that his guide represented all spiritual guides of the past ("thy bosom is endeared with all hearts")[46]:

> "Thy bosom is endeared with all hearts,
> Which I by lacking have supposed dead,
> And there reigns Love and all Love's loving parts,
> And all those friends which I thought buried.
> How many a holy and obsequious tear
> Hath dear religious love stol'n from mine eye,

---

[45] "Entanglement" (Shakespeare for the Seeker, Volume 2, Chapter 4.4)
[46] "Shakespeare's Sonnets or How heavy do I journey on the way" (Sonnet 31)

As interest of the dead, which now appear,
But things removed that hidden in thee lie.
Thou art the grave where buried love doth live,
Hung with the trophies of my lovers gone,
Who all their parts of me to thee did give,
That due of many, now is thine alone.
    Their images I loved, I view in thee,
    And thou (all they) hast all the all of me."
    (Sonnet 31)

All modes of evolutionary energies are encompassed within the guide's essence. Because of his spiritual ignorance, the poet was assuming that the guides of the past were gone. It seems that the poet used to follow a doctrine that was focused on an outdated teaching from previous times. He then discovered that all that he needed might be found in his guide. The poet referred to the previous guides as lovers, whose essence was preserved within his guide's heart. All the love that the poet offered them previously, was inherited by his guide. The poet recognized that all that he was looking for previously was contained within the heart of the presently living guide.

2.18 The Duckling who was brought up by a Hen

In the last story of Book 2, Rumi explains that ordinary man is like a duckling being nursed by a domestic hen:

> The duckling's nurse was an earthly and land-bound hen.
> The duckling picked-up his attachment to the land from
> his nurse. Because she was afraid of water, his nurse was
> not an appropriate counsellor. The duckling's real mother
> was a duck of the sea. In the duckling's heart was buried a

strong desire for the sea. In order to fulfil his desire, the
duckling had to leave his nurse and look for the sea.
(Book II, 3766-3810)

Rumi comments that man has to break his earthly attachment if he
desires to fulfill his evolutionary purpose. Man's body belongs to
the animal world; his inner being is angelic in nature. So man may
walk on the earth and also in the sky. His body is on the earth; but
his inner being is capable of reaching the heavenly spheres. To
arrive at the state of "angel", however, requires an extraordinary
personal effort. This means a personal struggle against the "shrew",
i.e., to free oneself from one's deceiving self and worldly
attachments.

Shakespeare used the character of young Prince Harry in his
History Plays to illustrate the transformation of "the ugly
duckling". Prince Harry, as a young man, spent most of his time in
taverns, hanging around vagrants and other shady characters.
Prince Harry's behaviour was a source of grief and disappointment
for his father. King Henry IV, Harry's father, like the duckling's
nurse, was afraid that his son was not fit to be a proper "hen", i.e.,
the future king of England. He even suspected that Prince Harry,
like the ugly duckling, was not from his own "nest":

> "Of my young Harry. O that it could be proved
> That some night-tripping fairy had exchanged
> In cradle-clothes our children where they lay."
> (Henry IV-Part 1, I.1)

At the moment of his father death, however, Prince Harry went
through a transformation that surprised all. Here is the Archbishop
of Canterbury's account of Prince Harry's transformation:

> "The breath no sooner left his father's body,
> But that his wildness, mortified in him,
> Seem'd to die too; yea, at that very moment

Consideration, like an angel, came
And whipp'd the offending Adam out of him,
Leaving his body as a paradise,
To envelop and contain celestial spirits.
Never was such a sudden scholar made;
Never came reformation in a flood,
With such a heady currance, scouring faults
Nor never Hydra-headed wilfulness
So soon did lose his seat and all at once
As in this king." (Henry V, I.1)

The transformation of young Harry affected his knowledge of theological matters, domestic policy, war strategy, and political topics. The rebirth of Harry was a puzzle to all, because the young Prince used to spend a lot of time drinking with uneducated, crude and superficial companions. He used to get drunk, seeking out entertainment, seemingly with no interest at all in learning or contemplation. In accordance with Rumi's allegorical language, this was a sort of organic transmutation. Such transformation may be compared to the appearance of a new flower, or a new tree that has taken root in the garden and is showing its first buds.

The transformation, however, could take place only once Prince Harry managed to detach himself from his "shrew", his deceiving self. Sir John Falstaff represented such a shrew. Sir John Falstaff had been Harry's close friend. He had been a jovial and drunken companion. But Shakespeare clearly indicates that those wild days served as preparatory training for Harry's transformation. Prince Harry knew very well that he was being trained. He knew that his purpose was to learn as much as possible about his "shrew". When the right time arrived, Harry was well prepared to leave behind his shrewish companion. After becoming king, Harry cut off his ties with him. Here are his last words to Falstaff:

"I know thee not, old man: fall to thy prayers;
How ill white hairs become a fool and jester!
I have long dream'd of such a kind of man,
So surfeit-swell'd, so old and so profane;
But, being awaked, I do despise my dream.
Make less thy body hence, and more thy grace;
Leave gormandizing; know the grave doth gape
For thee thrice wider than for other men.
Reply not to me with a fool-born jest:
Presume not that I am the thing I was;
For God doth know, so shall the world perceive,
That I have turn'd away my former self;
So will I those that kept me company.
When thou dost hear I am as I have been,
Approach me, and thou shalt be as thou wast,
The tutor and the feeder of my riots:
Till then, I banish thee, on pain of death,
As I have done the rest of my misleaders,
Not to come near our person by ten mile.
For competence of life I will allow you,
That lack of means enforce you not to evil:
And, as we hear you do reform yourselves,
We will, according to your strengths and qualities,
Give you advancement." (Henry IV-Part 2, V.5)

Harry had to leave his former companion behind because he was not able to perceive and understand the transformation that took place[47]. Therefore, he was not able to harmonize himself with this new phase of Harry's mission. Afterwards, as King Henry V, Harry was properly prepared to continue his journey.

---

[47] "Partial reformation" (Shakespeare for the Seeker, Volume 1, Chapter 1)

Book 3. Inner Being

In Book 3 Rumi illustrates various aspects of the inner being, without giving any specific description of it. Sometimes it is described as a beautiful mistress, a treasure, or a delectable prey. On other occasions it is referred to as an elephant, a falcon, or a camel. In his ordinary state man is not able to perceive the presence of his inner being. Nor does he have any idea about what it looks like or what it is capable of doing. At times, man gets this strange feeling that there is something within him, invisible but existing nevertheless.

Men, Rumi says, are like owls; they are waiting with one eye closed and one eye open, hoping that the delectable prey may appear. When the object of their chase appears from afar, they run towards it with all their might. When it vanishes from their sight, they become lost, "We wonder whether it was a real prey or a phantom". (Book III, 3724-3729)

3.1. The Travelers and the Young Elephant

An aspirant to higher knowledge is like a traveller who embarks upon a journey. During the journey he encounters many challenges. These challenges are the needed experiences that prepare him for the next stages of the journey. At the critical moments of his journey, the aspirant is provided with guidance and counsels. Only those who are able to perceive and act on those guidelines are able to continue their journey. The following story gives an example of the nature of such challenges.

> A party of travelers lost their way in a wilderness and were famished with hunger. While they were considering what to do, a sage came up and condoled with them on their unfortunate plight. He told them that he knew about their anguish, but warned them not to kill any young elephants that were in that area. He asked them to be content with herbs and leaves. He repeated that they should not go in chase of the young elephants, because the elephants' mother would track them down and revenge the killing of her offspring. Shortly afterwards the travelers saw a plump young elephant. They could not resist killing and eating it. Only one of the travellers refrained from eating it. Then they lay down to rest. But no sooner were they fast asleep, that a huge elephant made its appearance and proceeded to smell the breath of each one of the sleepers in turn. Those whom she perceived to have eaten of the young elephant's flesh she slew without mercy, sparing only the traveler who had been prudent enough to abstain. (Book III, 1-235)

A young elephant symbolizes the first trace of the manifestation of inner being. It is still too weak and too unstable to function correctly. Yet, it may seem to promise satisfaction for some desires. The travellers were advised by the sage to overcome their inner hunger and greed. Instead, they should be satisfied with that what was available to them at that time. But only one traveller was disciplined enough to follow the sage's counsel. He was able to perceive intuitively the importance of the sage's advice. So, his life was spared. He was able to continue his journey. As a matter of fact, it was the huge elephant that would carry him out of the wilderness and would deliver him to his next destination.

In "The Merchant of Venice", Shakespeare used the scene with the golden, silver and lead chests to illustrate how a disciple's intuitive perception was brought into operation. In this scene Bassanio had to choose the right chest[48]. Unlike the other contestants, Bassanio was able to put aside his rational and logical terms of reference ("gaudy gold" and "pale and common drudge"). He had to allow himself to be driven by his intuitive feeling ("thy paleness moves me more than eloquence"). Here is Bassanio's meditation while making his choice:

> "Therefore, thou gaudy gold,
> Hard food for Midas, I will none of thee;
> Nor none of thee, thou pale and common drudge
> 'Tween man and man: but thou, thou meagre lead,
> Which rather threatenest than dost promise aught,
> Thy paleness moves me more than eloquence;
> And here choose I; joy be the consequence!"
> (The Merchant of Venice, III.2)

It was his inner feeling that counted. This is why he was able to make the right choice ("And here choose I; joy be the consequence!") It was this inner quality that qualified Bassanio for discipleship.

3.2 The Villager and the Townsman

A disciple should pay attention to the moments when his inner being starts to operate. At such moments, the disciple should not mix-up the operation of the inner faculties with the ordinary faculties. Rumi compares the ordinary mind to a village. A town,

---

[48] "Bassanio's slip-ups" (Shakespeare for the Seeker, Volume 3, Chapter 6.4)

on the other hand, corresponds to the higher state of mind. In this context, following the promises of the ordinary mind is like abandoning the inner senses in order to enjoy the illusionary pleasures of the ordinary world.

> A certain villager paid a visit to the town and there received hospitality from one of the townsmen. At his departure the villager was profuse of thanks, and pressed the townsman to come and visit him with his family in his village. Having doubts as to the sincerity of the villager, the townsman hesitated long before accepting the invitation. But after ten years' solicitation he at length yielded. He set off with his family to the village. On his arrival the villager shut the door in his face. He said that he did not know the townsman. As the result, the townsman had to pass five nights in the cold and rain. At last, exhausted with suffering, he implored the villager to give him shelter, promising to render service in return. The villager granted it on condition that he would protect his garden from the wolves. The townsman accepted this condition, and taking a bow and arrows proceeded to patrol the garden. But because of the rain, the darkness and his own fears he ended up shooting the villager's pet ass mistaking it for a wolf. The villager abused him roundly, saying that he himself would not have taken an ass for a wolf, even on the darkest night. The townsman replied that the villager was a hypocrite because he could see his ass in the rain and in the darkness, yet he claimed that he could not recognize his friend of ten years' standing. (Book III, 236-720)

The Fool in Shakespeare's "King Lear" delivered a similar counsel to Kent, a nobleman at King Lear's court. The Fool warned Kent that he was being misguided by his ordinary senses[49]:

> "We'll set thee to school to an ant, to teach thee
> there's no labouring i' the winter. All that follow
> their noses are led by their eyes but blind men; and
> there's not a nose among twenty but can smell him
> that's stinking. Let go thy hold when a great wheel
> runs down a hill, lest it break thy neck with
> following it: but the great one that goes up the
> hill, let him draw thee after. When a wise man
> gives thee better counsel, give me mine again."
> (King Lear, II.4)

The Fool told Kent that he should use better senses than ordinary ones, because "that follow their noses are led by their eyes but blind men". Kent intended to follow the disgraced King Lear. The Fool told him that it would be foolish to do so. Because of his spiritual ignorance, King Lear could not discharge properly his evolutionary potentiality. Therefore, his role was downgraded. King Lear became like "a great wheel" that started to run down a hill. And it would be a waste of time to try to hold onto him, because he would "break thy neck with following it". Instead, there appeared a new opportunity that was going to move the process upwards. Therefore, Kent should follow "the great one".

---

[49] "The process" (Shakespeare for the Seeker, Volume 1, Chapter 3.1)

3.3 The Jackal who pretended to be a Peacock

The guides are exemplars of human perfection. They are like a perfected species among humans. They are not recognizable by ordinary men, because there is nothing special in their physical appearance. Yet, they are the custodians of the evolutionary process. They have been equipped with techniques, instruments, and methodologies allowing them to instruct men in how to fulfill their evolutionary potentiality. At the same time, they are the carriers of all available evolutionary energies. Sometimes a colour code is used to indicate the various modes of evolutionary energies. A multi-coloured robe is a symbolic indication of those various modes of energies. The jackal in the following story illustrates a pretender of such evolutionary capacity:

> A jackal fell into a dye-pit, and his skin was dyed in
> various colours. Proud of his splendid appearance, he
> returned to his companions, and desired them to address
> him as a peacock. But they proceeded to test his
> pretensions, saying, 'Do you scream like a peacock, or
> strut about gardens as peacocks do?' He was forced to
> admit that he did not, whereupon his pretension was
> rejected. (Book III, 721-839)

In accordance with the colour code, a man who has developed his inner being may be described as a man who is in control of all colours. In Shakespeare's Sonnet 99, the guide describes how roses of various colours were reflecting the poet's inner state:

> "The Roses fearfully on thorns did stand,
> One blushing shame, another white despair:
> A third nor red, nor white, had stol'n of both,
> And to his robbery had annexed thy breath,
> But for his theft, in pride of all his growth

A vengeful canker eat him up to death."
(Sonnet 99, 8-13)

The references to the roses are the symbolic indications of the evolutionary impacts to which the poet had been previously exposed[50]. The poet, like the jackal in Rumi's story, was not able to use these "colours" correctly. Namely, the red and white roses became just blushing and pale reflections of the poet's shame and despair. The yellow, i.e., the third rose, was a reflection of the poet's jealousy. It was this aspect that severely interfered with the process and prevented him from making the progress. This is why the third rose was also destroyed, i.e., "a vengeful canker eat him up to death".

3.4 Moses and Pharaoh

The ordinary, i.e., underdeveloped human mind is vulnerable to various "magical" tricks. The acceptance of the tricks reveals the weaknesses of undeveloped men. Through the development of his inner being, man becomes immune to magic. In other words, the effect of magic depends upon the state of mind of the participants. True miracles, on the other hand, are Divinely inspired. Only a spiritually developed man is capable of performing them. Rumi quotes an episode from the tradition of Moses to illustrate the difference between true miracles and magical tricks.

> Pharaoh saw in his dream the coming of Moses and that
> he would destroy his kingdom. Pharaoh's magicians
> promised him that they would thwart the conception of
> Moses. Their plot, however, failed. When Moses was

---

[50] "Shakespeare's Sonnets or How heavy do I journey on the way" (Sonnet 99)

conceived, a new star appeared in the sky. The Pharaoh accused his magicians of treachery and threatened to kill them. The magicians promised to trace down the newborn and kill him. But again, all their tricks failed to kill Moses. When Moses grew up, Pharaoh challenged Moses to combat with his magicians. By this demonstration he intended to make a fool of Moses in front of the entire population of Egypt. Pharaoh assembled his magicians and gave them robes of honours, presents, horses and money. He promised them more gifts if they would prevail over Moses. There were two young and very skilful magicians who heard Pharaoh's proclamation. They decided to challenge Moses. Before leaving to Egypt, they summoned their father's spirit and questioned him concerning the real nature of Moses. The father's spirit told them, 'O my dearest sons, it is not permitted to me to speak openly and freely, yet the mystery is not far from mine eye. I will tell you how you may find out about the nature of Moses' power. Go and seek the place where Moses sleeps. And when he is asleep, try to steal his magic rod. If you are able to steal it, then he is just a magician and you are both capable of dealing with him. But if you are not able to steal it, beware! Because this would mean that he is a Man of God and is Divinely guided'. The magician's sons kissed their father's grave and went away to Egypt to look for their fortune. In Egypt they sought for Moses and his house. It chanced that on the time of their arrival, Moses was asleep under a palm-tree. The magicians espied him but they did not realize that he was the fullest awake man in the world. For pleasure's sake he had shut his eyes, but all Heaven and Earth were under his gaze. Though his eyes were closed, his inner being was fully awake. The magicians approached saying, 'We must go behind him and snatch his rod from him'. When they got closer, the

rod began to shake. It started to tremble in such a way
that both magicians became petrified with terror. After
that, the rod turned into a dragon and attacked them.
They both fell on their faces panic stricken. They realized
that Moses was Divinely inspired. (Book III, 840-1258)

Pharaoh and the magicians represent aspects of a corrupted mind.
Their craft applies only to ordinary, i.e., underdeveloped men.
Rumi illustrates this further in the story of the snake-catcher:

A snake-catcher, who was following his occupation in the
mountains, discovered a large snake frozen by the cold.
He thought the snake was dead, but in reality it was alive.
It was frozen by frosts and snow. It only appeared to be
dead. Imagining that the snake was dead, the snake-
catcher tied it up and took it to Baghdad. He set up a
show on the bank of the Tigris. A tumult arose in the city
of Baghdad, 'A snake-catcher has brought a dragon; he
has captured a marvellous rare beast'. Myriads of
simpletons, who had become a prey to this foolish and
ignorant man, assembled. They were waiting to see the
dragon. And he was waiting for the large crowd of people
to come. In the meantime, thawed by the warmth of the
sun, the snake recovered life. The snake burst its bonds
and glided out roaring like a lion. The frightened
spectators started shrieking and fled en masse. Many of
them were killed in the rout. The snake-catcher became
paralysed with fear, crying, 'What have I brought from the
mountains and the desert?' The snake made one mouthful
of that blockhead. (Book III, 976-1064)

The snake-catcher, like a magician, uses snakes to amaze the
people. Rumi comments that man has an incredible potentiality for
development. But ordinary man does not recognize his own
potentiality. He does not know himself. Hundreds of thousands of

snakes and mountains are amazed at him: why then has he become amazed and fond of a snake? Every man contains within himself an inner Moses and an inner Pharaoh. Man's evolutionary potentiality corresponds to that of Moses. But his corrupted self, like Pharaoh, is driven by lust and earthly desires. Man must recognize these two competing forces within himself. The corrupted self may be asleep, but it is never dead. So long as that dragon remains frozen, all is well and good. But when the heat of lust strikes upon it, that vile dragon starts to flap its wings.

Shakespeare used the character of Prospero in "The Tempest" to illustrate the challenges of the struggle between the inner Moses and the inner Pharaoh. Prospero developed his inner being that gave him access to extraordinary powers. But he could use his power only for a specific evolutionary purpose against corrupted aspects. This put him in quite a challenging situation; he should not abuse his powers. At one point, however, he could not resist to show off his skills in front of his daughter Miranda and her beloved Ferdinand. Prospero called for the goddesses Ceres, Juno, and Iris to perform a masque celebrating the rites of marriage and the bounty of the earth[51]. The masque was a demonstration of Prospero's powers. By calling on Juno, Ceres, and Iris, he demonstrated that he could exercise his magic and control the goddesses. The masque, however, was not part of the process. Prospero arranged the masque simply to show off his powers in front of Ferdinand and Miranda. The masque marked Prospero's weakness. This is why during the masque the goddesses, like Pharaoh's magicians, were trying to trick Prospero and take advantage of his weakness. The goddesses brought the spirits called Naiads. The appearance of the Naiads was dangerous, because they could distract one's attention by their mystifying beauty. The Naiads arrived and danced. Prospero was greatly pleased with himself. He allowed himself to be driven by "some vanity":

---

[51] "Prospero's challenges" (Shakespeare for the Seeker, Volume 4, Chapter 8.1)

"… for I must
Bestow upon the eyes of this young couple
Some vanity of mine art: it is my promise,
And they expect it from me."
(The Tempest, IV.1)

Despite his relatively high developmental state and access to extraordinary powers, Prospero was not entirely free from egotistic desires. Because of this, he nearly lost his entire enterprise. At that very moment, Caliban, who like Pharaoh represents a degenerated inner self, was about to arrive and kill Prospero. At the last moment Prospero woke up from his fancies and managed to avoid making an error that could have turned his project into a complete fiasco. It was then that he realized that he needed his magical skills only as long as he was prone to his earthly desires. At the moment when he managed to free himself from such desires, he did not need his magic kit anymore:

"But this rough magic
I here abjure, and, when I have required
Some heavenly music, which even now I do,
To work mine end upon their senses that
This airy charm is for, I'll break my staff,
Bury it certain fathoms in the earth,
And deeper than did ever plummet sound
I'll drown my book."
(The Tempest, V.1)

Prospero broke his magic staff and drowned his secret book. These instruments of "rough magic" had a limited application. They were needed only while Prospero was still driven by his selfish desires. Prospero, like Moses, needed his magic staff only to deal with inferior forces. By breaking his staff and drowning his book, Prospero demonstrated that he purified himself from traces of egotistic desires.

By having Prospero "drowning" his secret book Shakespeare makes a reference to a similar episode from Rumi's life. When he met Shams of Tabriz, Rumi was sitting with his students by a fountain in Konya. On the fountain sill beside him were his books. Shams approached him and pushed the books into the water. When Rumi protested, Shams told him that it was now time for Rumi to experience what he was reading and talking about. But if he wanted to remain where he was right now, continued Shams, the books were still available to him. And Shams took out of the water one of the drowned books, which was completely dry. Like in the case of Prospero, this moment marked Rumi's transition onto the next phase of his spiritual journey.

3.5 The Elephant in a Dark House

The birth of a new man is realized through the development of his subtle faculties. The subtle faculties transcend the ordinary physical senses. Allegorically, the operation of the subtle faculties may be described as an experience that is beyond the eye, beyond the ear, beyond touch, beyond taste, beyond smell. But the activation of the subtle faculties is only a stage in the process. The next step requires fusing together the subtle faculties so they form the new inner being. The inner being is not perceivable by ordinary senses. In the following story, Rumi describes the inner being as the elephant in a dark room.

> Some travellers were exhibiting an elephant in a dark room. Many people arrived to see it. But the room was too dark to permit them to see the unknown to them beast. So they all tried to feel it with their hands to gain an idea of what it was like. One felt its trunk, and declared that the beast resembled a water-pipe. Another felt its ear,

and said it must be a large fan. Another touched its leg, and thought it must be a pillar. Another felt its back, and declared the beast must be like a great throne. According to the part which each of them felt, they gave a different description of the animal. (Book III, 1259-1404)

Ordinary sense-perception is only like the palm of the hand: the palm has no power to reach the whole of the elephant. In "Love's Labour's Lost" Shakespeare inserted a condensed version of "The Elephant in the Dark". Like Rumi, Shakespeare clearly states that the inner being is perceivable neither by the ordinary senses nor by the intellect. Shakespeare's description also provides a hint about the nature of the elephant and how it can be experienced[52]. The description was delivered by Berowne in his meditation on "Light". In this description, the elephant is compared to "the light of truth":

"As, painfully to pore upon a book
To seek the light of truth; while truth the while
Doth falsely blind the eyesight of his look:
Light seeking light doth light of light beguile:
So, ere you find where light in darkness lies,
Your light grows dark by losing of your eyes.
Study me how to please the eye indeed
By fixing it upon a fairer eye,
Who dazzling so, that eye shall be his heed
And give him light that it was blinded by.
Study is like the heaven's glorious sun
That will not be deep-search'd with saucy looks."
(Love's Labour's Lost, I.1)

In this quote Shakespeare says that the "elephant" ("the light of truth") is not learned from a book, because truth is incomprehensible to the ordinary intellect ("falsely blind the eyesight of his look"). The inner eye ("light seeking light") is

---

[52] "Technical background" (Shakespeare for the Seeker, Volume 2, Chapter 5.3)

needed, because the intellect is bewitched by truth ("doth light of light beguile"). So, before you find where wisdom is hidden ("where light in darkness lies"), your inner eye has to transcend the ordinary faculties ("by losing of your eyes"). Therefore, approach the "elephant" by focusing your attention upon the guide ("upon a fairer eye"). The guide is like a dazzling star, so the inner eye may recognize him ("that eye shall be his heed"). Then, he will pass onto you hidden wisdom ("give him light that it was blinded by"). This study is like looking at the heaven's glorious sun, which cannot be penetrated by the arrogant eyes ("will not be deep-search'd with saucy looks").

Berowne's meditation may also help to recognize Rumi's overall function. Namely, Rumi's function was encoded in his pen name. By using the system of equivalence of letters and numbers, the word RUMI may be substituted by the three letters NUR. "Nur" is the Persian word for "light". In other words, Rumi was "a fairer eye", therefore he was able to activate the "light of truth".

The system of equivalence of letters and numbers is often used in instrumental literature. For example, the episode with Scarus inserted by Shakespeare in "Antony and Cleopatra" may be explained by using that system. In this episode Scarus comes to Mark Antony and shows him the wound that he has received in the engagement. The wound was in the shape of the letter T; but then it changed its shape and became the letter H:

> "I had a wound here that was like a T,
> But now 'tis made an H."
> (Antony and Cleopatra, IV.7)

In this system the letters of the alphabet are assigned numerical values. For example, the letter H is equivalent to the number eight. The number eight corresponds to the geometrical figure of the octagon and it represents the "perfect balance":

"Here's eight that must take hands
To join in Hymen's bands,
If truth holds true contents."
(As You Like It, V.4)

In other words, the "eight" or the octagonal inner structure is needed "if truth holds true contents". Perfect balance means that the inner structure is based on purified and united inner faculties.

The letter T corresponds to the number nine and stands for inner or secret knowledge, sometimes represented by the enneagon, i.e., the octagon with a ninth point in its centre. Secret knowledge allows to access extraordinary powers. Extraordinary powers are available to man whose inner being has been transmuted in a certain way. The correct developmental sequence, therefore, requires achieving "perfect balance" as a necessary step leading toward "secret knowledge". This sequence is symbolically indicated as the transition of the letter H into the letter T. The above-quoted scene, however, shows the reverse sequence, i.e., the letter T changes into the letter H. This reverse sequence is used to indicate the danger associated with the attempt of employing secret knowledge before achieving inner harmony. Therefore, the message that was shown to Mark Antony was a warning that he was following the wrong way; his actions were going against the evolutionary sequence[53].

Shakespeare used the same system of equivalence of letters and numbers in the Dedication to the Sonnets. The dedication was addressed to Master W.H. It was signed by the letters T.T. In its symbolic meaning, the letters W and H indicate the first and the final stages of a spiritual journey, i.e., from initiation (W) to achieving inner balance (H). This means that the dedication is addressed to any traveler, who has entered onto the path. The symbolic meaning of the letter T is secret knowledge. It applies to

---

[53] "Rescue attempts" (Shakespeare for the Seeker, Volume 1, Chapter 2.3)

the custodians of the secret knowledge. In other words, the dedication was written by a guide[54].

3.6 The Poet and his Mistress

Rumi emphasizes the importance of recognizing the content from the container, i.e., essence from the form. A container may have many forms. In the case of poetry, it is its outward form, i.e., style, rhyme, composition, elegance, etc. The content, on the other hand, is the essence of truth, which may be stored or transmitted through poetry. In the following story, Rumi illustrates how preoccupation with the container has veiled the lover from recognizing his beloved.

> A lover was once admitted to the presence of his mistress but, instead of embracing her, he pulled out written sonnets. He started to read them to her, describing at length her perfections and charms and his own love towards her. His mistress said to him, 'You are now in my presence, and these lover's sighs and invocations are a waste of time. It is not the part of a true lover to waste his time in this way. It shows that I am not the real object of your affection, but that what you really love is your own effusions and ecstatic raptures. I see, as it were, the water before me which I have longed for and yet you withhold it. I am, as it were, in Bulgaria, and the object of your love is in China. One who is really loved is the single object of her lover, the Alpha and Omega of his desires. As for you, you are wrapped up in your own amorous ecstasy,

---

[54] "Shakespeare's Sonnets or How heavy do I journey on the way" (Dedication)

instead of being wrapped up in me'. (Book III, 1405-
1449)

Shakespeare used Malvolio in "Twelfth Night" as the caricature of
a lover who confused content with container. Malvolio also
misunderstood the principle of the Alpha and Omega. Malvolio is a
hypocrite, who expects that the supreme objective is to satisfy his
egotistic desires:

> "The devil a puritan that he is, or any thing
> constantly, but a time-pleaser; an affectioned ass,
> that cons state without book and utters it by great
> swarths: the best persuaded of himself, so
> crammed, as he thinks, with excellencies, that it is
> his grounds of faith that all that look on him love
> him." (Twelfth Night, II.3)

Malvolio dreams about getting married to Lady Olivia and
becoming a nobleman. Other members of Lady Olivia's household
decided to exploit Malvolio's self-love. They tricked Malvolio by
having him find a letter supposedly written to him by Olivia. Here
is Malvolio reading the letter:

> "Jove knows I love: But who?
> Lips, do not move;
> No man must know.
> 'No man must know.' What follows? the numbers
> altered! 'No man must know:' if this should be
> thee, Malvolio?"

> "I may command where I adore;
> But silence, like a Lucrece knife,
> With bloodless stroke my heart doth gore:
> M, O, A, I, doth sway my life."
> (Twelfth Night, II.5)

Malvolio easily falls into the trap. He convinces himself that Olivia's falling in love with him is:

> "Jove's doing, and Jove make me thankful!"
> (Twelfth Night, III.4)

His self-love does not allow him to see through the letter. Instead, Malvolio starts to believe that he himself is the one who "doth sway" Olivia's life. He naively imagines that the essence of truth can be transmitted through numerical or literary codes. He easily convinces himself that M, O, A, I is a code for his name:

> "M, -Malvolio; M,- why, that begins my name."

> "M, -but then there is no consonancy in the sequel; that suffers under probation A should follow but O does."

> "M, O, A, I; this simulation is not as the former: and yet, to crush this a little, it would bow to me, for every one of these letters are in my name."
> (Twelfth Night, II.5)

Shakespeare inserted a couple of clues that let the audience see through this "fustian riddle"[55]. The meaning of MOAI may be decoded by applying "the numbers altered!" and "no consonancy in the sequel". There are only two (Roman) numbers there, i.e., M and I. By removing these two numbers and then reversing the sequel of the remaining two letters, one may find out who "doth sway" Olivia's life: A and O. Like in Rumi's story, the Alpha and Omega, or the First and the Last, are a symbolic representation of the supreme priority. It is quite telling that the puritanical Malvolio, "that cons state without book and utters it by great swarths", corrupted this priority and entrusted it onto his earthly idol.

---

[55] "Malvolio" (Shakespeare for the Seeker, Volume 4, Chapter 7.1)

Incapable of understanding the spirit of the "letter", he corrupted its meaning and misused it to justify his own selfish desire.

3.7 The Man who prayed

Rumi stresses the fact that sincerity of intention is more important than the nature of the things asked for. The following story emphasizes the merit of sincerity.

> In the time of the Prophet David there was a man who used to pray day and night, saying, 'Thou hast created me weak and helpless; give me my daily bread without obliging me to work for it'. Thus he was praying for a long time, all day until night and all night until morning. The people were laughing at his words and at the folly of his hope and his approach. They were saying, 'What is this idiot saying?' They considered him to be a fool. But he still persisted with his prayers. At last a cow ran into his house of its own accord. The man killed it and ate it. (Book III, 1450-1509)

The same understanding of the merit of sincerity was illustrated by Shakespeare in "Henry V". Before the Battle of Agincourt, the Earl of Westmoreland expressed a wish that there would be more soldiers in King Henry's army:

> "O that we now had here
> But one ten thousand of those men in England
> That do no work to-day!" (Henry V, IV.3)

It was then that Henry V delivered his famous St. Crispin's Day speech in which he explained the merits of sincerity. King Henry declared that there was no place among his troops for insincere men:

> "No, faith, my coz, wish not a man from England:
> God's peace! I would not lose so great an honour
> As one man more, methinks, would share from me
> For the best hope I have. O, do not wish one more!
> Rather proclaim it, Westmoreland, through my host,
> That he which hath no stomach to this fight,
> Let him depart; his passport shall be made
> And crowns for convoy put into his purse:
> We would not die in that man's company
> That fears his fellowship to die with us.
> This day is called the feast of Crispian:
> He that outlives this day, and comes safe home,
> Will stand a tip-toe when the day is named,
> And rouse him at the name of Crispian.",
> (Henry V, IV.3)

There would be no advantage in having insincere men among the troops. Like insincere prayers, they would not be able to contribute constructively to the task at hand. Henry thus gave his soldiers the freedom to make the choice to fight with him or go home. But those who chose "to die with us" would be granted nobility. They would become brothers, and they would be elevated from their current lowly level of being[56]:

> "We few, we happy few, we band of brothers;
> For he to-day that sheds his blood with me
> Shall be my brother; be he ne'er so vile,
> This day shall gentle his condition:
> And gentlemen in England now a-bed
> Shall think themselves accursed they were not here,
> And hold their manhoods cheap whiles any speaks

---

[56] "Dawn of perfection" (Shakespeare for the Seeker, Volume 1, Chapter 1)

That fought with us upon Saint Crispin's day."
(Henry V, IV.3)

Henry's troops were able to rout the French despite the fact that they were outnumbered five to one. The Battle of Agincourt was used by Shakespeare to describe an example of the manifestation of Divine intervention. Only sincere men could experience it.

3.8 The Boys and their Schoolmaster

There is a difference between knowledge and imagination. Knowledge is like a bird with two wings. Imagination, or opinion, is like a one-winged bird: it is defective and curtailed in flight. The one-winged bird soon falls headlong; then again flies up some two paces or a little more. Just like that bird, opinion, by falling and rising, goes on with one wing in hope of reaching the nest. Those who have gained knowledge are delivered from imagination. They become two-winged: they spread their wings and fly straight to their destination. The following story illustrates the merit of knowledge as compared to the drawbacks of imagination.

> The boys in a certain school were suffering at the hands
> of their master from weariness and toil. They were trying
> to figure out how to get away from him. The smartest of
> them suggested that when the schoolmaster came into the
> school, each boy should condole with him on his alleged
> sickly appearance. The counsel of that boy was accepted;
> his intellect was superior to the other boys' wits.
> Following their plan, when the schoolmaster entered, one
> said, 'O master, how pale you are looking!' and another
> said, 'You are looking very ill today', and so on. The
> schoolmaster at first answered that there was nothing the

matter with him. But as one boy after another continued assuring him that he looked very ill, he was at length deluded into imagining that he must be really ill. So he returned to his house, making the boys follow him there. He told his wife that he was not well, bidding her mark how pale he was. His wife said, 'There is nothing wrong with you; this is only your vain imagination and opinion'. He responded angrily, 'O strumpet, are you disputing with me? Don't you see this change in my appearance?' His wife assured him that he was not looking pale, and offered to convince him by bringing a mirror. But he refused to look at it, and went to bed. He then ordered the boys to begin their lessons. The boys sat there, reciting their lesson, horribly disappointed. The clever boy said, 'O good fellows, recite the lesson and make your voices loud'. When they started to recite loudly, he said, 'Boys, the noise we are making will do the master harm. The master's headache will be increased by the noise'. The schoolmaster overhead the boy's comment and said, 'He is speaking the truth. My headache is getting worse. Get out of my house!' He dismissed them to their homes to the annoyance of their mothers. (Book III, 1510-1609)

Rumi takes the example of the smart boy to refute the opinion that all men are born with equal inner ability. According to that opinion, it is only experience and teaching that make men more or less capable. This is false, says Rumi, because the boy who had no experience in any course of action was able to devise a stratagem which the schoolmaster, with many years of experience, was incapable of detecting. The capacity that comes from one's inner nature is more valuable than the skills that are the result of experience and learning.

Shakespeare used the characters of Henry IV and his son, Prince Harry, to illustrate the difference between truth and opinion, and between innate capacity and acquired experience. Prince Harry, who appears in "Henry IV", spent most of his time in taverns, hanging around with a bunch of vagrants. King Henry was gravely concerned over the misbehaviour of his son. It is important to note that King Henry understanding of his son behaviour was not based on inner perception and knowledge. King Henry's evaluation of Prince Harry's actions was the result of his and others' opinions and his own previous experiences. Here is King Henry rebutting his son for not behaving correctly. In his rebuke, King Henry makes references to himself as Bolingbroke and he compares Prince Harry's behaviour to "the skipping king", i.e., the previous King Richard II:

"And art almost an alien to the hearts
Of all the court and princes of my blood:
The hope and expectation of thy time
Is ruin'd, and the soul of every man
Prophetically doth forethink thy fall.
Had I so lavish of my presence been,
So common-hackney'd in the eyes of men,
So stale and cheap to vulgar company,
Opinion, that did help me to the crown,
Had still kept loyal to possession
And left me in reputeless banishment,
A fellow of no mark nor likelihood.
By being seldom seen, I could not stir
But like a comet I was wonder'd at;
That men would tell their children 'This is he;'
Others would say 'Where, which is Bolingbroke?'
And then I stole all courtesy from heaven,
And dress'd myself in such humility
That I did pluck allegiance from men's hearts,
Loud shouts and salutations from their mouths,
Even in the presence of the crowned king.
Thus did I keep my person fresh and new;

My presence, like a robe pontifical,
Ne'er seen but wonder'd at: and so my state,
Seldom but sumptuous, showed like a feast
And won by rareness such solemnity.
The skipping king, he ambled up and down
With shallow jesters and rash bavin wits,
Soon kindled and soon burnt; carded his state,
Mingled his royalty with capering fools,
Had his great name profaned with their scorns
And gave his countenance, against his name,
To laugh at gibing boys and stand the push
Of every beardless vain comparative,
Grew a companion to the common streets,
Enfeoff'd himself to popularity;
That, being daily swallow'd by men's eyes,
They surfeited with honey and began
To loathe the taste of sweetness, whereof a little
More than a little is by much too much.
So when he had occasion to be seen,
He was but as the cuckoo is in June,
Heard, not regarded; seen, but with such eyes
As, sick and blunted with community,
Afford no extraordinary gaze,
Such as is bent on sun-like majesty
When it shines seldom in admiring eyes;
But rather drowzed and hung their eyelids down,
Slept in his face and render'd such aspect
As cloudy men use to their adversaries,
Being with his presence glutted, gorged and full.
And in that very line, Harry, standest thou."
(Henry IV-Part 1, III.2)

King Henry tells his son that he has almost completely alienated himself from the whole court and the other members of the royal family. The hopes and expectations that he had of his son have vanished. And every man secretly predicts Harry's downfall. King Henry says if he himself had appeared so often in public, so overly familiar to people, so freely accessible, so cheap and available to the common hordes, then public opinion, which helped him get the crown, would have stayed loyal to King Richard, the previous king. He would have stayed a banished man, with no reputation and no promise of success. But because he was so rarely seen in public, when he did appear they looked at him with amazement, as if he was a comet. Men would tell their children, 'That's him!' Others would ask, 'Where? Which one's Bolingbroke?' Then he assumed a courtly manner. He made himself look so humble that he won the loyalty of men's hearts. They even treated him as a royal in the presence of the crowned King Richard. He was like a ceremonial robe that is admired because it is so rarely seen. In the meantime, frivolous King Richard kept company with shallow and superficial companions. King Richard was quick with a joke but quickly out of jokes. He degraded his dignity, mixed his royalty with capering fools, had his great name disgraced with their scorn, and ruined his authority by laughing at the jokes of foolish boys. He spent his time in common places, surrendering himself to the pursuit of popularity. Soon, they saw him every day and it was like overdosing on honey: a little too much is as bad as far too much. So, when he wanted to appear as King, he was like the cuckoo in June, heard but not noted. Seen, but by eyes so used to seeing, that they took him for granted. They were stuffed, gorged, and full with his presence. And that is exactly, says King Henry, the way Prince Harry stands now. He says that Prince Harry has lost his princely dignity by associating with vile criminals. Everybody is sick of seeing him all the time.

Prince Harry, however, was driven by his inner perception. He did not rely on the opinion of his father or other courtiers. He was following his inner voice. He knew that he had to play an important role. He had to use a very different approach if he was to succeed. Here is how, right at the beginning of the play, he explained his strategy:

> "I know you all, and will awhile uphold
> The unyoked humour of your idleness:
> Yet herein will I imitate the sun,
> Who doth permit the base contagious clouds
> To smother up his beauty from the world,
> That, when he please again to be himself,
> Being wanted, he may be more wonder'd at,
> By breaking through the foul and ugly mists
> Of vapours that did seem to strangle him.
> If all the year were playing holidays,
> To sport would be as tedious as to work;
> But when they seldom come, they wish'd for come,
> And nothing pleaseth but rare accidents.
> So, when this loose behavior I throw off
> And pay the debt I never promised,
> By how much better than my word I am,
> By so much shall I falsify men's hopes;
> And like bright metal on a sullen ground,
> My reformation, glittering o'er my fault,
> Shall show more goodly and attract more eyes
> Than that which hath no foil to set it off.
> I'll so offend, to make offence a skill;
> Redeeming time when men think least I will.
> (Henry IV-Part 1, I.2)

Harry says that he knows what his vile associates are like. For a while, therefore, he will tolerate his lazy and rowdy companions. But in doing this he will be like the sun, who allows the clouds to hide temporarily its beauty from the world. When the sun wants to be itself again, it breaks through the mists and fog. Then it is more loved through its previous absence. And because people have missed the sun so much, they are that much more impressed when it finally appears. If every day of the year was a holiday, playing would be as dull as working. But when it's rare, it's looked forward to. Nothing is as precious as the unexpected occurrence. So when he puts a stop to his wild behaviour and accepts the responsibilities of being the king, he will look better and attract more people. Like a bright metal on a dark background, his reformation will shine even more brilliantly when it's set against his wicked past. For now, therefore, he will continue to be so wild that it will make wildness his art. But he will redeem himself when the world least expects it.

At first look, Harry's explanation is very similar to his father's approach. But there is a significant difference. In these two quotes Shakespeare describes three types of man, i.e., the stupid, the half-wise, and the wise. They represent three consecutive stages of the process leading to "kinghood" that is illustrated in the History Plays. The first stage is represented by the previous King Richard II. Richard II was a fool; neither had he "royal" quality nor wit to pretend that he did. Henry IV was witty enough to skilfully pretend that he was worthy. Prince Harry was witty enough to use his inner quality in an effective way.

Indeed, when the time was ripe Prince Harry went through an amazing transformation. The transmutation of his inner being was needed so he could discharge his evolutionary function. The divine intervention manifested during the Battle of Agincourt was the result of Prince Harry's inner transmutation.

3.9 The Dervish's Vow

Rumi says that taking an oath is a custom followed by wicked men. The wicked man is not able to know the true course of events. Therefore he cannot be sincere. He uses oaths as a shield to justify his actions. It is unavoidable that he will break his oaths at any time. The following story illustrates this aspect of insincerity:

> There was once a dervish who took up his abode in the mountains in order to enjoy perfect solitude. In that place were many fruit-trees and the dervish made a vow that he would never pluck any of the fruit. He would eat only what was given him by destiny, i.e., shaken down by the wind. For a long time he kept his vow. But a time came when there was no wind, and consequently no fruit fell down. The dervish was true to his vow for the first five days, but he could not endure the pangs of hunger any longer. He stretched out his hand and plucked some of the fruit from the branches. Shortly afterwards the chief of the police arrived with his troops in pursuit of a band of robbers, and arrested the dervish along with them. As punishment, the dervish's hand was cut off. When the chief of the police discovered that he had made a mistake he apologized very earnestly. But the dervish reassured him, saying that he was not to be blamed. It was evident that he was punished for breaking his vow. (Book III, 1610-1745)

A developed man, on the other hand, is able to see what is right and what is wrong. So he does not need to take oaths, because he knows the outcome of his actions. Rumi illustrates the operation of "sincerity" in the story of the Camel and the Mule:

> The mule said to the camel, 'O good friend! You do never fall but go happily along the way. But I am tumbling repetitively. I am falling on my face, whether it be in a dry or a wet place. Tell me, please, what the cause of this is so I may know how I must live'. The camel answered, 'My eye is clearer than yours. Furthermore, it is also looking from on high. When I come up to the top of a high hill, I

am able to see the end of the pass. Through my superior perception I can see all the obstacles and the way to avoid them. So that I take every step with clear sight and am delivered from stumbling and falling, whereas you do not see two or three steps in front of you. You see the bait, but you do not see the snare. (Book III, 1746-1771)

Rumi's story helps to understand the character of Shylock in Shakespeare's "The Merchant of Venice". Shakespeare used Shylock to explain further the relationship between sincerity and the habit of taking an oath[57]. Shylock demanded from the Venetian court his right to Antonio's flesh. Shylock justified his claim by the conditions spelled out in the bond that he and Antonio had signed. Because Antonio was not able to fulfil the financial obligation of the bond, therefore Shylock requested from the Venetian court to grant him the right to kill him. The degree of Shylock's insincerity was demonstrated by his response when he was requested to show mercy. According to Shylock, he could not show mercy because that would mean breaking his oath:

"An oath, an oath, I have an oath in heaven:
Shall I lay perjury upon my soul?
No, not for Venice."
(The Merchant of Venice, IV.1)

The fallacy of Shylock's reasoning was further explained by Shakespeare in "All's Well That Ends Well". Here is Diana's comment on the merit of taking an oath:

" 'Tis not the many oaths that makes the truth,
But the plain single vow that is vow'd true.
What is not holy, that we swear not by,
But take the High'st to witness: then, pray you, tell me,
If I should swear by God's great attributes,

---

57 "Villains" (Shakespeare for the Seeker, Volume 3, Chapter 6.4)

I loved you dearly, would you believe my oaths,
When I did love you ill? This has no holding,
To swear by him whom I protest to love,
That I will work against him: therefore your oaths
Are words and poor conditions, but unseal'd,
At least in my opinion."
(All's Well That Ends Well, IV.2)

Diana explains that it is sincerity that counts and not an oath. If an oath is driven by ill intention, then such oath has no value at all[58].

The intention of Shylock's oath was to kill Antonio. As such, his oath was not valid. Such a misuse of "holiness" is another example of spiritual usury. This is why Shylock was presented as a "usurer".

3.10 The Sheikh-Pir and his Lost Sons

As an introduction to the story about the Sheikh and his lost sons, Rumi briefly explains the function of a spiritual guide. In the following text Sheikh-Pir , i.e., Ancient-Sage, means a guide[59]:

"Rumi asks 'Who is a Sheikh-Pir?' And he answers, 'He is an old man', i.e., he has white-hair. The meaning of 'white-hair' is opposite to 'black-hair'. Black hair indicates 'self-existence'. In other words, he is not 'old' till not a single black hair of his self-existence remains. When his self-existence has ceased, he becomes old (Pir), whether he has black-hair or grey-hair. 'Black hair' is the attribute of men who are driven by sensual and earthly attractions;

---

[58] "Modulation of beauty" (Shakespeare for the Seeker, Volume 2, Chapter 5.1)
[59] The readers will notice that, coincidently, the pronunciation of the "Sheikh-Pir" is very close to "Shakes-peare".

it has nothing to do with the hair of the beard or the hair of the head. Just like Jesus, when still in the cradle, raised a cry, 'Without having become a youth, I am a Sheikh and a Pir'.

The guides are brought on to the earth because through them all created beings are able to experience mercy. Ordinary man may experience only partial mercy; universal mercy belongs to the guides. Through a guide, ordinary man is united with universal mercy. The mercy of the guide is like sea; it is unlimited. Man may move forward only by following a guide." (Book III, 1790-1813)

Then Rumi follows with the story of the Sheikh and his sons:

There was an old and wise man who was known for his sanctity. He lost all his sons. But he showed no grief nor regrets. His wife asked him, 'Tell me, why are you so hard-hearted? We are all mourning the death and loss of your sons. Why are you not weeping and lamenting?' The Sheikh said to her, 'Do not think that I have no pity and affection nor a compassionate heart. I have pity for all the wrongdoers, even though they are ungrateful. I have pity and forgiveness for dogs which is expressed by my thoughts: why do they suffer from the stones which are thrown at them? I pray for the dog that bites, crying: O God, deliver him from this evil disposition! I also keep these dogs in my thoughts, so that they may not be stoned by the people'. The wife said, 'Since you have pity on all, and you are like the shepherd watching his flock, why do you not mourn for your dead sons? The evidence of pity is shown by tears in the eyes. Why are your eyes without tears?' He turned towards his wife and said, 'Winter is not like summer. Whether they are dead or living, they are not absent and hidden from my heart. Since I see them distinctly before me, for what reason should I lament as you do? Although they are outside Time's revolution, they are with me and playing around me. Weeping is caused by severance or by parting. But I am united with my dear ones and embracing them. Other people see their dear ones in their dreams. I see them plainly in my waking state. I am able to remove myself for a moment from this world and escape from the captivity of my physical senses'.

Physical sensations and thoughts resemble weeds, which occupy the surface of pure water. The hand of the inner being puts these weeds aside and the pure water is then visible to the wise. But when the inner being is still latent, the weeds keep growing thick. The weeds are fed by earthly attachments and attractions. Through his inner being man is able to behold visions in his walking state. It is then that the gates of heaven are open before him.

(Book III, 1772-1834)

Feste in Shakespeare's "Twelfth Night" delivered a similar message to Olivia. Olivia was mourning her dead brother. Feste demonstrated to Olivia that she was a fool, because she was mourning her brother's soul that was in heaven:

Feste:

"Good madonna, why mournest thou?"

Olivia:

"Good fool, for my brother's death."

Feste:

"I think his soul is in hell, madonna."

Olivia:

"I know his soul is in heaven, fool."

Feste:

"The more fool, madonna, to mourn for your brother's
soul being in heaven. Take away the fool, gentlemen."
(Twelfth Night, I.5)

Both Rumi and Shakespeare refer to the transformation from the
waking state into a higher state as "dying before dying".
Shakespeare described the challenges of such a transformation in
"Othello". The process of dying before dying is illustrated as
Othello "killing" Desdemona[60].

Of course, the "killing" of Desdemona did not have anything to do
with physical harm. Shakespeare clearly emphasized that there was
neither shedding of blood nor wounding:

"Yet I'll not shed her blood;
Nor scar that whiter skin of hers than snow,
And smooth as monumental alabaster.
Yet she must die, else she'll betray more men."
(Othello, V.2)

Desdemona had to complete her transformation by killing her
attachments to worldly matters. Otherwise, she would not be able
to discharge properly her evolutionary function ("she'll betray more
men"). In other words, if Othello had not "killed" Desdemona, the
entire world would have ended up again in chaos:

"But I do love thee! and when I love thee not,
Chaos is come again." (Othello, III.3)

But Desdemona did not understand fully her situation. This is why
Othello had to help her. However, Othello could not disclose to
Desdemona his real purpose for "killing" her:

---

[60] "Transition" (Shakespeare for the Seeker, Volume 3, Chapter 6.2)

"It is the cause, it is the cause, my soul,
Let me not name it to you, you chaste stars!
It is the cause." (Othello, V.2)

Desdemona could not know the purpose. Because she would be too frightened to benefit correctly from that particular experience, just like the man who swallowed the snake (see Chapter 2.7).

In his confrontation with Desdemona in their bedchamber, Othello accused her of giving away a handkerchief, a present that she had received from him. Of course Desdemona knew that she did not give away the handkerchief. If she had had enough trust in Othello, she would have known that he would not lie to her. Desdemona's protestations, therefore, was a sign that she did not trust him. Desdemona's lack of trust was further manifested by her fears:

"And yet I fear you; for you are fatal then
When your eyes roll so: why I should fear I know not,
Since guiltiness I know not; but yet I feel I fear."

She could have "sacrificed" her attachments and fears by putting herself trustfully into Othello's hands. Because she was not able to do it, Othello had to "murder" her fears. This is why Othello said that instead of "a sacrifice", Desdemona had to experience "a murder":

"And makest me call what I intend to do
A murder, which I thought a sacrifice."

After passing through this very difficult experience, Desdemona was able to comprehend fully Othello's purpose for "killing" her. When Emilia asked who was responsible for her death, "dead" Desdemona answered:

"Nobody; I myself. Farewell
Commend me to my kind lord: O, farewell!"
(Othello, V.2)

Only then was Desdemona, like the Sheikh with his sons, was able
to experience a higher state.

3.11 The Fool and the Dervish

Rumi indicates that one of the critical characteristics of an aspirant
to higher knowledge is patience. He illustrates this in an episode
from the tradition of Luqman.

> Luqman went to King David and saw that he was making
> rings of iron, which he then was interfolding into each
> other. He had not seen the armourer's handicraft before,
> so he was astonished and curious. 'What can this be? I
> will ask him what he is making with the interfolded rings'.
> But then he thought, 'Patience is better. Patience is the
> quickest guide to the object of one's quest'.
> When one asks no question, the sooner is the secret
> disclosed to him. And if one asks, the slower will his
> object be obtained. What is easy will be made difficult by
> impatience.
> So, Luqman kept silent. In the meantime the making of
> the rings was finished. Then David fashioned a coat of
> mail and put it on in the presence of Luqman. 'This', he
> said, 'is an excellent garment for warding off blows on the
> battle-field and in war'. Luqman said, 'Patience too is of
> good effect, for it is the protection and defence against
> pain everywhere'. (III.1835-1883)

It is through patience that man might gain wisdom. The wise man is free from the pain and disappointment that are common for ordinary men. This is further explained in the story of the Fool and the Dervish.

The fool once paid a visit to a dervish, and asked him how he fared. The dervish replied, 'I fare like a man who directs the course of the world as he wills, to whom death and life are subservient, and whom the stars themselves obey'. The fool then pressed him to explain his meaning more clearly. The dervish replied, 'It is evident to any man that the world is subject to the command of God. Not a leaf falls from a tree without the decree and command of the Lord of lords. Not a morsel goes from the mouth down the throat without the Lord's approval. Desire and attachments, which are the reins of mankind, are themselves subservient to the rule of God. All action in the universe only comes to pass by the command of the Maker. When the predestination of God becomes the pleasure of His servant, the servant becomes the Man of God. His actions are not driven by hope of reward, but because his very nature is congruous with the Divine design. The Man of God does not even desire his own life for himself. Nor is he relying on the hope of reward in the life to come. Whatever path is taken by the evolutionary needs, whether it is life or death, it is all one to him. He lives for the sake of service, not for wealth. He dies for the sake of the evolutionary needs, not in fear and grief. His faith is based on his desire to comply with the Divine design and not on hope to gain paradise. His avoidance of mistakes is also for the higher purpose. It is not driven by fear of falling into the fire. Thus this attitude of his arises from his very nature, not from any discipline and endeavour of his own. At times he smiles when he contemplates God's pleasure. God's decrees are

to him as sweetmeats of sugar. Therefore I ask',
continued the dervish, 'does not the world follow the will
and commands of such a Man of God? Why, then, should
such a one make prayers and petitions? The Man of God
does not make prayers and invocations from self-pity. He
has consumed away his self-pity at the moment when he
was transmuted into a new man'. (Book III, 1884-1923)

In Sonnet 94 Shakespeare gave a similar description of the Men of
God:

> "They that have power to hurt, and will do none,
> That do not do the thing, they most do show,
> Who moving others, are themselves as stone,
> Unmoved, cold, and to temptation slow:
> They rightly do inherit heaven's graces,
> And husband nature's riches from expense,
> They are the Lords and owners of their faces."
> (Sonnet 94, 1-7)

In this Sonnet Shakespeare seconds Rumi in his explanation of the
nature of those who are charged with guiding humanity[61]. Such
men and women, says Shakespeare, have power to hurt others, but
they chose not to do so. They do not act in the way that others
expect them to. They are able to influence others, but themselves
are unswayable. They are inheritors and carriers of the entire
spectrum of evolutionary energy ("they rightly do inherit heaven's
graces"). They are charged with preserving nature's greatest
treasures ("husband nature's riches from expense"). They are in full
control of their moods.

---

[61] "Shakespeare's Sonnets or How heavy do I journey on the way" (Sonnet 94)

3.12 The Visions of Daqiqi

As indicated in the introduction, the Absolute emanates the cosmic matrix, i.e., a blue-print of evolutionary plans for mankind. The matrix is encoded onto rays of creation that percolate through the evolutionary transmission chain. Through several intermediary stages, this transmission chain links the Absolute with the level of ordinary man. The level immediately below the Absolute is described as the Realm or the "Garden". The Realm is the top level of the transmission chain. There is a three-level structure below the Realm, which consists of the higher worlds, the intermediate worlds, and the lower worlds that are linked to the world of ordinary men. In accordance with "as above so below", this cosmic structure is a reflection of the human mind. The above referred worlds correspond to various meditative or inspirational states of the mind.

Rumi illustrates such a multi-level structure in an episode with Daqiqi, a Persian poet who lived in the 10th century.

> Daqiqi was journeying with the purpose of meeting a Man
> of God. His wish was to become his servant. At one
> point he saw seven candles. As he watched them
> overwhelmed with awe, the candles united and became
> one candle. Then that one candle became seven once
> more. All the candles were linked together, but it was
> impossible for him to describe these links. Afterwards,
> the seven candles assumed the likeness of seven men.
> Then these seven men changed into seven trees standing
> within a deserted wilderness. They formed a garden that
> was providing shelter and happiness. What was even
> stranger was that there were hundreds of thousands of
> people passing through that deserted wilderness looking
> for the trees but they were not able to see the garden.
> Even though the trees were calling upon them, 'Come,

come towards us!'- none of those people saw the trees.
But if Daqiqi would have told them, 'Go in this direction,
so you may find happiness from these tress', they would
all have said, 'This poor and intoxicated wretch has
become mad; he is talking nonsense'. Then Daqiqi
noticed that the seven trees were bowing down in prayer.
Then the seven trees changed into seven men again and
they asked Daqiqi to lead them in their prayer. While he
was leading the prayer, Daqiqi saw a ship in great distress.
The people in the ship were terrified and were crying for
help. When Daqiqi heard their lamentation, he felt a
strong pity for them. At that moment he was in a state of
spiritual ecstasy. He started to pray for them and ask for
their safety. Through his prayers, the ship was spared. The
people in the ship, however, thought they were saved by
their own efforts. At the moment when the ship was
saved, the prayer was also finished. Daqiqi heard that his
companions began to murmur to one another, saying,
'Who was disturbing our prayer? Who was asking for
intercession?' Then they concluded that it was Daqiqi
who interfered with their devotion. When Daqiqi turned
back to take a look at his noble companions, he could not
see anyone; they all had gone. During many years
afterwards, Daqiqi was grieving for the loss of these Men
of God. He shed many tears longing for them. (Book III,
1924-2305)

The candle in the story allegorically represents the Light that
emanates from the Absolute, i.e., the Source of Everything. It is
that Light that percolates through the evolutionary transmission
chain. The seven trees correspond to the Realm or the Garden.
Daqiqi's companions, i.e., the Men of God, exist in the Realm.
During his inspirational vision, Daqiqi was in a state that
corresponded to the higher world. While in this state he was able to
witness the Realm, but he was not able to sustain the link. His pity

for the people in the ship showed some traces of his earthly attachments. This is why he was not able to sustain the link with the Men of God. The distressed people in the ship illustrate a state corresponding to the intermediate world. The blind people lost in the wilderness represent ordinary men in the physical world.

In the following episode, Rumi illustrates how the evolutionary matrix is linked to the ordinary world. This episode was taken from the story of the man who prayed to be fed without having to work (see Chapter 3.7). A certain intervention allowed the sequence of events to unfold that led to the killing of the cow. Here is the conclusion of the story:

> After the man had slain and eaten the cow, the owner of the cow showed up and accused him of theft. The man tried to excuse himself by saying that he was begging God for his daily bread and his prayer was answered. 'Your cow', he said, 'was my portion of daily bread'. But the owner of the cow did not listen to him. He seized him by the collar and dragged him before the judgment-seat of King David. When he stated his case, David ordered the accused to recompense the plaintiff, telling the accused that he must not break the law. When hearing the sentence, the accused raised laud lamentation and cries telling David that he was taking side with the oppressor. David was taken aback by the man's allegation. He decided to take more time and reconsider the case. During his solitary meditation the entire sequence of events that led to the killing of the cow was revealed to him. David returned to the court and reversed his previous sentence: he requested the plaintiff renounce his claim and acquit the man of his deed. The plaintiff, however, refused to do so. David said to him, 'O you stubborn and disobedient man, give the whole of your wealth to the accused immediately. Otherwise, your plight

will become grievous. I tell you to do so, so your crime may not be made manifest through him'. But the plaintiff did not pay attention to what David was saying. Instead, he started even louder protestations against David's injustice. At this point David ordered that all the plaintiff's goods be given to the accused. The reason for his decision was that David had discovered that the plaintiff had previously killed his master and stolen all his goods. That master was the father of the accused. David then led all those present at the court to a tree in the desert where the murder had been committed. He addressed the owner of the cow, 'You demanded the law: take then the law and go with it. You killed your master miserably, whilst he was crying for mercy on this very spot. In your haste you hid the knife under the tree, because of a terrible apparition which you beheld'. Then David turned to those present and told them, 'The master's body together with the murderer's knife is buried here. On the knife the murderer's name is written'. David ordered that people dig under the tree. When they did, they found the body and the knife. The murderer was put to death in the same place where he murdered his master. (Book III, 2306-2569)

Rumi explains that the murderer represents man's corrupted self faculty. The cow represents earthly attachments and sensuality. The corrupted self faculty is a claimant on account of the cow. It is this corrupted faculty that has made itself a master through robbery. The corrupted faculty prevents the inner being from growing. Such a state is an illustration of ordinary man whose being is entirely enclosed in the physical world. The slayer of the cow is the intellect faculty. The intellect is captive and craves of daily bread without toil. The daily bread without toil is the evolutionary energy that is at the guide's disposal. But access to that daily bread depends upon sacrificing the cow. The intellect may prevail over the self faculty only with the help of the guide. David represents the guide. Through his meditative states, he has access to the Realm. The Realm is the source of his inspiration. Through his inspiration he was able to see the true sequence of events and was able to intervene constructively into the affairs of the ordinary world.

Shakespeare in the scene of Shylock's trial at the Venetian court retells the story of the slayer of the cow. Like the plaintiff in that story, Shylock brought Antonio to the Venetian court. Shylock was seeking Antonio's death because Antonio was not able to fulfil the financial obligation of their bond (see the chapter 3.9: "The Dervish's Vow"). In reality, Shylock shrewdly planned to murder Antonio, so he would be able to protect and expand his business. In other words, he was driven by greed and revenge. Antonio's fate was to be decided by the court. Portia, like King David, was directing the court proceeding. And like King David, at first, Portia declared that Shylock's claim was valid:

> "For the intent and purpose of the law
> Hath full relation to the penalty,
> Which here appeareth due upon the bond."
> (The Merchant of Venice, IV.1)

Then, like King David, Portia asked Shylock to reconsider his claim and exercise mercy for Antonio. But Shylock, like the murderer, refused and declared that all he craved was the law:

> "My deeds upon my head! I crave the law,
> The penalty and forfeit of my bond."
> (The Merchant of Venice, IV.1)

So, again like King David's "you demanded the law: take then the law and go with it", Portia warned him:

"For, as thou urgest justice, be assured
Thou shalt have justice, more than thou desirest."
(The Merchant of Venice, IV.1)

At the end Shylock lost everything.

Portia was the guide. She had full access to the Realm. Like King David, she was capable of seeing the past, the present, and the future. She was able to arrange the entire sequence of events that allowed the city of Venice to be exposed to a remedying experience[62].

3.13 The Fools of Sheba

Rumi says that probation is a disease that brings Divine mercy. Folly, on the other hand, is a disease that brings Divine rejection. This is why there is no remedy for the fool. Therefore, Rumi advises us, 'Flee from the fools, my friend!' He illustrates this in the following story:

> Jesus, son of Mary, was fleeing to a mountain. A certain man was running after him and asking, 'Is everything well with you? There is no one in pursuit of you. Why do you flee?' But Jesus still kept running with haste and did not answer him. The man tried to keep up with Jesus, but he could not. So he started to cry, 'From whom art thou fleeing, O noble one? There is no lion pursuing you, no enemy, and there is no fear or danger'. Jesus answered him, 'I am fleeing from the fool. Be gone! I am saving myself. Do not disturb me anymore!' 'Why', asked the

---

[62] "Pilgrimage" (Shakespeare for the Seeker, Volume 3, Chapter 6.4)

man, "are you not the Messiah by whom the blind and the deaf are restored to sight and hearing?' Jesus said, 'Yes'. The other man continued, 'Are you not the King in whom the spells of the Unseen World have their abode? So that when you speak those spells over a dead man, he is returned to life'. Jesus answered, 'Yes, I am he'. The man then said, 'Do you not make living birds out of clay?' Again, Jesus answered, 'Yes, I do'. 'Why then', the man kept asking, 'do you run away as if you were afraid?' Jesus said, 'I swear that the spells and the Most Great Name which I pronounced over the deaf and the blind were able to restore their sight and hearing. By pronouncing a spell and the Most Great Name I tore apart the rocky mountain. By pronouncing spells over a dead corpse I returned it to life. I pronounced spells over the nonexistent and it became existent. But when I pronounce my spells hundreds of thousands of times over the heart of the fool - it does not cure his folly! The heart of the fool has become hard like rock and it cannot be changed from that disposition'. The man asked, 'What is the reason of that? Folly is like a disease, why then the Most Great Name has no effect?' Jesus answered, 'The disease of folly is the result of the wrath of God. Physical disease and blindness are not the result of Divine wrath. They are a means of probation. (Book III, 2570-2599)

Rumi adds that the flight of Jesus was not caused by fear, for he was safe from the mischief done by fools. His purpose was to teach others. In the following story, Rumi illustrates the nature of man's folly.

Once there were three fools. One was very far-sighted but blind. The second one was very sharp of hearing but extremely deaf. And the third was naked and bare, but his robe was long. The blind man said, 'Look, an army is approaching: I see what kind of people and how many they are'. The deaf man said, 'Yes, I hear their voices and know what they are saying'. The naked man said, 'I am afraid they will cut off my robe'. The blind man said, 'Look, they have come near! Arise and let us flee before it is too late'. 'Yes', said the deaf man, 'The noise is getting nearer; come on, my friends!' The naked man said, "Alas, from covetousness they will cut off my robe and I will be naked'. So, the three fools left the city and came forth and in their flight entered a village. In that village they found a fat fowl, but not a scrap of meat on it. It was a dried-up dead fowl, and its bones through being pecked at by crows had become bare. They were eating thereof as a lion eats of his prey. Each of them became surfeited with eating it. All three ate thereof and grew exceedingly fat. They became like three very great and big elephants. In such a way, that each man, because of fatness, was too big to be contained in the world. Notwithstanding such bigness, they sprang forth through a chink in the door and departed.

There are caravans of people following one after another through this chink in the invisible door. If one looks on the door for that chink, he will not find it because it is extremely imperceptible, though there are many caravans going through it continually. (Book III, 2600-2656)

Rumi explains that the deaf man is he who is driven by hope. He hears of other people dying, but has not heard of nor considered his own death. The blind man is driven by greed. He sees in great details other people's faults and considers himself to be a fault finder. But he himself does not perceive his own faults. Those who are attached to their wealth, or talents, or learning - are like the naked man. The naked man thinks that he knows a hundred thousand superfluous matters of sciences, but he does not have a clue about his inner being. He knows the properties of every substance, but in elucidating his own essence he is as ignorant as an ass. He knows the value of every merchandise, but does not know the value of himself. He became acquainted with fortunate and inauspicious stars, but has no idea about what is wrong and what is right. The naked man is afraid that his robe will be cut off. He does not realize that the naked man's robe cannot be cut-off. He possesses nothing, yet he dreads of thieves. Only at the hour of death, i.e., when they depart through that tiny chink in the invisible door, these fools will realize that whatever they had - it was only a loan. They were preoccupied with their false wealth, supposed learning, or shallow wits. The only thing that really matters is one's inner being.

Rumi illustrates this point further by telling the story of the fools of Sheba. And he remarks that although the story may seem to include some ridiculous things, he asks the readers to keep in mind that in all ruined places one may find a treasure.

> There was once a city called Sheba. It was very huge and great, but its size was the size of a saucer, no more than that. It was very huge and very broad and very long, ever so big, as big as an onion. There were many estates, orchards and meadowlands in Sheba. There was abundance of fruits; so much so that the fruits were falling to the ground. The scattered largesse of fruit would block the way. It would be hard to describe all the blessings bestowed upon the people of Sheba. And these blessing were increasing day by day. Many thousands of people were living there, but they all amounted to three fools. Accordingly, they did not appreciate what they enjoyed. So, thirteen prophets were sent to Sheba. They were ready to guide those who had lost the way. They told the people, 'Come on, the benefit has increased! Where is the thanksgiving? Is it not reasonable to give thanks to the Benefactor? Otherwise, the door of destruction will

be opened'. The fools of Sheba answered, 'We have become tired of giving thanks and receiving benefits. We have become so saturated and disgusted with the bounty that we are indifferent to piety or offence'. They became a foe to their bounty. Any sweet thing they touched, it was turned into sourness.

Such a morbid quality is one of the characteristics of mortality. If there is no spiritual light, everything changes into destructivity.

When they heard the counsel of the prophets, their foolishness turned it into meaningless prattle. They said, 'We have heard this many times; it has become old'. And they asked for something new, something more exciting. They did not realize that if something else fresh and new had been said, the next day they would consider it as old. Such impaired hearing is a symptom of foolishness. First, that foolishness would have to be cured. Then, that seemingly old tale would become new to them. It would lead them to new growth.

The prophets said that they were spiritual physicians; they were sent to help. They were inspired by the rays of Divine light.

These spiritual physicians looked into the inner heart. So they knew which deed would be beneficial, and which would derail the patient from the straight path. They themselves were a medicine for the spiritually sick.

But the fools of Sheba said, 'You are just impostors. Where is the evidence of your knowledge of medicine and your usefulness? Show us miracles! But since you are clad in a body, like ourselves, we will not listen to your grossly pretentious claims!' The prophets answered, 'This disbelief is the result of your blindness. You do not see the jewel that we hold in our hands. This jewel is a test: we show it in front of your eyes. If you ask for evidence, your words are the evidence that you do not see the jewel.

Therefore, you are beguiled by blindness'. The fools said,
'You are bringing bad luck to us. We are rejecting you and
your counsels. We were free from cares. But you have
cast us into grief and trouble. Through your evil presage
the delightful concord and agreement that existed
amongst us has been turned into a hundred separations.
Formerly we were parrots eating sugar for dessert; now
through you we have become birds that meditate on
death'. The prophets said, 'The foul and evil presage has
its origin within your hearts. If you are asleep in a perilous
place and a dragon is approaching you from a spot close
at hand, we are like a kindly person who makes you aware
of it. We are telling you that you have to jump up quickly,
or else the dragon will devour you. But you are telling us
that we are uttering an evil presage? What evil presage is
that? Is it not better to jump up and deliver yourself from
the midst of danger?' Then the fools told the prophets
that they, i.e., the prophets, were like a certain hare who
pretended that he was the ambassador of the Moon.
In that story, all the beasts of chase were in woe because
of a herd of elephants dwelling beside a spring. They were
all deprived of water and were kept far from the spring by
their dread of the elephants. So, they designed a plot.
From the mountain-top the old hare cried towards the
elephants on the first night of the new-moon: 'Come on
the fourteenth, O king elephant, that you may find within
the spring the proof that I am the ambassador of the
Moon. I am delivering this message to you. The message
says that the spring is mine; therefore leave it and be
gone! And if you do not depart, I will make you blind. In
order to demonstrate that my message is true, come to
the spring on the fourteenth night from today and put
your trunk in the spring. Then you will see how the Moon
will be angry with you and her image in the water will be
disturbed'. When on that night the king elephant put his

trunk in the water, the water was disturbed, and the Moon showed disturbance.

The fools concluded that they were not as stupid as the elephants. They were not going to listen to the stories told them by the prophets. The prophets answered, 'You fools! Know that the hidden nature of that hare is your corrupted self. It intends to interfere with your inner being. Its purpose is to deprive your soul of the Water of Life. Your interpretation is a reflection of your inner state. You imagine that the Moon may be disturbed by the limpid water. And that the hare is able to frighten the elephants'. But the fools of Sheba would not accept the Prophets' counsels. They refused to be convinced of the fallacy of their reasoning. So at last the prophets left them to their doom. (Book III, 2657-3092)

Shakespeare constructed the charismatic character of Sir John Falstaff to illustrate an attitude similar to that of the fools of Sheba. Here is a description of Falstaff given by Prince Harry in "Henry IV-Part 1":

"Thou art so fat-witted, with drinking of old sack
and unbuttoning thee after supper and sleeping upon
benches after noon, that thou hast forgotten to
demand that truly which thou wouldst truly know.
What a devil hast thou to do with the time of the
day? Unless hours were cups of sack and minutes
capons and clocks the tongues of bawds and dials the
signs of leaping-houses and the blessed sun himself
a fair hot wench in flame-coloured taffeta, I see no
reason why thou shouldst be so superfluous to demand
the time of the day." (Henry IV-Part 1, I.2)

Prince Harry says that Falstaff is so wasted from drinking booze and sleeping on benches all afternoon that he does not even remember how to ask for what he wants to know. There is no need for him to know what time it is. Unless, says Harry, hours were glasses of wine, minutes were chickens, clocks were whores' tongues, sundials the signs of whorehouses, and the sun itself were a hot woman in a flashy dress. In other words, Falstaff is "very far-sighted but blind, very sharp of hearing but extremely deaf, and naked and bare but his robe was long".

The inner being may be activated by absorbing the available evolutionary energy. Shakespeare refers to the evolutionary energy as "honour". In the following meditation we may recognize "the fool who is naked but worried about his robe being cut-off". Here is Falstaff's seemingly witty meditation on "honour":

> "Can honour set to a leg? no: or
> an arm? no: or take away the grief of a wound? no.
> Honour hath no skill in surgery, then? no. What is
> honour? a word. What is in that word honour? what
> is that honour? air. A trim reckoning! Who hath it?
> he that died o' Wednesday. Doth he feel it? no.
> Doth he hear it? no. 'Tis insensible, then. Yea,
> to the dead. But will it not live with the living?
> no. Why? detraction will not suffer it. Therefore
> I'll none of it. Honour is a mere scutcheon: and so
> ends my catechism." (Henry IV-Part 1, V.1)

Falstaff arrogantly asks, can honour set a broken leg? No. Or an arm? No. Can it make a wound stop hurting? No. Can't honour perform surgery? No. What is honour then? A word. What is in that word, honour? Air. Quite a bargain! Who has it? A guy who died last Wednesday. Does he feel it? No. Does he hear it? No. It can't be detected, then? Not by the dead. But it will not live with the living? No. Why? Slander will not allow it. This is why Falstaff does not want any part of it. And he concludes his meditation saying that honour is nothing more than a coat-hanger. Like the fools of Sheba, Falstaff completely misinterpreted his situation.

Falstaff's account of honour is so different from Prince Harry's[63]. In "Henry V" Prince Harry, as King Henry V, describes "honour" in the following way:

> "By Jove, I am not covetous for gold,
> Nor care I who doth feed upon my cost;
> It yearns me not if men my garments wear;
> Such outward things dwell not in my desires:
> But if it be a sin to covet honour,
> I am the most offending soul alive."
> (Henry V, IV.3)

The entire story of Falstaff is an illustration of the process described in the story of the Fools of Sheba. Prince Harry was continuously pointing out to Falstaff his foolishness. But Falstaff remained indifferent. He was incapable of changing his self. Despite his charismatic personality he was a parasite, living off other people's work and effort. When it became obvious that there was no chance for Falstaff's transformation, Prince Harry, as King Henry V, had to leave him behind to his doom.

3.14. The Miracle

In popular understanding, events, which are associated with breaking off the limitations of space and time, are called "miracles". Therefore, many happenings are considered miracles because they seem to defy the conventions of space or time or

---

[63] "Dawn of perfection" (Shakespeare for the Seeker, Volume 1, Chapter 1)

both. Hence, in some people miracles produce confusion, in others scepticism, fears, excitement, and so on. But what is important is the effect of the miracle. In all cases a miracle is an instrument of both influence and assessment of the people acted upon. Therefore, only certain audiences are qualified for exposure to miracles. As illustrated in the previous story, the Fools of Sheba were not qualified to witness miracles. In their case, it would have been a waste of time and effort. This was further underlined in the episode with Jesus, when he ran away from the fools.

The following story illustrates an episode where a miracle was used as a developmental instrument. We may note that there was someone among the audience who could benefit from it.

> After a meal, Anas, who was a companion of Mohamed, saw that a table-napkin was stained and filthy. Anas said to his maid-servant, 'Throw it into the oven at once'. Thereupon the maid threw it into the oven. The guests were expecting to see the smoke of the burning napkin. Instead, and to their great astonishment, the maid took the napkin out of the oven. The napkin was clean and white, completely purged of filth. The guests asked, 'Why did it not burn, and how did it become cleansed?' Anas told them that Mohamed often used to rub his hands with it. Then the guests asked the maid, 'You knew about the value of the napkin. Why then did you not hesitate to throw such a precious object into the fire?' She answered, 'I have confidence in my master. What is a piece of cloth? I would throw myself in the fire, not only this napkin, because of my confidence in a generous one who knows'. (Book III, 3093-3265)

Certain objects are capable of being spiritually charged. These objects may be "typed" for a specific person. In such a case they may be used as an instrument of both influence and assessment of the person acted upon. They can also be used as a protective tool. Bestowing such an object may indicate the selection of a guide's deputy in a given territory. In the episode with Anas, the napkin served such a purpose. Anas demonstrated to his guests that he was charged with certain responsibilities. His maid was perceptive enough to understand his role.

Shakespeare also used napkins in his plays to illustrate the operation of such an object. For example, in "Othello", it was a handkerchief "spotted with strawberries" that represented such a charged object[64]. At the beginning of the play, Desdemona was the holder of the handkerchief. However, after Desdemona and Othello departure to Mauritania, Cassio would be Othello's deputy in Cyprus. At one point, therefore, it was necessary for Othello to transfer the handkerchief to Cassio. At that time Cassio was not yet ready to fully comprehend the situation. Othello had to arrange the transfer in such a way that it would be entirely transparent to Cassio. Othello used Iago. Iago, who was driven by a completely different motivation, helped Othello to execute this task by placing the handkerchief in Cassio's apartment.

In Shakespeare's "As You Like It", Orlando was the holder of a napkin. Like Cassio in "Othello", at the beginning of the play Orlando was not aware of the importance of the napkin. The napkin became "active" only when Orlando's inner state had been transmuted. His advanced state was marked by Orlando overcoming a hungry lioness. After the fight with the lioness, Orlando sent his "blood-stained napkin" to Rosalind. It was a sign that Orlando was ready for her[65].

In "Hamlet" Queen Gertrude was the carrier of the napkin. The napkin, however, was intended for Hamlet. But Gertrude could

---

[64] "Developmental techniques" (Shakespeare for the Seeker, Volume 3, Chapter 6.2)

[65] "The process" (Shakespeare for the Seeker, Volume 2, Chapter 5.2)

pass the napkin to Hamlet only when he was ready for it. Hamlet's inner change took place during his fencing match in the final scene of the play[66]. During the fencing match Gertrude noticed that, finally, Hamlet started to behave in accordance with his royal stature. It was then that Gertrude gave him the napkin:

> "Here, Hamlet, take my napkin, rub thy brows;
> The queen carouses to thy fortune, Hamlet."
> (Hamlet, V.2)

In all cases, the transfer of a handkerchief marked a critical moment in the process. In "Hamlet", the transfer indicated the end of the allotted time for this particular developmental stage.

3.15 The Language of Animals

In the context of the following story, "the speech of animals" is a technical term for the deceptive self, i.e., the inner whisperer. The whisperer's messages may take the form of deceptive prophecies. The deceptive prophesies are constructed in such a way that they would affect the hearer according to this hearer's inner state. It is in this manner that the whisperer's prophecies may become self-fulfilled. The readers can clearly see how the man in the following story was influenced by such simplistic messages. We should notice that such prophecies have to be based on an accurate presentation of some future events. Yet, they convey only a part of the story.

> A certain man came to Moses and desired to be taught
> the language of animals. The man argued that men used
> their language only to get food and for purposes of

---

[66] "The fencing match" (Shakespeare for the Seeker, Volume 4, Chapter 7.3)

deception. Therefore, the knowledge of animals'
languages might stimulate his faith. Moses was not willing
to comply with this request, as he knew such knowledge
would prove destructive to the man. He advised the man
to seek knowledge from inner inspiration and not from
words. But the man insisted. Then Moses heard an inner
voice who told him, 'Grant him his wish. Let him have a
free choice between constructive and destructive'. Moses,
therefore, taught him the language of fowls and dogs. The
next morning, the man went amongst the animals and
heard a discussion between the cock and the dog. The
dog was abusing the cock for picking up the morsels of
bread, which fell from their master's table. The dog
argued that the cock could find plenty of grains of corn to
eat, whereas he could only eat the morsels of bread. The
cock, to appease him, said that on the next day the
master's horse would die, and the dog would have enough
food. The master, hearing this, at once sold his horse. The
dog, being disappointed of the loss of his meal, again
attacked the cock. The cock excused himself saying, 'His
horse died in another place. He sold the horse and
escaped from loss by passing his loss upon others'. 'But
do not worry', continued the cock, 'the mule will die
tomorrow'. Hearing this prediction, the covetous master
sold the mule. Then the cock foretold the death of a
slave, and the master again sold the slave. The master was
saved from loss and his face was lit up with joy. He was
giving thanks and making merry, saying, 'I have been
saved from three calamities in the world. Since I learned
the language of the fowl and the dog I have pierced the
eye of evil destiny'. The next day the disappointed dog
angrily approached the cock, 'O you deceiving cock,
where are the goodies that you promised me?' The cock
excused himself by telling that all three deaths had taken
place just as he had predicted. But the master had sold the

horse, mule, and slave, and in that way he had thrown the loss on others. Then he added, 'As punishment for his fraudulent dealing, the master will himself die tomorrow. Then there will be plenty for you to eat at the funeral feast'. Hearing this, the master ran to Moses in great distress and prayed to be saved. Moses told him, 'Go sell yourself and escape! Since you have become expert in avoiding loss, use your knowledge now. Escape from death by yourself'. Once more the man started to lament and ask for help. Moses told him that he would pray for him, so he may experience peace prior to his departure from this world. And he explained, 'Once you have experienced inner peace, you will be living forever'. (Book III, 3266-3398)

In "Macbeth", Shakespeare used the witches to illustrate the operation of the deceptive self. The witches, like the cock in Rumi's story, were able to predict future events. Namely, they whispered to Macbeth, thane of Glamis, that he would become thane of Cawdor and then King of Scotland:

First Witch:

"All hail, Macbeth! hail to thee, thane of Glamis!"

Second Witch:

"All hail, Macbeth, hail to thee, thane of Cawdor!"

Third Witch:

"All hail, Macbeth, thou shalt be king hereafter!" (Macbeth, I.3)

A moment later, Macbeth was informed that he indeed became thane of Cawdor. Banquo, Macbeth's friend, tried to warn him about the deceptive nature of "the instruments of darkness":

"And oftentimes, to win us to our harm,
The instruments of darkness tell us truths,
Win us with honest trifles, to betray's
In deepest consequence." (Macbeth, I.3)

Banquo told Macbeth that the destructive forces earn our trust by telling us the truth about little things, but then they betray us when it will damage us the most. (We may notice that Banquo's warning would have also applied to the covetous master who understood "the speech of animals" in Rumi's story). Macbeth, however, ignored Banquo's warning. He started to believe that he was destined to become the King of Scotland. In this way he fell into the witches' trap.

Shakespeare added a twist to this episode to further explain the operation of the deceiving self. Namely, he indicates that the destructive forces are not quite perfect in their operation[67]. Hecate, the goddess of witchcraft, was upset at the witches because they had not consulted with her before they approached Macbeth. Hecate was angry because the witches invested their charms in a rather weak character. From Hecate's perspective, Macbeth was not vicious enough. He was not able to serve evil efficiently enough. Macbeth was only after his own personal greed and simplistic wants. Here is Hecate berating the witches:

"Have I not reason, beldams as you are,
Saucy and overbold? How did you dare
To trade and traffic with Macbeth
In riddles and affairs of death;
And I, the mistress of your charms,
The close contriver of all harms,
Was never call'd to bear my part,
Or show the glory of our art?

---

[67] "Scotland: 11th century AD" (Shakespeare for the Seeker, Volume 1, Chapter 3.3)

And, which is worse, all you have done
Hath been but for a wayward son,
Spiteful and wrathful, who, as others do,
Loves for his own ends, not for you."
(Macbeth, III.5)

Hecate told the witches that the next time they encounter Macbeth they must summon visions and spirits whose messages would enhance Macbeth's viciousness. This could be done by filling Macbeth with a false sense of security and drawing him into a stronger determination towards his wicked quest:

"And that distill'd by magic sleights
Shall raise such artificial sprites
As by the strength of their illusion
Shall draw him on to his confusion:
He shall spurn fate, scorn death, and bear
He hopes 'bove wisdom, grace and fear:
And you all know, security
Is mortals' chiefest enemy."
(Macbeth, III.5)

Indeed, during the second encounter, the witches convinced Macbeth that he was invulnerable. They told him that he should not be afraid to be violent, bold, and firm. He might scorn and laugh at the power of other men, because nobody born from a woman would ever harm him:

"Be bloody, bold, and resolute; laugh to scorn
The power of man, for none of woman born
Shall harm Macbeth." (Macbeth, IV.1)

He did not have to worry about those who hated him. According to the witches, Macbeth would never be defeated until Birnam Wood marched against his Dunsinane Hill castle:

> "Be lion-mettled, proud; and take no care
> Who chafes, who frets, or where conspirers are:
> Macbeth shall never vanquish'd be until
> Great Birnam wood to high Dunsinane hill
> Shall come against him." (Macbeth, IV.1)

Macbeth became convinced of his invulnerability. He believed that he was protected because he knew that every man is born from a woman and forests do not move. After his second encounter with the witches Macbeth was transformed into a fully determined villain.

3.16 The Woman who lost her Infants

The higher worlds operate outside ordinary existence. In literary descriptions imaginary places are used to represent these worlds. Very often the higher world is compared to a garden. The higher world may be accessed after passing through a sequence of specific experiences. Such experiences involve breaking off the limitations of time and space. This is why such experiences may be presented as travel into the past and/or into the future. The higher worlds correspond to various meditative or inspirational states of the human mind. In practical terms this means that the activation of higher states of mind allows gaining access to the "Garden" or "heaven", i.e., arriving at the ultimate goal of human destiny. The following story is an example of such an experience.

> A woman used to bear a son every year, but he never
> lived more than six months. In great distress she cried to
> God, 'For nine months I have the burden of pregnancy,
> and for six months I have joy; my happiness is fleeter
> than the rainbow'. Till one night, she saw the vision of a

beautiful garden. There was a palace in the garden upon which was written her name. She knew that the palace belonged to her. And she was told, 'This palace and this garden are for those who have excelled in sincerity and self-development. You would have had to do much service in order to partake in such a feast. But since you have been negligent in doing the service, you have been given hardship instead'. 'O Lord', cried the woman, 'give me such hardship for a hundred years and more!' When she advanced into the garden, she saw there all her children. She understood that she thought that they were lost, but they were not.

Without inner eye no one may become a Man of God. The core of every fruit is better than its rind. The body is like the rind; the inner being is the core. Fear of death is really fear of losing one's ordinary self. (Book III, 3399-3684)

The woman's sons represent the steps of the ladder leading to the garden. Climbing each step required effort; arrival at each step was bringing her some joy. But then it was necessary to make more effort in order to reach towards the next step. Till the time when she was able to start to perceive the first sights of the garden.

The adventures of Pericles described by Shakespeare in "Pericles, Prince of Tyre" are an illustration of a similar sequence of experiences. Pericles transition into the higher world is presented as a sea journey during a tempest. At that time Pericles, like the woman in Rumi's story, did not yet understand what was happening to him. He thought that he was like a tennis ball being played by the forces of nature:

"A man whom both the waters and the wind,
In that vast tennis-court, have made the ball

For them to play upon."
(Pericles, Prince of Tyre, II.1)

It is important to point out, however, that Pericles was able to be obedient to these forces:

"Yet cease your ire, you angry stars of heaven!
Wind, rain, and thunder, remember, earthly man
Is but a substance that must yield to you;
And I, as fits my nature, do obey you."
(Pericles, Prince of Tyre, II.1)

By the force of nature, Pericles' ship was wrecked and Pericles was tossed upon the coast of Pentapolis. Pentapolis is an imaginary place that represents the higher world. In Pentapolis, Pericles met Thaisa whom he married. It was then that he experienced a first taste of true happiness. But he could not stay there for too long. By experiencing Pentapolis, Pericles learned the skills that he needed to discharge his evolutionary function within the ordinary world. Afterwards, he had to return back to the ordinary world to complete his mission. During Pericles' descent Thaisa gave birth to their daughter, Marina. But Thaisa died while giving birth. Pericles, like the woman who lost her infants, reacted angrily to what was happening to him:

"O you gods!
Why do you make us love your goodly gifts,
And snatch them straight away? We here below
Recall not what we give, and therein may
Use honour with you."
(Pericles, Prince of Tyre, III.1)

At the end of the play Pericles met "resurrected" Thaisa:

"This, this: no more, you gods! your present kindness
Makes my past miseries sports: you shall do well,

That on the touching of her lips I may
Melt and no more be seen. O, come, be buried
A second time within these arms."
(Pericles, Prince of Tyre, V.3)

Only then did he understand the nature and the purpose of Thaisa's "death"[68].

3.17. The Minister of the Prince of Bokhara

Man's life is like a journey. The important thing is to accept that fact, find out what the destination is and how it can be reached. The following story illustrates an example of such a journey. It helps to grasp the story's inner meaning to know that the city of Bokhara represents the source of knowledge. Therefore it may be said that everyone who has gained knowledge is a native of "Bokhara". Another aspect of being a native of Bokhara is to know that Bokhara is the place where one's heart is.

> The Prince of Bokhara had a minister who, through fear
> of punishment for an offence he had committed, ran
> away and remained concealed in the mountains and in the
> desert for ten years. At the end of that time, being unable
> to endure absence from his lord any longer, he decided to
> return to Bokhara and throw himself at his lord's feet. He
> was resolved to endure whatever punishment his lord
> might be pleased to inflict upon him. His friends did all
> they could to dissuade him, assuring him that the Prince's
> wrath was still hot against him. If he appeared in Bokhara
> he would be put to death, or at least imprisoned for the

---

[68] "Restoration of the transmission" (Shakespeare for the Seeker, Volume 2, Chapter 4.1)

rest of his life. He replied, 'O advisers, be silent, for the force of the love which is drawing me to Bokhara is stronger than the force of prudent counsels. When love pulls one way, then all conventional wisdom becomes impotent to withstand it. If it shall please my lord to kill me, I will yield up my life without reluctance, for this life of estrangement from him is the same as death. Release from this life will be eternal happiness. I will return to Bokhara'. Accordingly, he journeyed back to Bokhara, experiencing the very toils and discomforts of the trip as sweet and delightful, because they were steps towards his lord. When he reached Bokhara, his friends and relations all warned him not to show himself, for the Prince was still mindful of his offence and bent on punishing him. But he replied to them, as to his other advisers, that he was utterly unconcerned of his life. He was resolved to commit his entire being to his lord's good pleasure. All these people were following him with amazement, wondering whether the Prince was going to burn him or hang him. They thought that he was like the foolish moth that considered the flame to be the light: it fell in the flame and was cut off from life. But these people did not know that the candle of Love is not like that ordinary candle. In reality, the fire of Love is the reverse of burning candles. It only seems to be fire, while it is all sweetness. The minister went to the court and threw himself at his lord's feet. He fell on the ground senselessly. Like the moth, he cast himself upon candle. The Prince took the minister's hand and said, 'This man whose breath has departed will only come to life when I give him spiritual breath. Then this man, whose worldly attachments are dead, shall be united with my essence. Through this union he will gain access to a higher state'. The senseless man came to himself and turned his face in praise of the Beloved. (Book III, 3685-3921; 4377-4748)

Rumi adds that for lovers the only lecturer is the beauty of the Beloved. And the Lovers' only book and lecture is the Beloved's face.

Shakespeare illustrated the same theme in "Love's Labour's Lost". King Ferdinand of Navarre and his companions, including Berowne, decided to embark upon a journey leading to knowledge. In this way they intended to transform Navarre into the wonder of the world:

> "Navarre shall be the wonder of the world;
> Our court shall be a little Academe,
> Still and contemplative in living art."
> (Love's Labour's Lost, I.1)

However, the approach which they adopted and the methods that were supposed to lead them to their goal were overly naïve and simplistic:

> "Not to see ladies, study, fast, not sleep!"
> (Love's Labour's Lost, I.1)

Such an approach corresponded to that of uniformed mystics who immerse themselves in severe exercises and studies without understanding the overall process. Such an approach was based on using a similar medicine for every ailment without taking into account the question of proportion, and without making a proper diagnosis. In the following comment Berowne compared such approach to that of naive "earthly godfathers" who try to gain knowledge simply by inventing new terminology ("that give a name to every fixed star"):

> "These earthly godfathers of heaven's lights
> That give a name to every fixed star
> Have no more profit of their shining nights
> Than those that walk and wot not what they are.

Too much to know is to know nought but fame;
And every godfather can give a name."
(Love's Labour's Lost, I.1)

Berowne alluded to another and more effective way to learn in his meditation on women's eyes[69]:

"From women's eyes this doctrine I derive:
They sparkle still the right Promethean fire;
They are the books, the arts, the academes,
That show, contain and nourish all the world:
Else none at all in ought proves excellent.
Then fools you were these women to forswear,
Or keeping what is sworn, you will prove fools."
(Love's Labour's Lost, IV.3)

Berowne compares women's eyes to a purifying fire. Like in Rumi's counsel, Berowne states that the eyes of the Lover are the books, the arts, and academes. The Lover's eyes are the source of truth, which "contain and nourish all the world". And all those who are ignorant of that fact - are just fools.

3.18 The Guest-killing Mosque

There are two attractions placed in the nature of man. One of these attractions is to lift man up to higher spheres of functioning. The other attraction is to lower him down to a kind of low, bestial life. Therefore, two forms of external agencies are needed to bring these attractions into operation. The external agency that brings the attraction to higher spheres of living is often called an angel, and

---

[69] "The being of Navarre" (Shakespeare for the Seeker, Volume 2, Chapter 5.3)

the one which leads man astray is called a demon. In human life, however, there are many combinations of these two extremes that lead to the existence among the agents of many mixes, grades and shades. Therefore, when man enters on a spiritual journey, he encounters a sort of dichotomous situation. On one side, he is provided with new forms of protection, safety, and guidance. On the other side, he is exposed to new distracting challenges. These various attractions are very often described in traditional myths as fairies, spirits, and ghosts. The means of the distractive attractions are limited to a marginal degree of deception and biased presentation. This is illustrated in the story of the Guest-killing Mosque.

> In the suburbs of the city of Ray there was a mosque in which none could sleep a night and live. Some said it was haunted by a malevolent ghost; others claimed that it was under the influence of a magic spell. Some people proposed to put up a notice warning visitors not to sleep there if they wanted to stay alive. Some others advised that the door should be kept locked at night. At last a stranger came to that city. He desired to sleep in the mosque. He said that he did not fear to risk his life, because the life of his body was not of much value to him. The men of the city warned him again and again of the danger and rebuked him for his foolhardiness. They said that all those who spent a single night in that mosque died there. But the stranger told them that he would not stop his journey because of some idle fancies. For him death and leaving this earthly abode was as sweet as leaving the cage was for the captive bird. The people of Ray warned him that probably the whisperer was tempting him to his own destruction. The visitor, however, would not be dissuaded. He persisted in his purpose of spending the night there. Accordingly, he slept in the mosque. At midnight he was awakened by a terrible

and threatening voice. But instead of being dismayed, he confronted his unseen foe, challenging him to show himself, 'If you are a true man, come! Show yourself!' At these words the spell was dissipated. At this very moment the visitor was showered with gold that fell on all sides. So much gold poured down that the visitor feared that its abundance might block the doorway. Afterwards that valiant man took the gold out of the mosque and buried it. He was afraid that the gold would corrupt the mind of the people and turn them into gold-worshippers. (Book III, 3922-4376)

Rumi explains that by throwing himself into the killing-mosque, the visitor reached a state of certainty. In this context, materialistic knowledge is above opinion, but is inferior to certainty. Only through reaching a state of certainty can man escape from the pangs of death and time. A certainty corresponds to the condition of "being cooked", just like the boiled chick-pea in the following story:

At the time of its being boiled, the chick-pea comes up continually to the top of the pot and raises a hundred cries. It cries, 'Why are you setting the fire on me? Since you bought me, why are you torturing me?' The housewife goes on hitting it with the ladle and says, 'Boil nicely and don't jump away from one who makes the fire. I do not boil you because you are hateful to me. I boil you so you may get taste and savour. In this way you may become nutriment and mingle with the vital spirit. This affliction of yours is not on account of your being despised. When green and fresh you were drinking water in the garden. That water-drinking was for the sake of this fire. You have been parted from the garden of water and earth so you can become food and enter into the living. You will become nutriment and thoughts. The chickpea answered, 'Since it is so, O lady, I will gladly boil! In this boiling you are, as it were, my architect. Strike me with the skimming spoon, for you beat me very delightfully. In this way I may submit myself to the boiling to the end and may find a way to the embrace of the Beloved. Because man, in the state of independence, grows insolent and becomes hostile to his Beloved'. (Book III, 4160-4208)

The story of the Guest-killing Mosque may help to unfold the inner meaning of Shakespeare's "Hamlet". The Ghost of Hamlet's father plays the same role as the ghost of the mosque. The Ghost is an agent of the destructive forces. Shakespeare points out that the Ghost's impact depends on the person's attachment to and respect for Hamlet's father, i.e., the former King. Among the characters who are exposed to the Ghost are Hamlet, Hamlet's friend Horatio, the watchmen, and Gertrude, Hamlet's mother. Each of them reacts to the Ghost in a different manner. Their reactions are a reflection of their respect for the former King. The degree of their respect is a measure of the purity of their inner states. Namely, Horatio and the watchmen respected Hamlet's father. This is why they can see the Ghost. But the Ghost will not speak to Horatio because he approaches the apparition with a condition:

> "If there be any good thing to be done,
> That may to thee do ease and grace to me,
> Speak to me." (Hamlet, I.1)

Of course, "any good thing to be done" is not the Ghost's purpose. This is why Horatio is only partially effected by the Ghost. On the other hand, Hamlet was very strongly attached to his father. Therefore, his approach to the Ghost is unconditional:

> "Be thou a spirit of health or goblin damn'd,
> Bring with thee airs from heaven or blasts from hell,
> Be thy intents wicked or charitable,

Thou comest in such a questionable shape
That I will speak to thee." (Hamlet, I.4)

This is why the Ghost speaks to Hamlet. In this way the Ghost is able to corrupt him completely.

Gertrude knew very well her former husband. She did not have any illusions about him. This is why she can neither see nor hear the Ghost:

> Hamlet:
>
> "Do you see nothing there?"
>
> Gertrude:
>
> "Nothing at all; yet all that is I see."
>
> Hamlet:
>
> "Nor did you nothing hear?"
>
> Gertrude:
>
> "No, nothing but ourselves." (Hamlet, III.4)

In this way Shakespeare indicates that Gertrude is the only character of "Hamlet" that is immune to the Ghost's temptation[70].

The conclusion of the Guest-killing Mosque story parallels Timon's experience illustrated in Shakespeare's play "Timon of Athens". Similarly to the Guest of the Mosque, Timon was also showered with gold. Here is Timon's explanation of the function of "gold":

> "What is here?
> Gold? yellow, glittering, precious gold? No, gods,
> I am no idle votarist: roots, you clear heavens!
> Thus much of this will make black white, foul fair,

---

[70] "Ophelia's prophesies" (Shakespeare for the Seeker, Volume 4, Chapter 7.3)

Wrong right, base noble, old young, coward valiant."
(Timon of Athens, IV.3)

Timon described "gold" as capable of changing black into white, foul into fair, wrong into right, base into noble, old into young, and cowardly into valiant. In other words, "gold" is a substance allowing for the transmutation of ordinary man into a noble one. However, the Athenians, just like the people of the city of Ray, were not ready for such a transmutation. This is why Timon, like the Guest of the Mosque, had to hide his gold. The gold had to remain hidden till the time when the people would be correctly prepared for such an exposure. In the case of the Athenians, they had to wait three hundred years before they were ready to use the gold properly[71].

3.19 The Lover and his Mistress

A potential disciple who enters on the developmental path has to go through a series of trials. The important thing is that these trials are not for the purpose of testing his ability for discipleship. The guide already knows what is the candidate's potential and what are his or her abilities. These trials are used to expose the candidates to certain experiences from which they may start to learn. It is such a trial that is illustrated in the story of the Lover and his Mistress.

> A certain youth was madly in love in a woman. Fortune,
> however, did not give him an opportunity to meet her.
> Whenever he sent a messenger to the woman, the
> messenger would steal his letter. And if his secretary
> wrote a letter to be sent to the woman, his messenger

---

[71] "Targeted impact" (Shakespeare for the Seeker, Volume 2, Chapter 4.3)

would change the content of the letter while reading it to her. For seven years that youth was engaged in search and seeking. (Book III, 4749-4810)

Here Book 3 ends[72]. The story continues in Book 4:

The lover had no possibility of seeing even his Mistress' shadow. He was only hearing descriptions of her. Except for one brief meeting, during which his heart became enravished with love. Afterwards, however much effort he made, that cruel lady would give him no opportunity for another encounter. One night, as he was wandering through the city, he got scared by an approaching patrol. As there is no absolute evil in the world, evil is relative. This was the case with the night patrol. The night-patrol provided the means, so that in fear of it, the lover ran into the orchard. In the orchard he saw his beloved, who was searching with a lantern for a lost ring. The moment the lover found himself alone with his mistress, he attempted to embrace and kiss her. But his mistress pushed him away, saying, 'Do not behave so boldly, be mindful of good manners!' He said, 'Why, there is none present here. None is moving here but the wind. Who is present? Who will stop me from this conquest?' 'O madman', said she, 'you are a fool! You have not learnt from the wise. You are saying that the wind is moving. Tell me then, who drives the wind along? The wind is blowing and that shows that the Mover of the wind is also present'. The lover replied, 'It may be I am lacking in good manners, but I am not lacking in constancy and fidelity towards you'. His mistress replied, 'One must judge of the hidden by the manifest. I see for myself that your outward behaviour is bad, and thence I cannot but infer that your

---

[72] In this way Rumi indicates that there is no "gap" between Book 3 and the following ones.

boast of hidden virtues is not warranted by actual facts. You are ashamed to misconduct yourself in the sight of men, but have no scruple to do so in the presence of the Mover of the wind, and hence I doubt your supposed virtues'. The lover then proceeded to excuse himself by the plea that he had wished to test his mistress, and ascertain for himself whether she was a modest woman or not. He said that he of course knew beforehand that she would prove to be a modest woman, but still he wished to have a proof of it. His mistress reproved him for trying to deceive her with such false pretences. She told him that, after being found in fault, his only proper course should be to confess it. Moreover, she added that any attempt to put her to a test would have been an extremely unworthy approach. (Book IV, 1-387)

Bassanio in Shakespeare's "The Merchant of Venice" is another example of a lover who, at the beginning of the play, was not yet ready for Portia, his beloved woman. This is why Portia led him through a series of trials. Portia knew that Bassanio's financial situation was on the top of his priorities list. Therefore Portia put him through a test to demonstrate to him that his affection for her was still phoney. Bassanio was in hurry to go back to Venice to fix his problem:

"For as I am, I live upon the rack."
(The Merchant of Venice, III.2)

Portia, like the Mistress in Rumi's story, indicated to him that he was not quite honest with her:

"Upon the rack, Bassanio! then confess
What treason there is mingled with your love."

And when Bassanio came out with a silly explanation:

"None but that ugly treason of mistrust,
Which makes me fear the enjoying of my love,"

she clearly indicated to him that she knew that he was lying:

"Ay, but I fear you speak upon the rack,
Where men enforced do speak anything."

Then she gave him her ring:

"I give them with this ring;
Which when you part from, lose, or give away,
Let it presage the ruin of your love
And be my vantage to exclaim on you."

Portia knew that Bassanio would not be able to keep his word. In other words, her ring, like that of the mistress' ring in Rumi's story, would be lost[73]. (A lost ring symbolically indicates that a specific evolutionary potentiality is not ready for its actualization.) Therefore, the expected penalty was not so severe: "be my vantage to exclaim on you". All of this was lost on Bassanio. His answer to this challenge sounded phoney and even embarrassing:

"But when this ring
Parts from this finger, then parts life from hence:
O, then be bold to say Bassanio's dead!"
(The Merchant of Venice, III.2)

A guide knows his disciples very well. The readers can see how patient Portia and the mistress in the story had to be while dealing with their disciples. The developmental process takes a long time before it may be completed. However, what matters are the candidate's ability and his determination to follow such a challenging path.

---

[73] "Bassanio's slip-ups" (Shakespeare for the Seeker, Volume 3, Chapter 6.4)

Book 4. Evolutionary Cosmic Matrix

The latest phase of man's evolution is realized through the activation of higher states of mind and the unveiling of man's inner being. Allegorically, man's inner being may be referred to as the angelic soul.

The angelic soul opens the door to experiences of a cosmic nature, i.e., extra dimensional. In this way humanity has the capacity to perceive that which is beyond the range of conventionally experienced physics. A wise man, i.e., a Man of God, is an exemplar of humanity who has fully developed his inner being. Therefore, he is in a position to guide others on the journey leading to the Realm. It is only at the end of his journey that the evolutionary cosmic matrix can be fully perceived. The matrix contains the entire evolutionary plan for humanity.

In instrumental literature such a journey is described symbolically as a caravan of souls, a lover's quest, a search after truth, a treasure hunt, etc. In a teaching situation such descriptions are themselves transcended as the disciples gradually get behind and beyond the significance of the symbolism. At the beginning of the journey these symbols help. But at some point they have to be abandoned, otherwise they would hinder progress. This may be compared to the situation where one marches towards a visible point in order to keep on the right track. But he must abandon it as soon as he reaches that particular point and choose another marker, and if necessary yet another, until the goal is reached. In this way man may retrace the various stages of the evolutionary ladder and ascend towards the Realm.

4.1 The Most Remote Temple

In accordance with "as above so below", a more advanced structure serves as a template for the lower one. According to Rumi, the physical universe, the human body, the mind, spiritual matter, and spiritual essence consecutively represent substances in increasing degree of refinement. The universe, with its stars, galaxies, and bodies is the dwelling place of material substances. The human body is the dwelling place of the mind. The mind is the dwelling place of spiritual matter and of essence. In other words, the physical universe is a reflection of the human mind. This is why Rumi compares man to the macrocosm, while the physical universe is the microcosm. (Book IV, 521-524)

The story of the Most Remote Temple is an allegorical illustration of the formation of the macrocosm, i.e., the highest state of the human mind.

> King David intended to build the most remote temple. However, a Divine voice forbade him to do so. The voice told him that his deeds did not qualify him for such an honourable task. He was told that the building of the temple should be undertaken by his son Solomon. Because such a temple is not built out of bricks and mortar, but is fashioned out of accumulated good deeds and intentions. In this way David's deeds will become Solomon's deeds, because all sages form a single inner being. Accordingly, when Solomon came to the throne, he started to build the temple. Solomon's enterprise was met with many miraculous circumstances, e.g., the stones in the quarry were crying out and moving of themselves to the site of the temple. In order to complete the temple, Solomon needed Bilqis, the Queen of Sheba, to renounce her sovereignty and submit herself to him. Solomon, therefore, forwarded to the Queen his request. As answer

the Queen sent a gift of forty camels laden with bricks of gold. When the Queen's envoy arrived in Solomon's land, he saw a carpet made entirely of solid gold. He rode on the carpet for a distance of forty stages, till gold had no more esteem in his sight. He thought to himself, 'Let us take the gold back to the Queen's treasury; what a fruitless quest are we engaged in! This is a spacious land of which the soil is pure gold. To bring gold here as a gift is folly'. When Solomon saw that gift he laughed and said, 'I did not ask you to bring me gifts. I asked you to be worthy of the gifts which I give. O shamefaced envoy, turn back! Take the gold back with you. And bring me a pure heart instead! Go to Bilqis and bid her come here with all speed'. And he charged the envoy to urge the Queen to renounce her sovereignty and present herself in all humility at his court. As she was delaying her arrival, Solomon again sent her a message assuring her that he desired her attendance at his court solely for her own benefit. At last Bilqis renounced her royal state and cast away all care for worldly things. Impelled by earnest desire to learn Truth, she presented herself at the court of King Solomon. But she still felt a strong desire for her throne. No wealth, no treasury, and no goods were being coveted by Bilqis except her throne. When Solomon became aware of her attachment, he commanded that the throne of Bilqis should be brought from Sheba. He said, 'In order that she may not feel hurt at the time of meeting with me, let her throne be brought here. So that she may know from what low places to what a high place she has arrived'. The throne of Bilqis was brought immediately. Solomon turned his eyes towards the throne and said, 'It is this that catches fools, like a tombstone'. Afterwards Solomon proceeded with completing the temple. He was assisted by men and fairies; some of them from good-will, and others on compulsion. One day a demon placed himself on the throne. He was imitating Solomon. This false King took over the kingdom and subjected to himself the entire empire. People, however, noticed that there was a great difference between this King and the previous one. They said, 'The former King was like wakefulness, this one is like sleep'. The false King impersonated Solomon for a while. Afterwards, Solomon regained his kingdom. Having completed the temple, he began to pray there every day. One day Solomon observed that a weed had sprung up in a corner of the temple. He was greatly distressed because he thought it foretold the ruin of the building. But he took comfort from the thought that, while he himself lived, he would not allow the temple to fall into ruin. So long as he lived, at least, he would root up all evil weeds that threatened the safety of the temple. (Book IV, 388-1489)

Rumi described the throne as "this that catches fools, like a tombstone". In "Richard II" Shakespeare used the term "the hollow crown that ... keeps Death his court" to convey the same meaning. Here is King Richard's comment about it:

"For God's sake, let us sit upon the ground
And tell sad stories of the death of kings;
How some have been deposed; some slain in war,
Some haunted by the ghosts they have deposed;
Some poison'd by their wives: some sleeping kill'd;
All murder'd: for within the hollow crown
That rounds the mortal temples of a king
Keeps Death his court and there the antic sits,
Scoffing his state and grinning at his pomp."
(Richard II, III.2)

According to Shakespeare's presentation, the spiritual status of "King" is not determined by the crown, but by the inner being of a person. As long as the King's priority is focussed on the crown, he is like a fool caught by a tombstone. Richard's crown was "hollow" because he had not arrived yet at the state of true King[74]. The entire series of the History Plays is an illustration of the process that gradually leads to the development of true "kinghood".

The most remote temple represents the highest state of the human mind. King David and Solomon are symbolic links of the transmission chain. They illustrate the leading aspects of the intellect faculty. At the time of King David it was not possible yet to activate the highest state of mind. At that time, humanity did not absorb efficiently enough the creative energy, i.e., a lower mode of evolutionary energy that was needed for the completion of the spiritual purification. The Queen of Sheba represents the leading aspect of the heart faculty. As long as this particular faculty was maculated by its attractions to an earthly "throne", the most remote temple could not be sustained. Her throne is a symbol of earthly and egotistic attachments; it represents spiritual impurities. In order to be able to complete the temple, Solomon had to make a compromise. He allowed for the presence of her throne, i.e., some impurities in his temple. This is why, later on, an aspect of the destructive forces was able to interfere with the process. As a result, Solomon lost his kingdom for some time. Afterwards, these impurities manifested themselves as weeds, which had to be removed daily. Solomon knew that the temple would be ruined after his death.

In the play entitled "Pericles, Prince of Tyre" Shakespeare illustrates the continuation of the story of the most remote temple. Let's recall that the entire canon of Shakespeare's plays is an illustration of the process of activation, formation, and maintenance of these various inspirational states of mind. Some of these states are only partially operational; some are on the verge of becoming active; and some are still latent. This corresponds to

---

[74] "Preliminary realization" (Shakespeare for the Seeker, Volume 1, Chapter 1)

certain experiences that are somehow familiar but still not quite comprehensible; possible but not encountered yet; seemingly impossible. Shakespeare illustrates such experiences as a series of events taking place in somewhat familiar environments; remote locations and at other times; imaginary places and times. By creating such settings it is possible to illustrate, as a journey, man's struggle towards the fulfillment of his ultimate evolutionary purpose. But, as Rumi points out, "such a journey is not like the ascension of an earthly being to the Moon. It is rather like the ascension of a cane into sugar or of an embryo to rationality" (Book IV, 553-554).

In "Pericles, Prince of Tyre" Shakespeare describes the evolutionary process implemented in Western Europe. The process is illustrated as Pericles' journey through various levels of the evolutionary ladder. It is important to emphasize that in 7th century AD, i.e., at that time of the initiation of Pericles' journey, the evolutionary process was seriously disrupted. This disruption was indicated by Rumi as the presence of weeds, which caused the collapse of Solomon's temple. Pericles' journey was a form of evolutionary corrective action. This corrective action may be compared to the rebuilding of "the most remote temple". It had to be taken in the planetary future in such a way as to short-circuit a fault that interfered with the process in the planetary past. As this required the correction of something already actualized in time, it could be accomplished only by an agency which was not only outside time but also outside existence. This would imply that the corrective action was initiated at the level of the Realm. A higher-order corrective projection was triggered. A corrective signal was sent from the Realm to an earthly receptacle of the evolutionary transmission chain. Pericles, whose name in Greek means "Surrounded by Glory", was the recipient of this Divine call. As a result, Pericles embarked on his mission of traveling towards "the farthest temple".

Pericles' mission is presented as a multi-stage journey. The time span of Pericles' journey encompasses two historical millennia. Shakespeare had to implement several chronological gaps to accommodate such a long time span. He used Gower as the chorus to fill-in the time gaps between the various stages of Pericles' journey:

> "From to bourn, region to region.
> By you being pardon'd, we commit no crime
> To use one language in each several clime
> Where our scenes seem to live. I do beseech you
> To learn of me, who stand i' the gaps to teach you,
> The stages of our story."
> (Pericles, Prince of Tyre, IV.3)

The conclusion of Pericles' journey marked the restoration of "the most remote temple". Shakespeare points out that it was this event that led to the birth of the European Renaissance and the Reformation[75].

Rumi inserted an anecdote that illustrates another aspect of building the temple. It emphasizes the difference between ordinary and inspirational knowledge.

> Every morning Solomon was visiting the temple. Each time he saw that a new plant had grown there, he would ask, 'Tell me what is your name and use. What kind of medicine are you? To whom you are hurtful and for whom are you useful?' Then each plant would tell its effect and name, saying 'I am life to that one, and death to this one. I am poison to this one, and sugar to that one. This is my name that was inscribed on the Tablet by the pen of the Divine decree'. Thus physicians and herbalists have derived their knowledge of the virtues of plants

---

[75] "Conclusion" (Shakespeare for the Seeker, Volume 2, Chapter 4.1)

from the instructions originally given by King Solomon
when he classified the plants that grew in the court of the
temple. By hearing from Solomon about those plants, the
physicians learnt and became authorities on medicine.
Afterwards they compiled medical books. The ordinary
intellect is not capable of producing this sort of
knowledge. The ordinary intellect is only the receiver of
such knowledge and teaching. It is capable of being
taught and of apprehending. But only the subtle aspects
of the mind are capable of being Divinely inspired. It is
through Divine inspiration that all crafts and professions
were derived. (Book IV, 1287-1314)

Friar Laurent in Shakespeare's "Romeo and Juliet" alluded to this
type of derivative knowledge. Here is Friar Laurent's comment on
the various properties of plants and flowers:

"O, mickle is the powerful grace that lies
In herbs, plants, stones, and their true qualities:
For nought so vile that on the earth doth live
But to the earth some special good doth give,
Nor aught so good but strain'd from that fair use
Revolts from true birth, stumbling on abuse:
Virtue itself turns vice, being misapplied;
And vice sometimes by action dignified.
Within the infant rind of this small flower
Poison hath residence and medicine power:
For this, being smelt, with that part cheers each part;
Being tasted, slays all senses with the heart.
Two such opposed kings encamp them still
In man as well as herbs, grace and rude will;
And where the worser is predominant,
Full soon the canker death eats up that plant."
(Romeo and Juliet, II.3)

Friar Laurence was an expert in derivative knowledge. He did not have any inspirational wisdom. Yet, he took upon himself the function of spiritual counsellor of Romeo. He considered Romeo to be his pupil. Friar Laurence introduced Romeo to the concept of love. He indicated to Romeo the difference between sensual obsession and true love. He was also familiar with the overall sequence of the evolutionary process and with the experience of "to die before dying" Or, as said by Rumi, "Oh, happy he that died before death" (Book IV, 1372). Friar Laurence hoped to use the formula "to die to live" to reconcile the two feuding families of Verona through their children's union. Friar Laurence's knowledge, however, was not coupled with a true understanding of the process. This is why his stratagem did not work according to his intention.

Friar Laurent's state of understanding is explained in Rumi's next anecdote. This anecdote illustrates the fact that the ordinary intellect cannot know truth, unless it is inspired by divine wisdom:

> A man, deeply in meditation, was sitting in a garden. One
> of his friends told him, 'Lift up your head and open your
> eyes so you may enjoy the garden and the sweet herbs and
> flowers'. The contemplative replied, 'O man of vanity, the
> real orchards and fruits are within the heart. Only their
> reflection is visible in the ordinary world. If it were not
> the reflection of that true beauty, then this world would
> not be called the abode of deception. This abode of
> deception derives its existence from the reflection of the
> heart and the intellect of the wise men. Oh, happy he that
> died before death: because he got scent of the origin of
> this garden. (Book IV, 1358-1373)

Friar Laurent is like the friend of that contemplative man. He was not capable of seeing the evolutionary design. He was blindly copying a formula without understanding its implications. Friar

Laurence acted similarly to those mystics, who simply repeat mechanically certain procedures from the past without understanding the entire process and are unaware of the current projection of the evolutionary matrix[76].

4.2 The Slave who complained

There is a specific methodology to deal with destructive aspects. Namely, the destructive aspects are not confronted directly. Instead, a negative aspect is allowed to manifest itself in its fullest strength. This leads to a situation where the negative aspect cannot help but turn against others, usually weaker aspects. At the same time it is cut off from any access to evolutionary energies. This may be compared to denying him "spiritual oxygen". When it is weakened by its self-induced destructive behaviour, it can be diminished more effectively. The following story illustrates an example of an initial step towards identifying and then weakening such a negative aspect.

> A certain slave was in the service of a great king. This slave was one whose sense perception was dead and whose lust was alive. He was neglectful in his duties. So the king decided to reduce his allowance. When the slave saw that his allowance was reduced, he became violent and disobedient. Instead of reflecting on his behaviour, he went to the kitchen-steward and reproached him about his stinginess. The steward told him that by reducing the slave's allowance he followed the king's orders. He added that the orders were for the good cause and not on account of the king's stinginess. But the slave would not

---

[76] "Trials and errors" (Shakespeare for the Seeker, Volume 3, Chapter 6.6)

listen. Instead, he wrote a flattering letter to the king. Though the outward form of the letter was praise, because of the way in which the praise was expressed it was possible to scent traces of the slave's anger. On receiving this letter, the king observed that it concerned meat and drink. It did not have any marks of aspiration for spiritual attainments. Therefore, the king decided that the letter did not deserve his answer, because 'the proper answer to a fool is silence'. When the slave received no answer, he was much surprised. He blamed the messenger and accused the steward of envy. The slave did not recognize that his own folly was the real reason that his letter was left unanswered. Then he wrote five more letters, in which he accused the courtiers of concealing his letters. But the king persisted in his refusal to reply, saying that having any dealings with a fool would pollute his own nest. Fools only regard meat and drink, whereas the food of the wise is divine inspiration. (Book IV, 1490-2101)

Rumi quotes an episode from the famous love story of Layla and Majnun to further illustrate man's struggle with destructive aspects. Rumi compares Majnun, the lover, to a spiritual aspirant. His desire is to be united with Layla, his beloved. The she-camel represents Majnun's fleshly indulgences; she is only concerned with running after a young foal:

Since Majnun was full of love and passion, he had no recourse but to become beside himself. But the she-camel was very regardful and alert. Whenever she saw her toggle slack, she would at once perceive that he had become heedless and dazed. At such moments, she would turn and go back to the foal without delay. In these conditions Majnun remained going to and fro for years on a three days' journey. He said, 'O camel, we both are lovers. But thy affection and tendency are not in accord with me. We

are unsuitable fellow-travellers. Therefore, I have to part
from your companionship'.
These two fellow-travellers are brigands waylaying each
other: lost is the soul that does not dismount from the
body. The soul, because of separation from the highest
heaven, is in a great need. The body, on account of
passion for sensual pleasures, is like a she-camel. The soul
unfolds its wings to fly upwards. The body, on the other
hand, has stuck its claws in the earth. (Book, IV, 1533-
1546)

As was pointed out in Chapter 2.7, Shakespeare described in
Sonnet 50 a very similar experience with his own "beast".

"The beast that bears me, tired with my woe,
Plods dully on, to bear that weight in me,
As if by some instinct the wretch did know
His rider lov'd not speed being made from thee."
(Sonnet 50, 5-8)

The poet describes his situation while travelling from the ordinary
state to the higher state. He is having difficulties with overcoming
the "injurious distance" separating these two states. The ordinary
state, like the foal in Majnun's story, is where the guide's physical
form is present.

4.3 Bayazid

A spiritually developed man or woman is free from egocentric
judgment. His inner senses are clear and unclouded. In such a state
he can see a new colour, smell a new fragrance, and hear "some
heavenly music". Such a man can see the past and the future. A

developed man is called upon to plunge into the ordinary world to assume a function. It is this function and responsibility that is central to the process illustrated in the following episodes from the life of Bayazid Bistami.

> Bayazid predicted the birth of Abul Hassan Kharagani.
> Bayazid told his disciples, 'The scent of a friend is coming
> from this quarter; a spiritual monarch is coming into this
> village'. Bayazid specified the date of Kharagani's birth,
> his height, complexion, and the colour of his hair. He also
> stated that Kharagani would be Bayazid's spiritual
> inheritor and would receive his lessons by visiting
> Bayazid's tomb. Kharagani was born more than 80 years
> after Bayazid's death. His features and character were
> exactly as foretold by Bayazid. Accordingly, Kharagani
> would visit Bayazid's grave every morning. And either the
> apparition of Bayazid would come to him or, without
> saying anything, his questions would be answered and his
> difficulties solved. One day he visited the tomb as usual
> and found it covered with fresh snow. A voice was heard
> saying, 'I am calling you! Follow me and forsake the
> world! Even if the world is full of snow, do not turn your
> face away from me'. On that day Kharagani arrived at a
> perfected spiritual state; his heart became as white as
> snow. (Book IV, 1802-1934)

Bayazid's prediction of the birth of Kharagani was a message that spiritual power was transmitted through an invisible link, which is not subject to the limitations imposed by space and time.

Shakespeare indicated that his guide used the same technique to put him in contact with the previous guides of the transmission chain. Shakespeare admitted that his guide advised him to look at some previously written poetry as a template for his own writing. It was then that Shakespeare was exposed to and influenced by

Rumi's writings. Rumi is referred to in Sonnet 78 as one of Alien pens ("as every *Alien* pen hath got my use and under thee their poesy disperse"). In Sonnet 80 Shakespeare referred to Rumi as "a better spirit". Initially Shakespeare was discouraged and jealous when he realized that Rumi's poetry was more adequate than his own[77] ("O how I faint when I of you do write, knowing a better spirit doth use your name"). He felt intimidated by Rumi's talent and skills ("and in the praise thereof spends all his might, to make me tongue-tied speaking of your fame"). Afterwards, Shakespeare adopted Rumi's imagery of the ocean to represent infinitive love. He described himself as a humble bark, which was much inferior to the other ship ("the humble as the proudest sail doth bear, my saucy bark, inferior far to his, on your broad main doth wilfully appear"). Shakespeare recognized that he could be sustained only through his guide's infinitive love. He hoped that his own poetry might keep him floating, at least over the shallowest regions of his guide's love ("your shallowest help will hold me up afloat, whilst he upon your soundless deep doth ride"). Shakespeare humbly compared himself to a worthless boat ("being wrecked, I am a worthless boat"), and Rumi's poetry to a mighty and majestic ship ("he of tall building, and of goodly pride"). Here is the full text of Sonnet 80:

> "O how I faint when I of you do write,
> Knowing a better spirit doth use your name,
> And in the praise thereof spends all his might,
> To make me tongue-tied speaking of your fame.
> But since your worth (wide as the Ocean is)
> The humble as the proudest sail doth bear,
> My saucy bark (inferior far to his)
> On your broad main doth wilfully appear.
> Your shallowest help will hold me up afloat,
> Whilst he upon your soundless deep doth ride,

---

[77] "Shakespeare's Sonnets or How heavy do I journey on the way" (Sonnet 80)

Or (being wrecked) I am a worthless boat,
He of tall building, and of goodly pride.
> Then if he thrive and I be cast away,
> The worst was this, my love was my decay."
(Sonnet 80)

Later on Shakespeare established an invisible but tangible link with Rumi and Rumi's companions, whom he calls "his compeers" (Sonnet 86). Then he also discovered that Rumi and "his compeers" were guides from the past[78]. They acted as links of the evolutionary transmission chain. This is why Shakespeare's guide asked him to study their writings.

Let's return to Bayazid's story. Bayazid indicated that the evolutionary state of people at his time and place was such that he was not able to pass on to them his spiritual attainment. They had to wait some 80 years or so for the arrival of the next guide. The next episode further explains the limitations of Bayazid's disciples:

> One day, while in an ecstatic state, Bayazid told his disciples, 'I am God'. When his ecstasy had passed, the disciples said to him, 'Yesterday you said such and such words, and this was repugnant impiety'. Bayazid answered them, 'Next time I utter such words you must dash knives into me. God transcends the body, and I am with a body. Therefore, you must kill me when I say a thing like this'. When their spiritual guide gave them such instructions, each disciple made ready a knife. Then again, Bayazid was taken over by spiritual ecstasy; his reason became distraught. And he spoke even more impiously than before, 'Within me is nothing but God'. His disciples all became mad with horror and struck with their knives at his body. Each one, without fear aimed at the body of their guide. But no stroke took effect on that man of

---

[78] "Shakespeare's Sonnets or How heavy do I journey on the way" (Sonnet 86)

spiritual gifts. Each stroke that was aimed at Bayazid was reversed and wounded the striker. Whoever aimed a blow at Bayazid's throat saw his own throat cut, and died miserably. And whoever inflicted a blow on his breast, his own breast was split and he died for ever. And those who were not able to strike heavily at him, only wounded themselves. And their lives were saved. (Book IV, 2102-2187)

Rumi emphasizes the fact that there is a time when nothing can be done; a time when something can be done; and a time when most things are achievable. At the time of Bayazid it was not possible to advance the evolutionary process. By comparing Rumi's and Shakespeare's writings, it is possible to realize that Rumi was faced with a situation similar to Bayazid's. Namely, Rumi could not disclose everything that he knew, because his contemporaries were not ready yet for such an exposure.

As illustrated in the episodes with Bayazid, it is possible to develop an inner sense that allows one to discern the different qualities of time. Shakespeare provided examples of such an inner sense. These examples are described as episodes involving past-present-future interventions in the process. For example, the action of "Cymbeline" is placed in 1st century Rome and Britain at the time of Caesar Augustus. However, one of the scenes is placed in 16th century Renaissance Rome. It is a scene where Postumus, the leading character of the play, meets a Frenchman, a Dutchman, and a Spaniard at Philario's house in Rome. Then, there is a scene where Posthumus awakens in a prison in Wales and finds on the ground beside him a richly decorated book:

"What fairies haunt this ground? A book? O rare one!
Be not, as is our fangled world, a garment
Nobler than that it covers: let thy effects
So follow, to be most unlike our courtiers,

As good as promise."
(Cymbeline, V.4)

This particular episode belongs to the 9th century Celtic tradition. By placing Posthumus in various historical times Shakespeare illustrates how a certain experience in the future may be used to resolve a situation in the present. Namely, certain advanced developmental techniques were first mastered in 16th century Italy, so they could be applied to a specific situation in 9th century Wales and then passed over to 1st century Britain. Such an intervention was possible, because, as stated earlier, at the level of the Realm there is no such thing as past, present and future. Shakespeare clearly emphasizes, however, that such an "intervention" requires the presence of either a highly developed individual or super-corporal aspects of the Realm. It may help to comprehend such past-present-future relationships to recall that Posthumus' travels occurred during his banishment[79]. In Shakespeare's vocabulary "banishment" refers to certain meditative experiences associated with the activation of higher states of mind. During "banishment" the mind is forced out of its routine operation and is opened to new types of experiences.

4.4 The Three Fishes

As far as the evolutionary process is concerned, there are three types of man. These three "men" may be described symbolically as a wise man, a half-wise man, and a stupid one. The wise man is the guide. The guide is Divinely inspired and follows the Divine design. He may be compared to the leader of a caravan. The second man, i.e., the half-wise man, is perceptive enough to recognize the guide

---

[79] "Time factor" (Shakespeare for the Seeker, Volume 1, Chapter 3.2)

and his function. His sincerity allows him to understand the guide's instructions. He, like a blind man, clings to his guide and through him is able to follow the path. The stupid one is one who relies on his own intellect and emotional reflexes. He refuses to accept the role of the guide. He is like a traveller lost in the wilderness. These three types of travelers are illustrated in the story of the three fishes.

> There was in a secluded place a lake, which was fed by a running stream. In this lake were three fishes, the wise, the half-wise, and the foolish one. One day some fishermen passed by that lake, and having espied the fish hastened home to fetch their nets. The fish also saw the fishermen and were sorely disquieted. The wise fish said, 'I will not debate with the others, for assuredly they will dispute with me. And there is no time for arguments and persuasion. They love their native place so much that they will not be ready to come with me'. Without any delay the wise fish left the lake and took refuge in the running stream, which was linked to it. In this way he escaped the impending danger. The half wise fish delayed doing anything till the fishermen returned and threw their nets. The half wise fish was quite distressed. He said, 'I have lost the opportunity! Why did I not follow the guide? He has gone towards the sea and is freed from sorrow. Such a good comrade has been lost to me! But I will not think of that and will attend to free myself. I will become dead. I will turn my belly upwards and will commit myself to the water. To die before death is to be safe from torment'. So he floated upon the surface of the water, pretending to be dead. A fisherman seized him and flung him on the ground. The half wise fish, rolling over and over, managed to jump into the stream. In this way he gained his freedom. The foolish fish remained where he was, moving to and fro in agitation. That simpleton kept

leaping about, right and left, in order that he might save himself by his own efforts. He was easily caught and killed by the fishermen. (Book IV, 2188-2300)

Shakespeare described such three "men" in "The Merchant of Venice". These three "men" intended to "marry" Portia, the heiress of Belmont. Portia is the guide[80]. To "marry" her means to be accepted into Portia's "school". To be accepted by Portia, the candidates have to pass through a series of trials. The first trial is to demonstrate that a candidate is able to commit himself to the discipline of the school. This is spelled out in the oath that each candidate has to make:

> "I am enjoin'd by oath to observe three things:
> First, never to unfold to any one
> Which casket 'twas I chose; next, if I fail
> Of the right casket, never in my life
> To woo a maid in way of marriage: Lastly,
> If I do fail in fortune of my choice,
> Immediately to leave you and be gone."
> (The Merchant of Venice, II.9)

From an ordinary human point of view these requirements may sound too exaggerated and even ridiculous. However, when they are considered in the context of a spiritual training, then this difficulty disappears. If someone wishes to enter a spiritual path, it is obvious that he or she is expected to abandon other approaches. Only those who are able to commit themselves entirely to the chosen path may be allowed to follow it. The others are better off looking for "marriage" somewhere else.

There are three groups of candidates who wish to become Portia's disciples, i.e., a group of Western aristocrats, the Prince of Morocco and the Prince of Aragon, and Bassanio. The group of

---

[80] "Pilgrimage" (Shakespeare for the Seeker, Volume 3, Chapter 6.4)

aristocrats corresponds to the stupid fish in Rumi's story. After all, they are just spiritual tourists. They all shy away from taking the test and choose to leave Belmont (see Chapter 1.10).

Although the Prince of Morocco and the Prince of Aragon decide to take the test, they cannot pass it. They cannot pass it because they are driven by their inferior attachments. The Prince of Morocco places too much importance on his upbringing and his blood heritage:

> "I do in birth deserve her, and in fortunes,
> In graces and in qualities of breeding."
> (The Merchant of Venice, II.7)

The Prince of Aragon considers himself to be better than the others:

> "I will not choose what many men desire,
> Because I will not jump with common spirits
> And rank me with the barbarous multitudes."
> (The Merchant of Venice, II.9)

Morocco and Aragon also belong to the group of the stupid fish. This is why Portia calls them "these deliberate fools":

> "O, these deliberate fools! when they do choose,
> They have the wisdom by their wit to lose."
> (The Merchant of Venice, II.9)

Only Bassanio is able to pass the test. Bassanio is able to respond correctly to the entire environment of Belmont that was prepared by Portia. The impact of the environment and the presence of Portia induce in Bassanio an inner feeling that allows him to make the right choice. It is this inner quality that qualifies Bassanio for discipleship. In this sense Bassanio is a symbolic illustration of the half wise fish.

4.5 Pharaoh and Asiya

Rumi states that inner perception is the opposite of emotion; emotion feeds imagination. Therefore, imagination is the counterfeit of inner perception. A sort of touchstone is needed to distinguish between imagination and inner perception. The guides are such a touchstone. They can easily recognize the counterfeit coin from true gold. Rumi uses the characters of Moses and Pharaoh to illustrate the difference between these two types of understanding. Pharaoh is an example of man driven by imagination. Moses, on the other hand, is guided by his inner perception.

> Moses appealed to Pharaoh to abandon idolatrous life
> and enter onto the spiritual path. Pharaoh, however, tried
> to ridicule Moses with his sorceries by changing Moses'
> staff into a serpent. The pharaoh's sorcerers were also
> able to transform their own rods into serpents. But
> Moses' serpent swallowed them all. And then Moses
> explained, 'I have brought a serpent so I may destroy your
> serpent. This is my message for you, which means that if
> you enter onto the true path you will be freed from two
> serpents. Otherwise, your serpent will drag you into
> nothingness'. Pharaoh then proceeded to take counsel
> with his wife Asiya. He asked her whether it would be
> advisable to believe in the promises of Moses. Asiya urged
> him to do so. But Pharaoh said he would also consult his
> vizier Haman. Asiya knew Haman to be as blind to
> spiritual truth as Pharaoh himself. She did her best to
> dissuade Pharaoh from consulting him. To illustrate
> Haman's spiritual blindness, she told the story of a royal
> falcon who fell into the hands of an ignorant old woman.
> This old woman knew nothing of the virtues of a falcon
> and was displeased at the falcon's appearance. She said to
> the falcon, 'Where has your mother been that your claws

and beak are so long?' Following her ignorance the
woman clipped its talons, beak and wings. In this manner
she spoiled the falcon for all purposes of falconry.
Pharaoh, however, would not be diverted from his
purpose of consulting Haman. Haman persuaded
Pharaoh to reject Moses' appeal. (Book IV, 2301-2932)

Shakespeare illustrated a similar confrontation between
constructive and destructive forces in "Julius Caesar". In
Shakespeare's presentation, the characters of Julius Caesar, Cassius,
Brutus, and Brutus's wife Portia correspond to Rumi's Moses,
Haman, Pharaoh and Asiya, respectively.

Julius Caesar's role as spiritual King of Rome corresponds to that
of Moses of Egypt (see Chapter 1.16). Brutus, like Pharaoh, is
entirely driven by self-importance. He apparently places the good
of Rome above his own personal interests or feelings. In reality,
Brutus is rather a naive man who imagines that he is capable of
knowing what is good for Rome. Brutus' gullibility makes him an
easy target for Cassius, the "whisperer". Cassius harbours no
illusions about his own intention or his role as the whisperer:

> "Well, Brutus, thou art noble; yet, I see,
> Thy honourable metal may be wrought
> From that it is disposed: therefore it is meet
> That noble minds keep ever with their likes;
> For who so firm that cannot be seduced?
> Caesar doth bear me hard; but he loves Brutus:
> If I were Brutus now and he were Cassius,
> He should not humour me."
> (Julius Caesar, I.2)

Cassius is like Haman in Rumi's story. By using tricks he slyly leads
Brutus to believe that Caesar has become too powerful and must
die. Brutus accepts Cassius' false presentation of Caesar. Portia,
Brutus' wife, is a wise woman who is conscious of the damaging

influence of Cassius. Like Asiya in Rumi's story, Portia tries to warn her husband against Cassius. But Brutus disregards her counsel:

> "I have a man's mind, but a woman's might.
> How hard it is for women to keep counsel!"
> (Julius Caesar, II.4)

Brutus is one of Caesar's closest friends. Yet, Brutus becomes one of Caesar's assassins. If Brutus could not comprehend the evolutionary opportunity offered to Rome, then there was no place for a spiritual king there. The assassination of Caesar represents a serious failure that impinged on the universal plan:

> "...great Caesar fell.
> O, what a fall was there, my countrymen!
> Then I, and you, and all of us fell down,
> Whilst bloody treason flourish'd over us."
> (Julius Caesar, III.2)

Such a rejection was allowed by the measure of freewill that Rome had and its consequences could not be annulled by *force majeure*, no matter how much was at stake[81]. Nevertheless, this rejection disturbed higher-level forces. This was the reason why Rome, similarly to Egypt, was plagued with violent weather and a variety of bad omens, walking dead, and lions stalking through the city.

4.6 The Courtier who delayed his Friend's Death

A man who hears his inner voice within himself has no need to listen to spoken words. Consequently, what seems to be mercy and

---

[81] "Rejection" (Shakespeare for the Seeker, Volume 1, Chapter 2.2)

kindness to the ignorant, can be perceived by the wise as wrath and vengeance. Ordinary man must endure many ordeals and pain before he is able to perceive the difference between true inspiration and deceptive whispering. These different degrees of perception are illustrated by Rumi in the story of the courtier who saved his friend's life.

> A king was enraged against one of his courtiers and drew his sword to slay him. The bystanders were all afraid to interfere, with the exception of one who boldly threw himself at the king's feet and begged him to spare the offender. The king at once halted his hand and laid down his sword, saying, 'As you have interceded for him, I would gladly pardon him, even if he had acted as the very demon. I cannot refuse your entreaties, because they are the same as my own. In reality, it is not you who make these entreaties for him, but I who make them through you. I am the real actor in this matter and you are only my agent. The mercy you show to this offender is really shown by me, the king'. The offender was accordingly released and went his way. But, strangely enough, he showed no gratitude towards his protector. He refused to recognize the favour he had received through him. On the contrary, he omitted to greet him when he met him. People were surprised by his ingratitude. Then a certain mentor reproached him and asked, 'Why are you acting so unjustly towards a loyal friend?' He replied, 'I had offered up my life to the king. I desire no mercy but the blows of the king. If the king had cut off my head he would have given me eternal life in return for it. My duty is to sacrifice my life; it is the king's right to take life. The intercession of that courtier prevented me from experiencing death'. (Book IV, 2933-3084)

The offender did not understand that he was not ready yet to experience "to die before dying". His desire for "dying" was driven by the prospect of reward and not by service. This is why the king had to delay his death. Unlike Desdemona in Shakespeare's "Othello", the offender was not ready for such a transition (see Chapter 3.10). Desdemona was ready to travel to Mauritania, which corresponds to the "eternal life" that is referred to by the offender.

Shakespeare illustrated a similar situation in "Measure for Measure". In order to form an octagonal inner structure within the Bohemian branch, the Duke of Vienna needed to save Claudio's life[82]. According to the Duke's plan, a drunken inmate of the Viennese prison named Bernardine was to be executed instead of Claudio. In this way Claudio's life would be saved. When Barnardine was told that he should prepare himself for execution, he answered that he was not going to die because he was not ready for it:

> "… I have been drinking hard all night,
> and I will have more time to prepare me, or they
> shall beat out my brains with billets: I will not
> consent to die this day, that's certain."

It was at this very moment that, as in Rumi's story, an intervention took place. The Provost of the prison delivered the following message to the Duke:

> "There died this morning of a cruel fever
> One Ragozine, a most notorious pirate,
> A man of Claudio's years; his beard and head
> Just of his colour."

The Duke exclaimed:

---

[82] "Conclusion" (Shakespeare for the Seeker, Volume 4, Chapter 7.2)

"O, 'tis an accident that heaven provides!"
(Measure for Measure, IV.3)

The Duke's exclamation is equivalent to the king's pronouncement: "it is not you who make these entreaties for him, but I who make them through you". Indeed, Bernardine in his current state of drunkenness was not ready to die. But the pirate Ragozine was well prepared to deliver the required service. The timely death of Ragozine provided the needed solution: Claudio's life was spared. The "accident that heaven provides" allowed for the formation of the octagonal union within the Bohemian branch of the modern evolutionary cycle.

4.7 The Prince who was married to a Dervish's Daughter

At a certain stage of the spiritual journey a disciple is subjected to a trial. Such a trial tests to what degree the disciple has been able to overcome his worldly attachments. This is because at this stage, the sensitivity of his inner faculty may be partially awakened - but not its discriminatory power. As a result, the disciple may still be too blind to recognize the spiritual force of a genuine impulse to which he has been exposed. If, on the other hand, the disciple has been sufficiently developed, then his just awakened inner faculty will guide him through such an experience. This experience will lead him to the completion of the journey. Rumi illustrates this particular experience in the following story.

A certain king dreamed that his dearly beloved son, a
youth of great promise, had come to an untimely end. On
awaking he was rejoiced to find that his son was still alive;
but he reflected that an accident might carry him off at
any moment. Therefore he decided to marry him without

delay, in order that the succession might be secured. Accordingly he chose the daughter of a poor dervish as a bride for his son, and made preparations for the wedding. But his wife did not approve of the match. She thought that it was below the dignity of the prince to marry the daughter of a beggar. The king rebuked her, saying that a dervish who had renounced worldly wealth is spiritually rich. The king insisted on the consummation of the marriage. After the marriage, however, the prince refused to have anything to do with his wife. Instead, he carried on an affair with an ugly old woman, who had bewitched him by sorcery. The desperate king was praying for help. After a year a master physician was sent to him. The physician succeeded in breaking the spell. It was then that the prince's inner eye was opened and he recognized the superior qualities of his wife. He fell in love with her. (Book IV, 3085-3374)

The prince in the story represents a disciple. The old ugly woman represents attractions to the ordinary world. The beggar's daughter is an impulse of evolutionary energy. This impulse is designated for the prince. Because of his attraction to the ordinary world, the prince cannot correctly assimilate the impulse. The master physician is the guide.

In his play "All's Well That Ends Well" Shakespeare used a similar story to illustrate how a seed of European Renaissance was planted within the French evolutionary branch during the Middle Ages. The seed was in the form of a specific impulse of evolutionary energy. It is represented by Helena, "a poor physician's daughter". Bertram, a young count of Rousillon, represents a 13th century European man. Bertram is the intended recipient of the impulse. At the beginning of the play Bertram was too blind to see Helena's inner beauty. As the result, he was incapable of recognizing her function. Bertram's blindness was expressed by his attitude towards Helena:

> "I know her well:
> She had her breeding at my father's charge.
> A poor physician's daughter my wife! Disdain
> Rather corrupt me ever!"
> (All's Well That Ends Well, II.3)

As in Rumi's story, the king forced Bertram to marry Helena. Immediately after the marriage ceremony, Bertram left Helena and fled the country. While abroad, he was attracted to another woman. Then he went through quite an elaborate set of experiences that brought him back to Helena. In the final scene Bertram recognized Helena's wisdom and promised to be her faithful husband:

> "If she, my liege, can make me know this clearly,
> I'll love her dearly, ever, ever dearly."
> (All's Well That Ends Well, V.3)

"All's Well That Ends Well" symbolically illustrates a tiny fragment of the efforts aimed at evolutionary gains in Medieval Europe[83]. As illustrated by Bertram's experiences, it was a gradual and very complex process.

4.8 The Mule and the Camel

The final stage of man's evolution leads to the formation of a new organ of perception. This organ of supracognitive perception allows him to perceive and act in accordance with the cosmic matrix, i.e., beyond ordinary space-time limitations. This extra

---

[83] "Rousillon" (Shakespeare for the Seeker, Volume 2, Chapter 5.1)

dimensional capacity is illustrated by Rumi in the story of the mule and the camel (this is the continuation of the story from Chapter 3.9):

> One day a mule was placed in a stable where he met a camel. The mule said to the camel, 'How is it that I am always stumbling and falling down, whilst you never make a wrong step?' The camel replied, 'My eyes are always directed upwards, and I see a long way before me, while your eyes look down, and you only see what is immediately under your feet'. The mule recognized the truth in the camel's statement. The mule wept awhile and then said, 'O camel, you have spoken the truth'. He asked to be allowed to be the camel's servant. The camel agreed, saying 'Since you have sincerely asked, you may become my servant. In this way you will be saved from the pangs of devouring time'. (Book IV, 3375-3543)

Rumi remarks that the ordinary intellect cannot see beyond the grave, but the inner senses give insight into other worlds. The inner senses allow one to steer a better course in this world. Therefore men, following their ordinary intellect or their own opinions, are certainly confused. But those who have developed deeper perceptions are able to get a glimpse of truth. This is illustrated in the story of the husband and his adulterous wife:

> An adulterous woman, desiring to carry on an affair with her lover, climbed up a pear-tree to gather the fruit. When she had reached the top she looked down and pretended that she saw her husband misconducting himself with another woman. The husband assured her there was no one but himself there, and desired her to come down and see for herself. She came down and admitted there was no one there. Her husband then, at her request, ascended the tree. She at once called her lover and began to amuse

herself with him. Her husband saw her from his post in the tree and began to abuse her. But she declared there was no man with her. She said, 'Those illusions appear to you from the top of the pear-tree, for the top of that pear-tree causes the human eye to see such things. Come down from the top of the pear-tree, so those illusions may vanish. You see double, just as I saw double previously'. (Book IV, 3544-3636)

Rumi explains that the pear-tree in the story represents egoism and self-centeredness. People, who are driven by their corrupted self, have a limited capacity to perceive certain things. Such a limited ability causes their thoughts to be awry and makes their eyes squint. But when they manage to come down from their own pear-tree, then their thoughts and eyes may regain clarity. And in this manner, this pear-tree may become a tree of fortune.

Shakespeare indicates that the evolutionary process was disrupted in antiquity. There was interference in the evolutionary transmission. As a result, man lost access to the cosmic matrix. A corrective action was needed to short-circuit the fault that had appeared in the planetary past. In "Pericles, Prince of Tyre" Shakespeare illustrated the corrective action that was implemented in order to rectify the process. The corrective action was realized through Pericles' mission[84].

Pericles' mission led him from the ordinary world to Pentapolis. Pentapolis is a symbolic representation of the most remote temple, i.e., the higher world (see Chapter 4.1). Pentapolis, therefore, represents an entity that exists beyond the limitations of time and space. On his journey towards Pentapolis, Pericles had to travel back in time in order to pass through the intermediate worlds that had been corrupted in the past. The cities of Antioch and Tarsus represent such corrupted worlds. When he reached Pentapolis,

---

[84] "Pericles' mission" (Shakespeare for the Seeker, Volume 2, Chapter 4.1)

Pericles acquired some new skills. Namely, he was granted a vision that corresponded to that of the camel in Rumi's story. He was able to act in accordance with the design of the cosmic matrix, i.e., the requirements of the Realm. While in Pentapolis, his future challenges were presented to him symbolically by the five knights whom he had to fight in a tournament. Each of the knights was associated with one of the five cities that were on Pericles' descending route, i.e., Tarsus, Antioch, Tyre, Mytilene, and Ephesus. When he reached the city of Ephesus, Pericles was like the man who managed to come down from the pear-tree. Pericles' mission led to the restoration of the evolutionary transmission chain.

The transmission chain restored by Pericles allowed for the transmission of the entire spectrum of evolutionary energy. The transmission included the supracognitive energy, which is the highest energy available in the galaxy. This was the most significant event in the evolutionary history of mankind. However, neither supracognitive nor unitive energy was released to humanity at large. At the end of Pericles' mission the entire spectrum was made available only to a select group of people. This group was symbolically represented by those who were present in Ephesus at the time of Pericles' return. They witnessed Pericles' account of his experiences. Since then, this group of people, and their successors, have been acting as the guides and the custodians of the evolutionary process. Their role is to act at critical stages of the process, contriving results necessary to keep the whole evolution of the earth in step with events in the galaxy. Since that time, the custodians have supervised and directed the evolutionary process. Some of the characters in Shakespeare's plays characterized by their supracognitive perception and extraordinary skills are illustrations of the custodians.

Book 5. Barriers

In the preface to Book 5, Rumi emphasizes the limitations of the laws and other prescriptions as a means of guiding men along the path. Rumi compares the laws to a candle that allows one to see the path. "Unless you gain possession of the candle", he says, "there is no path. But when you have embarked upon the path, your path becomes the journey. And when you have reached the journey's end, you meet the Truth".

Shakespeare used Feste, the Fool who appears in "Twelfth Night", to express a similar concept:

> "Journeys end in lovers meeting,
> Every wise man's son doth know."
> (Twelfth Night, II.3)

But there are many barriers that stand in man's way. These barriers are man's distinctive tendencies which affect his behaviour. Rumi indicates that there are four main disturbing tendencies that interfere with man's journey. These tendencies may be symbolically compared to the duck, the peacock, the crow, and the cock. The duck is greed, the cock is lust, ambition and flamboyance are like the peacock, and the crow represents worldly desires.

5.1 The Prophet and the Gluttonous Guest

Rumi tells the following story to illustrate how gluttony may block understanding. At the same time he explains how this particular barrier may be removed:

> One day some visitors came to Mohamed and begged him for food and lodging. They said, 'We have come here as visitors seeking hospitality. You are the entertainer of all the inhabitants of the world. We are destitute and have arrived from afar. We are asking of you to shed your grace and light upon us!' Mohamed was moved by their entreaties. He asked each of his disciples to take one of the visitors to his house and feed and lodge him. So each disciple selected one of the visitors and took him to his house. But there was one big and coarse man, whom no one would invite. It was Mohamed who took him to his own house. In his house he had seven she-goats to supply his family with milk. But the hungry visitor devoured all the milk, to say nothing of the bread and the other foods. He left not a drop for Mohamed's family, who were therefore much annoyed with him. When the visitor retired to his chamber, one of the servant-maids locked him in for she was angry with him. During the night the visitor felt sick from overeating and tried to get out into the open air. But he was unable to do so, because the door was locked. He became very sick and defiled his bedding. Mohamed was aware of what had happened. In the morning Mohamed opened the chamber but hid himself behind the door, because he did not want to put the man to shame. The moment the door was opened, the man ran away. After he had gone a servant saw the mess the visitor had made. This meddling servant brought the dirty bed-clothes to Mohamed saying, 'Look at what your guest has done!' Mohamed smiled and said, 'Bring the pail here, so I may wash with my own hands'. His friends were shocked at the thought of Mohamed soiling his hands with such filth, and tried to stop him. But he

persisted in doing it. While he was engaged in the work the visitor came back to look for an amulet, which he had left behind him in his hurry to escape. Though he was ashamed, greed for his amulet took away his shame. Seeing Mohamed's cleaning the filth he had made, the amulet vanished from his mind and a great rapture arose in him. The visitor burst into tears and bewailed his own conduct. Mohamed consoled him, saying that his sincere weeping would purge the offence. The visitor thanked him and asked to be accepted as his disciple. Afterwards, Mohamed invited the visitor to have dinner with him. During the dinner the visitor drank only a small portion of milk and steadfastly refused to take more, saying he felt perfectly satisfied with the little he had already taken. The other guests were amazed to see his gluttony cured so quickly. (Book V, 1-394)

Shakespeare presented a similar example showing how greed and gluttony may be overcome by coming into contact with developmental activities. For this purpose Shakespeare used the character of Pistol, who appears in "Henry IV", "Henry V", and "The Merry Wives of Windsor". Pistol appears for the first time in "Henry IV-Part 2", i.e., in the play that is set in England at the beginning of the 15th century. At that time Pistol is described as:

> "...swaggering rascal! let him not come
> hither: it is the foul-mouthed'st rogue in England."
> (Henry IV-Part 2, II.4)

Then Pistol appears in "Henry V". At that time, Pistol, and his two companions Nym and Bardolph, went with the King's troops to war in France. A boy, who was as a servant to Pistol, described him and his two companions as thieves and liars. According to the boy, these three would steal anything and call it a trophy. Instead of fighting, they would keep themselves busy stealing. For example,

Bardolph stole a lute case, carried it for thirty-six miles, and sold it for a penny and a half. While in Calais, Nym and Bardolph stole a fire shovel. The boy complains that they would like him to join them in their mischief. He refused, because for him taking something from someone's pocket and putting it into his own would be just plain stealing. Such villainies nauseated him:

> "As young as I am, I have observed these three
> swashers. I am boy to them all three: but all they
> three, though they would serve me, could not be man
> to me; for indeed three such antics do not amount to
> a man. [...] They will steal
> any thing, and call it purchase. Bardolph stole a
> lute-case, bore it twelve leagues, and sold it for
> three half pence. Nym and Bardolph are sworn
> brothers in filching, and in Calais they stole a
> fire-shovel: I knew by that piece of service the
> men would carry coals. They would have me as
> familiar with men's pockets as their gloves or their
> handkerchers: which makes much against my manhood,
> if I should take from another's pocket to put into
> mine; for it is plain pocketing up of wrongs. I
> must leave them, and seek some better service:
> their villany goes against my weak stomach, and
> therefore I must cast it up." (Henry V, III.2)

Yet, it was possible for Pistol, like the gluttonous guest, to go through inner transformation. Shakespeare indicates, however, that it took nearly 200 years before the particular aspect that was symbolically represented by Pistol, could be transformed. Pistol reappears in the company of Sir John Falstaff, Bardolph and Nym in "The Merry Wives of Windsor", i.e., the play that is set-up at the end of the 16th century. At that time Pistol refused to serve Falstaff, because he recognized Falstaff's villainy. In his characteristically garbled way of speaking, Pistol expressed his decision to inform

Mr. Ford about Falstaff's mischievous intention to seduce Mr. Ford's wife:

"And I to Ford shall eke unfold
How Falstaff, varlet vile,
His dove will prove, his gold will hold,
And his soft couch defile."
(The Merry Wives of Windsor, I.3)

Shakespeare used Pistol's anachronistic reappearance to indicate a significant change in the projection of evolutionary energy that was implemented in Europe at that time. As a matter of fact, the play was dedicated to the illustration of that change[85]. Previously, the members of the upper class were serving as the main channel of the evolutionary transmission. For whatever reason, that previously used channel became sterile. At the end of the 16th century that particular channel could not fully discharge its evolutionary function. This is why, at that time, it was necessary to shift the evolutionary transmission to certain individuals within the middle and the working classes. Pistol's parting from Falstaff was an indication that the England of "The Merry Wives of Windsor" represented a different developmental state than the England at the time of "Henry V". Sir John Falstaff is the only "nobleman" among the main characters who appear in "The Merry Wives of Windsor". And he is utterly corrupted. He marks the end of the line of "knights". Shakespeare inserted a brief episode to show how an ordinary person may get into contact with developmental activities. In this episode Pistol meets Mistress Quickly. He immediately recognizes that there is something special about her:

"This punk is one of Cupid's carriers:
Clap on more sails; pursue; up with your fights:
Give fire: she is my prize, or ocean whelm them all!"
(The Merry Wives of Windsor, II.2)

---

[85] "Being of Windsor" (Shakespeare for the Seeker, Volume 4, Chapter 8.2)

At the end of the play Pistol is a different person. This is symbolically indicated by his miraculously improved way of speaking. Instead of his usual garbled manner of speaking, during the masque Pistol delivers his poetical invocation flawlessly:

> "Elves, list your names; silence, you airy toys.
> Cricket, to Windsor chimneys shalt thou leap:
> Where fires thou find'st unraked and hearths unswept,
> There pinch the maids as blue as bilberry:
> Our radiant queen hates sluts and sluttery."
> (The Merry Wives of Windsor, V.5)

The masque was the kind of event that may be compared to Mohamed's feast to which the gluttonous visitor was invited. During that feast everyone noticed the change in the guest's behaviour. The audience watching the performance of "The Merry Wives of Windsor" may witness a similar transformation in Pistol.

The story of the gluttonous guest is then followed by Rumi's reflections on the peacock of ambition and flamboyance.

> Now we come to the double-faced peacock, who displays himself for the sake of name and fame. His desire is to catch people. He is ignorant of good and evil, of constructive and destructive, and of the result and the use of his prey. The peacock catches his prey ignorantly, like a trap. What knowledge has the trap concerning the purpose of its action? What harm comes to the trap, or what benefit, from catching its prey? It is idle catching. 'So what', asks Rumi, 'can you get from the pursuit of people and throng of friends? From vain glory and self existence? Most of your life is already gone and it becomes quite late. Yet you are still busy in pursuit of trivia. You are going around catching one thing and releasing another from the trap. And then, like a madman, you are pursuing another attraction. Such a game is good

for heedless children! Keep in mind that night is coming and you have caught nothing valid in your trap. Your trap is nothing but affliction and your own shackle. In reality you have been catching yourself with the trap, for you are imprisoned and disappointed with your own catches. Is any owner of a trap such a dolt, like you, that he would try to catch himself?' (Book V, 395-476)

In Sonnet 29 Shakespeare meditates on the same theme. The poet describes his difficulties that are caused by the importance that he still gives to his ambition and flamboyance[86]:

"When in disgrace with Fortune and men's eyes,
I all alone beweep my out-cast state,
And trouble deaf heaven with my bootless cries,
And look upon myself and curse my fate.
Wishing me like to one more rich in hope,
Featured like him, like him with friends possessed,
Desiring this man's art, and that man's scope,
With what I most enjoy contented least,
Yet in these thoughts my self almost despising,
Haply I think on thee, and then my state,
(Like to the Lark at break of day arising)
From sullen earth, sings hymns at Heaven's gate,
    For thy sweet love remembered such wealth brings,
    That then I scorn to change my state with Kings."
(Sonnet 29)

The poet says that he sits alone and cries when he is out of luck or when disgraced by his friends. And he curses himself and pesters heaven with his useless complains. Then he lists a number of worldly pleasures that are still important to him, i.e., promising hope, good looks, having more friends, having certain skills and having new opportunities. Yet, he admits, he is least content with

---

[86] "Shakespeare's Sonnets or How heavy do I journey on the way" (Sonnet 29)

things he enjoys most. The poet discovers that he may distance himself from these destructive attachments by focussing his attention on the guide. During such moments his inner state changes, like a lark at daybreak that starts to sing hymns to heaven. At such moments the poet is able to bypass by his inner barriers and experience a different kind of riches, which he would not exchange for anything else.

5.2 The Arab and his Dog

In the story of the Arab and his Dog, Rumi gives another example of the workings of the personal "peacock", i.e., vanity. And he advises the readers, "Do not admire your peacock-feathers but look at his ugly feet, so that your vanity may not lead you astray".

> A certain Arab had a dog to which he was much attached. But one day the dog died of hunger. At once he began sobbing, shedding tears, and crying, 'This dog hunted for me by day and kept watch by night; he was catching prey and driving off thieves'. He was reciting poetry and lamenting over the dog. A beggar passed by and asked, 'What is this sobbing? For whom is thy mourning and lamentation?' On hearing that the dog had died of hunger, he asked the Arab why he had not fed him from the bag of food which he still had in his hand. The Arab replied that it was his bread and food left over from last night, which he was keeping for himself. The beggar asked, 'Why did you not give some bread to the dog?' The Arab replied, 'I am not at liberty to do so. Bread cannot be obtained by a traveler on the road without money, but tears from the eyes cost nothing'. The beggar exclaimed, 'You are a fool! In your opinion a piece of bread is better

than tears'. The beggar rebuked him for his hypocrisy,
and went on his way. (Book V, 477-535)

Sobbing and shedding tears, when caused by the Supreme Cause,
are developmentally constructive. But when man's heart is full of
envy and vanity, then his grief and his tears are destructive.
Shakespeare pointed out how it is possible to recognize and avoid
such idle grievances. In Sonnet 30, Shakespeare indicates that he
has learned about the nature of such idle grievances during his
meditation[87]. He refers to his meditations as "Sessions of sweet
silent thought":

> "When to the Sessions of sweet silent thought,
> I summon up remembrance of things past,
> I sigh the lack of many a thing I sought,
> And with old woes new wail my dear time's waste:
> Then can I drown an eye (unused to flow)
> For precious friends hid in death's dateless night,
> And weep afresh love's long since cancelled woe,
> And moan the expense of many a vanished sight.
> Then can I grieve at grievances foregone,
> And heavily from woe to woe tell o'er
> The sad account of fore-bemoaned moan,
> Which I new pay as if not paid before.
>> But if the while I think on thee (dear friend)
>> All losses are restor'd, and sorrows end."
> (Sonnet 30)

If during his meditations the poet allows his thoughts to wonder
freely, they go back into the past and bring up memories of all
kinds of unfulfilled desires. This makes him depressed and tearful.
He laments about old grievances and sadly recounts each woe of
the past. He realizes that this is like paying again for something that
has already been paid for. Then he discovers that the only way to

---

[87] "Shakespeare's Sonnets or How heavy do I journey on the way" (Sonnet 30)

free himself from such idle commemorations is to focus his attention on his guide. Only then can the poet's meditation lead to a constructive outcome ("but if the while I think on thee, dear friend, all losses are restor'd, and sorrows end").

5.3 The Sage and the Peacock

Rumi points out that paying too much attention to worldly accomplishments and wealth endangers man's evolutionary growth. He compares such attractions to the plumage of the peacock. A self-restrained man deems his "feathers" to be of no value, so that his feathers may not get him into trouble. His feathers are not harmful to him, therefore he does not have to tear them out because in moments of vanity he will be able to deal with them. But to those, whose beauteous feathers are of great importance, if they are not able to restrain themselves from displaying them, it is better to get rid of them. Rumi illustrates this in the story of the Sage and the Peacock.

> A sage went for a walk and saw a peacock busily engaged in tearing out his own plumage with his beak. At seeing this insane self-destruction the sage could not refrain himself. He cried out to the peacock to forbear from mutilating himself and spoiling his beauty in so reckless a manner. When the peacock heard this counsel, he looked at the sage and began to lament and weep. The long lamentation and weeping of the sorrowful peacock caused everyone who was there to weep with him. The peacock then explained that his bright plumage which he admired so much was a source of continuous danger to him. He said to the sage, 'Begone, for you are in chains of appearances. Do you not perceive that on account of

these feathers a hundred afflictions approach me from every side? Oh, many pitiless hunters always lay traps for me everywhere for the sake of these feathers. How many archers, for the sake of my plumage, shoot arrows at me when I am in the air! It is my plumage that leads me to being constantly pursued by hunters, whom I have no strength to contend against. I have therefore decided to get rid of it myself with my own beak'. This is why the peacock was making himself ugly so that no hunter would pursue him in the future. (Book V, 536-844)

Prospero, a character who appears in Shakespeare's "The Tempest", experienced such a moment of vanity when he called for the goddesses to perform a masque for his daughter Miranda and for Ferdinand (see Chapter 3.4). He used the masque to show off his beautiful plumage and his extraordinary skills. The masque exposed Prospero's weakness. This is why during the masque the goddesses were trying to take advantage of Prospero's weakness and trick him. According to Caliban, the goddesses were Prospero's enemies and "rootedly" hated him[88]:

> "Remember
> First to possess his books; for without them
> He's but a sot, as I am, nor hath not
> One spirit to command: they all do hate him
> As rootedly as I."
> (The Tempest, III.2)

At the last moment Prospero awoke from his fancies and managed to avoid making an error that could turn his project into a complete fiasco:

> "I had forgot that foul conspiracy
> Of the beast Caliban and his confederates

---

[88] "Prospero challenges" (Shakespeare for the Seeker, Volume 4, Chapter 8.1)

Against my life: the minute of their plot
Is almost come."
(The Tempest, IV.1)

Ferdinand and Miranda were surprised by Prospero's aggravation:

Ferdinand:

"This is strange: your father's in some passion
That works him strongly."

Miranda:

"Never till this day
Saw I him touch'd with anger so distemper'd."
(The Tempest, IV.1)

Prospero's ill temper was caused by the fact that by allowing himself to be driven by vanity, he nearly lost his entire enterprise. The important thing is that he avoided this mistake. Prospero, like the peacock in Rumi's story, was able to recover from his vanity and fancy.

5.4 Mohamed Shah and the People of Sabzawar

Rumi emphases the fact that the whole human community, not just a flock of followers, continues to exist in physical form because of the work and the life of the guide (see Introduction to Book 1). He illustrates this again in an episode from the life of Mohamed Shah of Khorasan. Mohamed Shah was the last prince of the Khorasan dynasty of Balkh, to which family both Rumi's mother and grandmother belonged. His family descended from Abu Bakr, the First Caliph. Mohamed Shah was the reigning prince in 1209, i.e., the year in which Rumi's father fled from Balkh.

In one of his campaigns Mohamed Shah captured the city of Sabzawar, which was inhabited by people who were sworn vicious enemies of all the descendants of Abu Bakr. After the city was taken, the inhabitants came out and proceeded with all humility to beg their lives, offering to pay any amount of ransom and tribute that he might impose upon them. But the prince replied that he would spare their lives only on one condition, i.e., that they would find in Sabzawar a man bearing the name Abu Bakr. The people of Sabzawar explained to him that it would be impossible to find in the whole city a single man bearing a name so hateful to them. But the prince was unswayable and refused to change his demand. So they went and searched the entire neighbourhood. After three days and three nights of searching, they found a traveler lying at the roadside at the point of death, whose name was Abu Bakr. As he was unable to walk, they placed him on a bier and carried him into the prince's presence. The prince reproached them for their contempt and neglect of this pious man, who was the only true heart amongst them.

In this parable, says Rumi, Sabzawar represents the world; the pious man is the Guide living among ordinary men but he is unrecognizable by them. Only through his presence, however, can the people of Sabzawar be saved. (Book V, 845-1118)

Shakespeare also alluded to this astonishing fact. In Sonnet 11, for example, Shakespeare's guide explains that if no one was taking care of the evolutionary growth of humanity, then time would end and the entire world would collapse within the life-time of a man. Here is the interpretation of the Sonnet[89] followed by its full text:

---

[89] "Shakespeare's Sonnets or How heavy do I journey on the way" (Sonnet 11)

The guide tells the poet that he may grow as fast as his body declines ("as fast as thou shalt wane so fast thou grow'st"). He specifies that the poet's growth refers to the development of his inner being, from which his physical body will be separated ("in one of thine, from that which thou departest"). The poet may think about his inner being as his new self, when he will be no longer young ("and that fresh blood which youngly thou bestow'st, thou mayst call thine, when thou from youth convertest"). This is why it is said that within man there is a seed of knowledge, beauty, and growth ("herein lives wisdom, beauty, and increase"). Without this seed, there would be only ignorance, destruction, and death ("without this folly, age, and cold decay"). If none was taking care of the seed, then time would end and the entire world would collapse within the life-time of a man ("if all were minded so, the times should cease, and threescore year would make the world away"). The guide tells the poet that those who do not make any effort to develop themselves will perish ("let those whom nature hath not made for store, harsh, featureless, and rude, barrenly perish"). But to those whom Nature endowed with beauty, she also gave a valuable gift ("look whom she best endowed, she gave the more"). The poet is such a man. Therefore, the poet is obliged to use this gift correctly ("which bounteous gift thou shouldst in bounty cherish"). Nature made the poet as her stamp so he may preserve her ("she carved thee for her seal"). The guide emphasizes that this stamp should be preserved and used; it should not be wasted ("and meant thereby, thou shouldst print more, not let that copy die").

> "As fast as thou shalt wane so fast thou grow'st,
> In one of thine, from that which thou departest,
> And that fresh blood which youngly thou bestow'st,
> Thou mayst call thine, when thou from youth convertest,
> Herein lives wisdom, beauty, and increase,
> Without this folly, age, and cold decay,
> If all were minded so, the times should cease,

And threescore year would make the world away:
Let those whom nature hath not made for store,
Harsh, featureless, and rude, barrenly perish,
Look whom she best endowed, she gave the more;
Which bounteous gift thou shouldst in bounty cherish,
    She carved thee for her seal, and meant thereby,
    Thou shouldst print more, not let that copy die."
    (Sonnet 11)

This counsel also served as an indication of why and what the poet should write about. By developing himself, the poet would be capable of recording his own experiences. In this way, he would be able to pass his experiences on to the future generations. But as long as the poet remained in his underdeveloped state, he would not be able to produce anything of true value.

5.5 The Man who claimed to be a Prophet

Rumi says that to explain the evolutionary nature of spirituality is as difficult as trying to convince a mountain to move. Whatever one would say, the mountain would echo back; the mountain would mock it like a scoffer. Similarly, the concept of conscious evolution of man's mind is entirely lost on worldly men, i.e., those who only desire to hear promises about riches or other pleasures. They cleave to the present life so strongly that they hate those who tell them of another. They say, 'You are telling us old fables and raving idly'. Rumi illustrates this situation further in the story of the man who claimed to be a prophet.

A man cried out to the people, 'I am a prophet; Yea, I am superior to all the prophets'. The people gathered round him, shouting, 'What deceit and imposture is this? If you claim that you are a prophet because you come from the realm of non-existence, we all are prophets. We also came here as strangers from that place. Why should you be any different or special?' He replied, 'Did not you come like a sleeping child? You were ignorant of the way and the destination. You passed through the different stages asleep, unconscious of the way and its ups and downs. But we prophets set out in wakefulness and well aware from beyond the five senses and the six directions to this world. We have perceived all the stages from the source, we are possessed of experience, and we have known the way like skilled guides'. On hearing that, the people seized him and took him to the king, saying, 'This man says he is a prophet. Put him to the torture, so he may never again speak such words'. The king saw that the man was very weak and fragile, and would not survive a single blow. So he decided to speak to him. He took him away from the crowd and asked him where his home was. The man replied, 'O king, my home is the house of peace, and I come from there into this house of reproach. I have neither home nor any companion; when has a fish made its home on the earth?' Then the king, as a jest, asked him what he had been eating for breakfast that made him pronounce such boastful statements. The man answered that if he ate mere earthly bread and water he would not have claimed to be a prophet. The king then said to him, 'What is this inspiration of yours, and what profit do you derive from it?' The man answered, 'What profit is there that I do not derive from it? I am not rich in worldly wealth, yet my inspiration is surely as precious as that of bees. Bees are so inspired that their dwelling place is filled with honey. He who has his face made joyful by that celestial wine is a prophet, and he who is unaffected by that spiritual drink is to be accounted as lost'. (Book V, 1119-1241)

Shakespeare implemented such challenges of recognizing the guides and their function by making them invisible to a merely rational mind or a speculative intellect. In Shakespeare's plays the guides appear as a king, a queen, a husband, a wife, a rogue, a fool, a prince, a maiden, a nobleman, a bastard, a magician, a craftsman, a general, or a clown; in the Sonnets the guide is presented as a young handsome man. Unlike Rumi, Shakespeare does not identify the guides. He leaves it up to the reader to recognize them through their effect on the other characters of the plays. In other words, there is no rational or intellectual means to identify the guides and their function. Neither is it possible to identify the inner structure of the plays by applying scholarly methods based on aesthetic or linguistic criteria. This is why any interpretation that explores the evolutionary aspects of Shakespeare's writings is incomprehensible to ordinary thinking patterns. In several of his plays, Shakespeare illustrated this kind of incomprehension. For example, the reaction of the young lovers who ridiculed the mechanicals' performance of "Pyramus and Thisby" inserted in "A Midsummer Night's Dream" is an example of such incomprehension. Prior to the mechanicals' presentation of "Pyramus and Thisby", Theseus explained the modus operandi of Shakespeare's plays:

Theseus:

"The best in this kind are but shadows; and the worst are no worse, if imagination amend them."

Hippolyta:

"It must be your imagination then, and not theirs."

Theseus:

"If we imagine no worse of them than they of themselves, they may pass for excellent men."
(A Midsummer Night's Dream, V.1)

Theseus says that even seemingly bad performances can produce a constructive effect if a play contains the required ingredients, its inner structure is based on the evolutionary matrix and it is presented to the right audience, in the right place and at the right time. Things that seem to be errors, omissions, and other deficiencies are intentionally introduced to provide gaps and inconsistencies to force the viewers' minds to amend them accordingly ("if imagination amend them"). In this way, the play may induce its intended impact on the audience.

In his prologue to "Pyramus and Thisby", Peter Quincy clearly spelled out the intent of the mechanicals' performance:

> "If we offend, it is with our good will.
> That you should think, we come not to offend,
> But with good will. To show our simple skill,
> That is the true beginning of our end.
> Consider then we come but in despite.
> We do not come as minding to contest you,
> Our true intent is. All for your delight
> We are not here. That you should here repent you,
> The actors are at hand and by their show
> You shall know all that you are like to know."
> (A Midsummer Night's Dream, V.1)

The players' intention is not to please but to tell the audience "all that you are like to know". The audience, however, may be offended by what they will find out about themselves. Nevertheless, the performance will fulfil its purpose by helping the audience realize their ignorance, and "that you should here repent you".

To overcome the limitations of the rational mind and speculative intellect, an extraordinary effort is needed. Rumi summarizes such an effort in the following anecdote about a lover and his mistress:

> A certain lover recounted to his mistress all the services
> he had done, and all the toils he had undergone for her

sake. He said, 'For your sake I did such and such, in this war I suffered wounds from arrows and spears. My wealth, strength and fame are gone. On account of my love for you many a misfortune has befallen me. No dawn found me asleep or laughing; no evening found me with money or means to live'. What he had tasted of bitterness and sorrow he was recounting to her in detail, point by point. Not for the sake of reproach. He was displaying a hundred testimonies of the trueness of his love. For men of reason a single indication is enough, but how should the longing of lovers be removed thereby? The lover repeats his tale unworriedly: how should a fish be satisfied with a mere indication so as to refrain from the limpid water? There was a fire in him. He did not know what it was, but on account of its heat he was weeping like a candle. The beloved said, 'You have done all this; yet open your ear wide and apprehend well. For you have not done what is the root of the root of love and duty. This what you have done is only the branches'. The lover said to her, 'Tell me, what is that root?' She said, 'The root thereof is to die and become nothing. You have done all else, but you have not died, you are still living. You have to die if you are a self-sacrificing friend!' The lover accordingly gave up his life: like the rose, he played away his head, laughing and rejoicing. (Book V, 1242-1270)

According to the story of the lover, "to die before dying" is the required condition for "a good marriage". Shakespeare further elaborated on the same theme in "Romeo and Juliet". Here is a quote from Friar Lawrence's comment on "a good marriage":

"She's not well married that lives married long;
But she's best married that dies married young."
(Romeo and Juliet, IV.5)

In this quote "marriage" means an unconditional commitment to the spiritual path; "death" refers to the spiritual state of "to die before dying" or "die to live"[90]. In other words, Shakespeare points out that, as in Rumi's story, "a good marriage is completed with death".

5.6 The Disciple who blindly imitated his Guide

Rumi emphasizes the fact that intuitive and theoretical knowledge is not sufficient enough to understand a wise man's actions. A wise man's actions are driven by a true understanding of the situation. Therefore, copying his sayings and acts may even be damaging to the well-intentioned but ignorant imitators.

> An ignorant young man entered an assembly of disciples who were being addressed by their Sheikh. He saw the Sheikh weeping and lamenting, and in mere blind and senseless imitation copied the Sheikh's behaviour. He started to weep though he understood not a word of the discourse. In fact, he behaved just like a deaf man who sees those around him laughing, and laughs himself just to conform with them, though he knows not the subject of their enjoyment. Hence the mere imitator of a Sheikh resembles a deaf man. After he had wept for some time, he made due salutations to the Sheikh and departed. One of the Sheikh's disciples followed him and thus addressed him, 'Do not go and tell others that you visited the Sheikh, saw him weeping, and wept. Your ignorant and mere imitative weeping is totally unlike the weeping of that man. Such weeping as his is only possible to one who

---

[90] "Trials and errors" (Shakespeare for the Seeker, Volume 3, Chapter 6.6)

has, like him, waged a war on himself for thirty years. His weeping is not caused by worldly sufferings, but by deep concerns for humanity. You cannot perceive by intellect or emotion the spiritual reality that is open and plain to his vision. Fools like you are ignorant of the motive of the Sheikh's actions. Therefore they only harm themselves if they try to imitate them without understanding their meaning'.

In like manner parrots, are taught to speak without understanding the words. The method is to place a mirror between the parrot and the trainer. The trainer, hidden by the mirror, utters the words, and the parrot, seeing his own reflection in the mirror, fancies another parrot is speaking, and imitates all that is said by the trainer behind the mirror. Similarly, the disciple who is still driven by his untamed self sees himself in the mirror of the Sheikh's presence. He does not perceive the Realm that is behind the mirror. He supposes that a man is speaking, but the essence of that interaction is beyond his perception. The disciple is only a parrot. He learns the words, but their inner meaning is still beyond his comprehension. (Book V, 1271-1472)

Shakespeare inserted in "Othello" an episode with a Clown to illustrate the action of a guide that is beyond his disciples' perception. Othello is a general and a guide. Cassio is his deputy. Othello, however, stripped Cassio of his rank because Cassio got drunk and got into a fight. In an attempt at reconciliation, Cassio goes with some musicians to play beneath Othello's window. It is then that the Clown appears. He delivers the following message:

"If you have any music that may not be heard, to't again: but, as they say to hear music the general does not greatly care." (Othello, III.1)

The Clown indicates that Cassio has been using a wrong approach. Instead of conventional means such as playing music, he should use his subtle faculties, i.e., "music that may not be heard". When the musicians responded:

> "We have none such, sir",

they are told to go away:

> "Then put up your pipes in your bag, for I'll away:
> go; vanish into air; away!"

Then the Clown tells Cassio that he is not honest in his approach:

> Cassio:
>
> "Dost thou hear, my honest friend?"
>
> Clown:
>
> "No, I hear not your honest friend; I hear you."
> (Othello, III.1)

The Clown tells Cassio that he should communicate with his guide through "music that may not be heard". But Cassio does not understand the message[91]. The meaning of the Clown's message is beyond his comprehension.

Rumi quotes another story that illustrates another aspect of a disciple's behaviour when he is still incapable of grasping his guide's actions. This is the story about a man and his sons.

> A man was giving to the poor four times the legal amount
> of alms due from his growing crops. Thus, instead of
> paying one-tenth of his crop, which is the legally required
> amount, he paid one-tenth of the green ears of corn,

---

[91] "Developmental techniques" (Shakespeare for the Seeker, Volume 3, Chapter 6.2)

another tenth of the ripe wheat, a third tenth of the threshed grain, and a fourth tenth of the bread made from the grains. And he used the same formula for grapes and other fruits of his garden. He would never omit to give one-tenth of any of his products. All this time his field and garden yielded abundant amounts of crops and fruits. The other owners of orchards were in need of him, both for fruit and money, while he needed nothing from any of them. But his sons, who were blind to their father's actions, saw only his lavish expenditure upon the poor. They were not able to see the link between their father's generosity and the yield of his field and garden. Therefore, they rebuked him for his supposed extravagance. (Book V, 1473-1555)

Shakespeare further elaborated on the theme of generosity in his play entitled "Timon of Athens". Timon is the title character. Timon seems to have access to an almost magical amount of gold. He enjoys giving presents to his friends and helping those who are in need. But he, like the generous man in Rumi's story, does not give presents out of a desire for return. He believes that generosity means giving, without expecting something in return. Most of the Athenians are amazed that Timon continues to be so generous, as it seems to them that Timon must have some magical power to possess such an unending bounty. Among his friends are a whole lot of people who stick around to try to benefit from his company. However, there is a time limit for such generous occasions. Such occasions are arranged to serve as teaching lessons. The "gifts" may have a constructive and developmental effect only when there are people who are capable of learning. Otherwise, the distribution of "gifts" would be meaningless. It may even have a degenerating effect on the recipients and their environment. Therefore those who are driven by greed will not be able to benefit from it[92]. At one

---

[92] "Athens: 3rd century AD" (Shakespeare for the Seeker, Volume 2, Chapter 4.3)

point it was necessary to test the effect of Timon's generosity on the Athenians:

"For by these shall I try friends." (Timon of Athens, I.2)

It was then that Timon's bounty ran out. But the city of Athens as a whole was not able to respond correctly to the impact of Timon's gifts. The Athenians turned out to be just greedy, selfish, and unkind. Here is Timon's assessment of the Athenians:

> "Breath infect breath,
> at their society, as their friendship, may
> merely poison! Nothing I'll bear from thee,
> But nakedness, thou detestable town!
> Take thou that too, with multiplying bans!
> Timon will to the woods; where he shall find
> The unkindest beast more kinder than mankind."
> (Timon of Athens, IV.1)

Therefore, Timon left the city and went to a forest.

5.7 How Adam was created

Ordinary men attach themselves to concepts and beliefs without being able to see that these derivative things are only stages, sometimes barriers, to understanding. This is why they remain at the stage of secondary things. In this way they create a sub-culture of emotional stimulus, fantasy, and quasi-truth. Because ordinary men take images, forms, and secondary effects as their aims, they are not able to find what lies beyond them. Rumi illustrates this in the following story.

When the Almighty determined to create mankind, the angel Gabriel was sent to bring a handful of earth for the purpose of forming Adam's body. Gabriel accordingly proceeded to the Earth to execute the Divine commands. But the Earth, being apprehensive that the man so created would rebel against the Maker and draw down a curse upon her, remonstrated with Gabriel. She was asking him to leave her and go away. At last Gabriel granted her wish and returned to heaven without taking a handful of earth. Then God sent the angel Michael on the same errand. When Michael reached the Earth, he put forth his hand to seize some clay from her. The Earth trembled and started pleading with him, shedding tears and making similar excuses. Michael also listened to her crying and returned to heaven with empty hands. Then God said to the angel Israfil, 'Go, fill thy hand with that clay and come back'. But Israfil also was diverted from the execution of the request. At last God sent Azrael, the angel of firm resolution and strong mind. Again, the Earth pressed him with arguments to take pity on her request. Azrael, who was of sterner disposition than the others, resolutely ignored the Earth's entreaties. He told her that in executing this order, painful though it might be, he was to be regarded only as a spear in the hand of the Almighty. On the return of Azrael to heaven with a handful of earth, God said he would make him the angel of death. Azrael was worried that this would make him very hateful to men. But God said that Azrael would operate indirectly, i.e., through disease and sickness, and men would not look for the prime cause beyond these secondary effects. Moreover, death is in reality a boon to the wise men. Only fools would demand that there were no such thing as death. (Book V, 1556-1854)

Shakespeare summarized this particular condition of man in a single sentence, which he inserted into "Henry IV, part 1":

"Why, thou owest God a death." (Henry IV-Part 1, V.1)

These words were spoken by Prince Harry to Falstaff.

5.8 The Secret Room of Ayaz

Rumi underlines the fact that it is characteristic of wrongdoers to think evil of the wise, because they judge their conduct by their own nature. He illustrates such behaviour in the story of Ayaz, a slave of the King of Ghazna.

> Mahmud, the celebrated king of 11th century Ghazna, had a favourite slave named Ayaz. Ayaz was greatly envied by the other courtiers. One day they came to the king and informed him that Ayaz was in the habit of retiring to a secret chamber and locking himself in. They suspected he had concealed there some stolen gold and silver from the treasury. The fact was that Ayaz had placed in that chamber his sheepskin robe and rustic shoon, which he used to wear before the king had promoted him. He used to retire there every day and wear them for a time in order to remind himself of his lowly origin, and to prevent himself from being puffed up with pride. The king was well assured of the loyalty of Ayaz. But in order to refute those who suspected Ayaz, he ordered them to go by night and break open that chamber and bring away all the treasure and other things hidden in it. Accordingly the courtiers proceeded to the chamber of Ayaz at night, broke open the door, searched the floor and the walls but

found only the old shoes and the ragged dress. They then returned to the king discomfited and shamefaced. They asked the king to pardon their offence. But the king refused, saying that their offence had been committed against Ayaz, and that he would leave it to Ayaz to decide whether they should be punished or pardoned. (Book V, 1855-2134)

In this story, the "sheepskin robe and rustic shoon" were used as instruments helping Ayaz to stay on the right course. The reference to a "rustic shoon" may help one to understand Shakespeare's "Hamlet". Namely, Shakespeare also used the symbolic meaning of old shoes and a ragged dress to indicate a man on the path. It was Ophelia, a character that appears in the play, who delivered this important clue. While addressing Queen Gertrude, Hamlet's mother, Ophelia disclosed to the audience who Gertrude's "true love" was:

"How should I your true love know
From another one?
By his cockle hat and staff,
And his sandal shoon."
(Hamlet, IV.5)

According to Ophelia, Gertrude's true love wears a pilgrim hat, staff and sandals ("his cockle hat and staff and his sandal shoon"). In other words, he is a man on a spiritual path. There is only one character in the play that fits this description: Hamlet[93]. In the case of Hamlet, however, this is only an indication of his evolutionary potentiality and not of his actual state. Nevertheless, Ophelia's comment is very important because it helps the audience to understand Gertrude and her actions. Gertrude knows what Hamlet's true potentiality is and the role he is capable of playing. Gertrude's only concern, therefore, is Hamlet's future. Her

---

[93] "Ophelia's prophesies" (Shakespeare for the Seeker, Volume 4, Chapter 7.3)

objective is to protect Hamlet against the machinations of the Danish court and make him the future King of Denmark. This is why she took advantage of Claudius' attraction to her to achieve her objective. After the death of the previous king, Gertrude knew that it would be too dangerous for the young Hamlet to be elected king, because he was still too young, naïve and immature. Therefore, she agreed to her marriage to Claudius on the condition that Hamlet would be declared the "most immediate" heir to the throne. Claudius, the present King of Denmark, accepted her condition.

5.9 The Repentance of Nasuh

In the following two stories, Rumi explains how remorse works. The stories point out that sincere regret is more developmentally constructive than pretentious acts of devotion.

> A certain ascetic had a very jealous wife. He also had a beautiful maid servant. The wife used to watch her husband jealously and not let him be alone with the maid. For a long time the wife watched them both, for fear that an opportunity should occur for their being alone. One day the wife was in the bath-house. Suddenly she remembered that her wash-basin had been left at home. She asked her maid servant, 'Go quickly to our house and fetch the silver basin'. On hearing this, the maid rejoiced for she knew that now she would be able to be alone with her master. So she ran joyously to the house. For six years the maid had been longing to find the master alone. She found him at home and alone. Desire took possession of both so strongly that they had no time to think about bolting the door. During that time the wife reflected and

asked herself, 'Why did I send her back to the house? I have set the cotton on fire with my own hand. I have brought the lusty ram to the ewe'. She ran in pursuit of the maid. When the wife arrived home, she opened the door. The maid jumped up in consternation; the husband was visibly embarrassed. The wife noticed that the maid was confused and excited. She saw her husband engaged in a ritual prayer, but with his pants down. His overall appearance gave evidence of his bogus pretence. (Book V, 2135-2225)

Rumi advises the husband, 'O master, strive earnestly to repentance so you may be saved!' And then he quotes the story of Nasuh.

Nasuh, in his youth, disguised himself in female attire and obtained employment as attendant at the women's bath-house. He enjoyed tremendously touching and massaging the women who frequented the bath-house. He was envied by all because he was in higher favour with the princess. He often felt remorseful and was trying to change his behaviour. But he was not able to do it. So, finally he went to a wise man and said, 'Please, say prayers for me'. The wise man knew Nasuh's secret, but he would not divulge it. The man prayed. His prayer produced a means that protected Nasuh from shame and prosecution. It happened that when Nasuh returned to the bath-house, a jewel belonging to the king's daughter had been lost. The king gave order that all persons connected with the bath-house should be stripped and searched. When the officers came to the bath-house to execute this order, Nasuh was overwhelmed with fear. He knew that if his sex were discovered he would certainly be put to death. He swooned with fear and became beside himself. His natural self was annihilated so that he became a new creature, even like a corpse rising from the grave. When he came to himself he was told that the lost jewel had been found. Those who had suspected him came and begged his pardon. Shortly afterwards the king's daughter sent for him to come and wash her head. But, in spite of her demands, he refused to place himself again in that compromising situation. He said, 'I died to my selfish self once and for all; then I came back to a new life. I tasted the bitterness of death and non-existence. After such an experience only a fool would go back to his previous life'. (Book V, 2226-2325)

Shakespeare presented a similar experience of "dying before dying" in the concluding scene of "Hamlet". It is only after going through a series of very difficult situations that Hamlet, like Nasuh, was able to experience the state "to be". The moment of his "awakening" is clearly defined. It commences when Hamlet "dies before dying":

"I am dead, Horatio." (Hamlet, V.2)

It is a very brief moment that lasts till Hamlet's physical death. This moment is the quintessence of the play. At this moment the distinction between past, presence, and future disappears. Hamlet is able to perceive the meaning of all that has happened to him.

5.10 The Lion, the Fox, and the Ass

Rumi observes that men without understanding are not really men at all, but only the likeness or form of men. Then he quotes an anecdote of Sheikh Mohamed of Ghazna as an example of a man of true understanding.

Sheikh Mohamed dwelt for a long time in the desert and was there miraculously sustained. One day he was inspired by an inner voice to travel to Ghazna and become a beggar. He was to beg money of the rich and distribute it to the poor. After he had done this for some time, a second inspiration came to him. He was to beg no longer, as the money for his charities would be supplied to him miraculously. He had attained to such a degree of insight that he knew, before they uttered a word, the wants of those who were coming to him for aid. The reason for this discernment was that he had purified his heart of all earthly desires. Therefore, whenever thoughts of anything of earthly matter occurred in his mind, he knew that it must have been in some way suggested to him by the person approaching him. (Book V, 2667-2811)

Rumi then introduces the function of the Pole, i.e., the Sage of the Age. This title reflects the fact that the Sage of the Age is like the Magnetic Pole toward which all turn. The Pole has access to all evolutionary energy available in the galaxy. His role is to protect and advance the evolutionary process on this planet. The whole human community only continues to exist in physical form because of the presence and the work of the Pole. The Pole perceives the currently operating evolutionary matrix, which he then applies to a select group of men. As a result, these men are capable of absorbing a critical mass of evolutionary energies. In this way humanity is sustained. There is never an age in which the Pole is not in existence. Yet, because of his endowment, he may remain unknown.

Rumi illustrates further the function of the Pole in the story of the lion, the fox, and the ass. Rumi says that the Pole is like the lion, and it is his business to hunt. The other animals, i.e., the people of the world, live from the Pole's leavings:

A lion had been wounded in a fight with a male elephant. Because of his wounds, the lion was unable to hunt for some time. Some smaller animals were deprived of their meal for they used to eat the lion's leavings. So, when the lion became ill they suffered distress. The lion gave orders to a fox, saying, 'Go and hunt an ass for me. If you find an ass, beguile him with your charming talk and bring him here. As soon as I gain enough strength from eating the flesh of the ass, I will seize another victim. I will eat only a little, so you shall have the rest'. The fox answered, 'I will serve you obediently. I will rob the ass of his wits. Cunning and enchantment is my business'. The fox went and searched the neighbourhood and, at last, found a lean and hungry ass who was grazing in a stony place where there was little or no grass. The fox expressed his sympathy for the ass unfortunate condition. But the ass replied that it was his Divinely appointed lot, and that it would be improper for him to complain. The ass gave the example of another ass who worked hard for a water-carrier. He said, 'After having starved in its master's service, by chance that ass was taken to the king's stables. He was struck by the magnificent appearance of the horses. He started to lament and complain about his fate and wished to be as happy as those royal horses. But one day the horses were taken to battle. When they returned they were in a most miserable condition. Some were wounded, and others were dying. After seeing this sight, the ass determined that his own hard life was preferable and he returned to its master'. The fox replied that the ass was wrong in his refusal to better his condition. He added that if the ass would come with him, he would take him to a delightful meadow where he would never lack grass all year round. The ass replied that desire to strive for sustenance was only a mark of the weakness of one's faith. The fox replied that an exalted faith was a privilege

granted only to a few great men. The ass answered that
the fox was wrong because all men have been provided
according to their needs. And to illustrate that fact he told
the anecdote of a devotee who determined to put the
matter to the test.

'The devotee went out into the desert, trusting that
Divine provision would supply his needs. He laid down
on the ground and went to sleep. It happened that the
next day, by the Divine providence, a caravan of travelers
got lost in the desert and ended up where the devotee was
sleeping. The travellers found him and forced him to eat.'
The fox again pressed the ass to try to better his
condition. The ass answered that he knew of no
occupation and exertion better than trust in God; because
those worldly occupations often led to ruin. Although the
ass was repeating all these excellent precepts, all the time
he was feeling a strong craving for the pleasant grazing
ground the fox had told him about. He was making
objections in a parrot-like manner, repeating precepts
heard about, but not thoroughly understood nor
absorbed. Finally, the ass yielded to the fox's enticement
and went with him to the lion's lair. The lion, being
famished with hunger, sprang upon him the moment the
ass appeared. Being, however, weakened with sickness
and fasting, he missed his aim, and the ass escaped. The
fox blamed the lion for failing to kill the ass. The lion,
after excusing himself, persuaded the fox to try to
convince the ass to come into his lair a second time.
Assuming that the ass probably would have forgotten his
previous experience, the fox consented to try. The fox
was received by the ass with many complains for having
deceived him. But at last the fox managed to persuade the
ass that what he had seen was not a real lion, but only a
magic spell. The spell was used to protect the delightful
meadow from the unworthy. The ass argued strongly, but

greed prevailed. His self-restraint was too weak. So the silly ass allowed himself to be deluded again. He followed the fox to the lion's lair, where the lion tore him to pieces. After the lion had slain the ass, he went to the river to quench his thirst. Meanwhile, the fox ate the ass' heart and liver, which were the most delicate parts. When the lion returned and inquired for them, the fox assured him that the ass had possessed neither a heart nor a liver, for if he had he would never have shown himself so stupid. (Book V, 2326-2666; 2812-2911)

The temporary physical limitation of the lion was induced by the Supreme Being that is symbolically referred to as the elephant. Such a limitation was needed to induce the manifestation of the true nature of the ass and the fox. The ass represents the self faculty. It turns out that the ass always behaves like an ass; there are no means to change its nature. The fox is a symbolic representation of the ordinary intellect. The fox's nature cannot be changed either. He may be useful in subduing the ass. But as demonstrated in the story, he will also try to outsmart his guide. Of course, the lion is fully aware of the true nature of the ass and the fox.

In the play "Julius Caesar", Shakespeare illustrated a similar interaction between the guide, the intellect, and the self. This particular situation is a representation of the evolutionary state of Rome in the 1st century BC. Brutus, Julius Caesar's friend, is like the ass. He allowed himself to be beguiled by Cassius into joining the conspirators who planned the assassination of Julius Caesar. Shakespeare used the historical figure of Julius Caesar to symbolically illustrate a spiritual guide. Julius Caesar indicated this by referring to himself "as the northern star" (see Chapter 1.16). As a guide he was charged with the incredibly difficult task of facilitating the utilization of a newly released evolutionary impulse[94]. But Rome could benefit from the presence of this

---

[94] "Spiritual king" (Shakespeare for the Seeker, Volume 1, Chapter 2.2)

spiritual "king" only if the Romans were capable of recognizing his role and his function. The Romans, however, were not capable of comprehending the need for such a king. The status of Rome was such that it was incapable of benefiting constructively from the presence of a spiritual king. Such an incapacity was further indicated in the episode in which Julius Caesar asked some priests to carry out an animal sacrifice to find out what the current status of Rome was. The priests performed the sacrifice and they found out that:

> "Plucking the entrails of an offering forth,
> They could not find a heart within the beast."
> (Julius Caesar, II.2)

In other words, Shakespeare also used the absence of a physical heart as a symbol of a certain inner state of man. At that particular time, Rome was like a beast without a spiritual "heart". Of course, Julius Caesar did not need the priests to know this. Like Sheikh Mohamed of Ghazna, and like the lion in the story, he knew very well what the spiritual state of the Romans was and he was fully aware of the planned assassination. The assassination was the manifestation of the true nature of the Romans. The assassination seriously affected the evolutionary plan.

5.11. The Moslem and the Magian

One of the most difficult concepts to grasp is the operation of free will and causality. Rumi used some of his stories to illustrate and clarify this concept. The following dispute between the Moslem and the Magian is an example of such an illustration.

A Moslem pressed a Magian to embrace the true faith.
The Magian replied, 'If God wills, I shall become a true
believer and gain access to inspirational truth'. The
Moslem replied, 'God certainly wills that your soul be
developed; but your own lust and earthly desires hold you
back'. The Magian replied, 'O reasonable man, since these
desires are predominant I shall be on the side of the
stronger. I can side only with him who is predominant. I
must fall if I do not allow myself to go in the direction to
which the predominant force is pulling me. If my earthly
desires are predominant, this means it was God's will that
they are my dominant characteristics. Those desires are at
God's command. They are like a dog guarding the
owner's house. The children of the house are allowed to
play with the dog; they keep pulling his tail, but the dog is
harmless to them. If, however, a stranger passes by, the
dog will rush at him like a fierce lion'. The Moslem
continued his arguments saying that the choice resides in
man's soul. Before the choice is made, both dispositions
towards good and towards wrong are activated. Then it is
up to man to make his choice. The choice towards good
is constructive; the choice towards wrong is destructive.
And he told the anecdote of a man caught robbing a
garden. The man was defending himself saying that his
stealing was predetermined. The owner of the garden
administered him a severe beating. When the thief
protested and cried for mercy, the owner assured him that
this beating was also predestined. He continued his
arguments explaining that prescripts and rules were not
inconsistent with the existence of freewill. He cited the
story of a devotee who was admiring the splendid apparel
of the slaves of the Chief of Herat. He cried to Heaven,
'Ah! Learn from this Chief how to treat faithful slaves!'
Shortly after the Chief was deposed, and his slaves were
put to the torture to make them reveal where the Chief

had hidden his treasure. But none of the slaves would betray his secret. Then a voice from heaven came to the devotee, saying, 'Learn from them how to be a faithful slave, and then, look for recompense'. The unconvinced Magian, again, presented further arguments, and the discussion continued with the usual result of leaving both the disputants of the same opinion as when they began. Rumi remarks that this type of dispute about man's freewill and causality will endure till the last day. Because no debate, but only true experience can resolve these difficulties. (Book V, 2912-3438)

Causality at the level of ordinary man is the field of operation of the Will of the Realm. The Realm transmits its Will through intermediary levels all the way down to the level of ordinary man. On the level of ordinary man, the needs of the evolutionary process are manifested as a series of intertwined opportunities that appear in different places and at different times. Because the operation of the Realm and the transmission chain are beyond the grasp of the intellect, it is impossible for an ordinary man to recognize and respond constructively to these opportunities. This is the reason why the evolutionary process is often interrupted and delayed. Such situations are allowed by the measure of free will that man has and its consequences may not be annulled by evolutionary forces, no matter how much is at stake. All that may be done is to arrange situations that provide other opportunities for man to choose differently.

Shakespeare gives a compelling illustration of such an operation in his plays. For example, in accordance with the Will of the Realm, the timing of the release of unitive energy on the earth was dictated by the evolutionary needs of the galaxy. Therefore, the conditions on the earth had to be correctly prepared if the event was to fulfil the galactic requirements. According to Shakespeare's illustration, the preparations for this event were initiated within the Celtic evolutionary branch in the 10th century BC.

The Celtic branch offered a series of opportunities for overcoming errors made previously by free-willed man. Each of these opportunities provided man with a new chance to make a constructive choice. As presented by Shakespeare in "King Lear", 10th century BC Britain was not able to fulfil that evolutionary requirement[95]. The process had to be delayed till the time of "Cymbeline", i.e., the 1st century AD[96].

Posthumus is the main character of the play. When Posthumus got into serious trouble, his dead ancestors were pleading with Jupiter, the king of gods, to take pity on their descendant and restore his fortunes. It was then that Jupiter arrived and berated the spirits for troubling him. He grudgingly told them, and the audience, that Posthumus' affairs were in the care of "the fingers of the powers above" and that Posthumus' trials "well are spent". In other words, Posthumus' adventures were part of the divine design and he served as a marker of a new evolutionary opportunity:

> "No care of yours it is; you know 'tis ours.
> Whom best I love I cross; to make my gift,
> The more delay'd, delighted. Be content;
> Your low-laid son our godhead will uplift:
> His comforts thrive, his trials well are spent.
>
> Our Jovial star reign'd at his birth, and in
> Our temple was he married. Rise, and fade.
> He shall be lord of lady Imogen,
> And happier much by his affliction made.
> This tablet lay upon his breast, wherein
> Our pleasure his full fortune doth confine."
> (Cymbeline, V.4)

---

[95] "Concluding remarks" (Shakespeare for the Seeker, Volume 1, Chapter 3.1)
[96] "Techniques" (Shakespeare for the Seeker, Volume 1, Chapter 3.2)

But it took a series of such challenging situations before King Cymbeline was finally able to emulate and implement the evolutionary template that was projected from the Realm. However, as illustrated by Shakespeare, the evolutionary gains achieved at the time of "Cymbeline" were lost at the time of "Macbeth", i.e., in the 11th century AD.

5.12. The Emir's Wine

The projection of various modes of evolutionary energies is realized in accordance with the formula which states that a new impulse is activated long before the organism has fully deployed the previous ones. In other words, an evolutionary energy X can be fully accommodated only in terms of a struggle towards digesting energy $X + 1$. The release of each new impulse of evolutionary energy was manifested by the appearance of a prophet. Rumi indicates that the release of the unitive energy of love was marked by the appearance of Jesus. In the language of instrumental literature, unitive energy is symbolically compared to wine. Its effect on the deeper consciousness is equated with drunkenness. The important thing is that such spiritual "drunkenness" is an intermediate step, which has to be experienced first before the next step can be taken. In other words, this drunkenness is not the objective of spiritual training. At first, drinking is forbidden. Then, drinking is required. At a specific time, the drinking of wine has to be abandoned. Therefore, there is a time when drunkenness is needed; and there is a time when such drunkenness may impede one's progress. Rumi illustrates this in the following story.

> There was an Emir with merry heart who was exceedingly
> fond of wine. He lived in the epoch of Jesus, when wine
> was permissible and lawful. The Emir was a

compassionate man, kind to the poor and just. One day
the Emir called his servant and told him, 'Go and fetch
me wine from such-and-such a Christian monastery. They
have an excellent wine that may release my soul from its
inconstancy. In that wine there is a hidden substance.
This substance is like a treasure hidden in a ruin. One
drop from that Christian's cup has the same effect as
thousands of wine-jars and wine-cellars'. The servant
went and bought the wine. He paid with gold for the
purchased wine, i.e., he gave some stones and bought
jewels in exchange. This was a wine that would fly to the
head of kings and put a golden crown on the cupbearer's
head. As he was returning with the wine, he passed the
house of an ascetic. This ascetic called out to him, 'What
have you got there?' The servant said, 'Wine that belongs
to the Emir'. The ascetic cried out, 'What! Does a seeker
after truth indulge in wine? The seekers after truth should
have nothing to do with pleasure and drinking, because
wine is a very evil that steals men's wits'. And he broke
the wine-jar with a stone. The servant ran away from him.
He went back home and told his master what had
happened. The noble became furious. He took a thick
stick and went to the ascetic's house to chastise him. The
devotee heard of his approach and hid himself under
some wool. He said to himself, 'One would need to have
a face as hard as a mirror made of steel to tell an angry
man of his faults. Only then would he reflect his ugliness
without fear'.

This situation is further illustrated in the story about the
Shah of Tirmid. The Shah was once playing chess with a
courtier. When checkmated, the Shah got into a rage and
threw the chessboard at his courtier's head. Afterwards,
the courtier was ordered to play a second time. This time,
before checkmating the Shah, the courtier ran away and
covered his head with rugs and cushions. The Shah

exclaimed, 'What are you doing? What is this?' The courtier replied, 'Checkmate, checkmate, checkmate, O excellent Shah!' And Rumi adds, 'How can one tell you the truth except under cover!'

Rumi then continues the story of the Emir:

Hearing noise, the neighbours of the ascetic came out and interceded for him with the Emir. They were telling the Emir that he should pardon his act and consider his ill-fortune. The Emir refused to be pacified. But the neighbours kept repeating their entreaties. They were arguing that the Emir had so much pleasure in his sovereignty that he could well dispense with the pleasure of wine. The Emir strenuously denied this, saying that no other pleasure of sovereignty, or what not, could compensate him for the loss of wine. For there was no other pleasure for him who has experienced spiritual intoxication. (Book V, 3439-3829)

In instrumental literature the term "cupbearer" applies to the spiritual guide, i.e., the keeper of "wine". It is such "a wine that would fly to the head of kings and put a golden crown on the cupbearer's head". This means that the guide is able to fill his disciple's heart with the unitive energy of love. The Persian word for the cupbearer is "Saki". The ceremonial salutation to the Saki in Persian language may be reproduced phonetically by the following French phrase: "Honi soit qui mal y pense". This phrase was adopted as their slogan by the Knights of the Order of the Garter. The salutation to the cupbearer would usually mark an event within an activity of evolutionary nature. Shakespeare described such an event in "The Merry Wives of Windsor" as the Queen Fairy masque[97]. Here is Mistress Quickly's invocation in which she makes a reference to the slogan of the Knights of the Order of the Garter:

---

[97] "Queen Fairy masque" (Shakespeare for the Seeker, Volume 4, Chapter 8.2)

"And nightly, meadow-fairies, look you sing,
Like to the Garter's compass, in a ring:
The expressure that it bears, green let it be,
More fertile-fresh than all the field to see;
And 'Honi soit qui mal y pense' write
In emerald tufts, flowers purple, blue and white;
Let sapphire, pearl and rich embroidery,
Buckled below fair knighthood's bending knee:
Fairies use flowers for their charactery."
(The Merry Wives of Windsor, V.5)

In this quote Mistress Quickly appeals to the fairies to use flowers to write their salutation to the cupbearer.

In his Roman tetralogy, Shakespeare illustrated the environment and overall conditions prior to and immediately after the release of the unitive energy of love. Similarly to Rumi, Shakespeare used wine and drunkenness to describe this particular mode of evolutionary energy and its effect on certain individuals. "Coriolanus", i.e., the first play of the tetralogy, is set-up in the 5th century BC. We may notice that at that time "wine" was not available yet. At that time man was not ready yet to be "awakened" by wine[98]:

"I am weary; yea, my memory is tired.
Have we no wine here?"
(Coriolanus, I.9)

"Wine, wine, wine! What service
is here! I think our fellows are asleep."
(Coriolanus, IV.5)

At the time of "Antony and Cleopatra", i.e., the third play of the Roman tetralogy, "wine" was made available. The effect of unitive

---

[98] "Rome: 5th century BC" (Shakespeare for the Seeker, Volume 1, Chapter 2.1)

energy is manifested during the triumvirs' party. The effect of "wine drinking" symbolically illustrates the spiritual capacity of the triumvirs, Lepidus, Mark Antony and Octavius, to absorb unitive energy effectively[99]. Lepidus' developmental state is such that he is not able to withstand the impact of unitive energy. Lepidus gets drunk. Therefore, he has to go. Indeed, Lepidus makes only one more appearance before being eliminated by Octavius Caesar. Mark Antony is also having difficulties with the effect of "wine". When Octavius Caesar interrupts the wine drinking festivities to remind Mark Antony that now is the time for more serious business to be done, Mark Antony's answer is most telling in describing his inner state:

"be a child o'th' time."

Mark Antony tries to persuade Octavius Caesar to forget duty and urges his men to drink until they reach complete lethargy:

"Come, let's all take hands,
Till that the conquering wine hath steep'd our sense
In soft and delicate Lethe."
(Antony and Cleopatra, II.7)

In this particular context, "lethargy" indicates spiritual intoxication. The main purpose of the availability of such inspirational states is not their enjoyment but gaining capacity for carrying on additional responsibilities. However, Mark Antony preferred to enjoy the moment. He, like the Emir in Rumi's story, neglected his duties in order to enjoy "drunkenness". Mark Antony's tendency to live for the moment, with little regard for the overall process, was the main factor in his failure.

---

[99] "Meeting of the triumvirs" (Shakespeare for the Seeker, Volume 1, Chapter 2.3)

5.13 The Portrait of the Slave-girl

The unitive energy of love, which is the second highest energy available in the galaxy, enables the inner layers of the manifest faculties to unite to form man's angelic soul. In this way man is able to overcome the limitations of time and space; he may access higher worlds. It is in this sense that the unitive energy of love is the principle of all motion towards universal perfection and completion. Rumi refers to this in the following lines:

> "The wheeling heavens are turned by waves of Love:
> were it not for Love, the world would be frozen.
>
> Every mote is in love with that Perfection and hastening
> upward like a sapling." (Book V, 3854, 3858)

"Love" here refers to objective love, and not its echo in emotional attachments and sensual attractions. In the following quote from "The Merry Wives of Windsor", Shakespeare indicated the distinction between ordinary and objective love:

> "O powerful love! that, in some
> respects, makes a beast a man, in some other, a man
> a beast."
> (The Merry Wives of Windsor, V.5)

In this quote Falstaff, representing a witty but underdeveloped mind, addresses himself as a man who was turned into a "beast" while chasing after fictitious love. The other part of the quote "O powerful love! that, in some respects, makes a beast a man" applies to objective Love that can transmute an ordinary man ("beast") into a fully developed man[100].

This is further illustrated in the story of the Caliph and the portrait of the slave-girl.

---

[100] "Impurities" (Shakespeare for the Seeker, Volume 4, Chapter 8.2)

An informer said to the Caliph of Egypt, 'The king of Mosul is wedded to a beautiful damsel. He holds in his arms a girl like whom there is no other beauty in the world'. When the Caliph saw a portrait of the girl he conceived a passionate desire for her. Immediately he dispatched to Mosul a captain with a very mighty army. He gave him orders to take the girl by force and bring her to Egypt. When the king of Mosul saw that mighty army, he sent an envoy to the captain with a message. In the message he asked, 'What do you wish to obtain by shedding the blood of innocent people?' The captain sent him the portrait of the girl with the following message, 'Look on the portrait: this is what I require. Give her up, or else I will take her by force, for I am the conqueror'. When the king saw the message, he said, 'Take her away at once. I am not an idolater. It looks that it is more fit that the idol should be in the hands of the idolater'. When the girl was brought to the captain, he straight away fell in love with her. He became distraught and kept saying, 'What should I care about the Caliph? Since I am in love, life and death are the same to me'. To his fiery eye a hundred Caliphs seemed less dangerous than a fly. On the way back to Egypt, the captain encamped in a wooded meadowland. His desire for the girl was so strong that he went straight to her tent. He took off his pants and approached the girl with his penis fully erected. At this very moment he saw a fierce black lion coming from the jungle and rushing upon the camp. The captain rushed out of the tent and smote the lion with his sword. Then, at once he returned back to the tent. When the girl saw him coming back with his penis still erected, she did not resist him at all. Full of astonishment and admiration, the girl happily fell into his arms. For a while they were absorbed in their love-affair. But afterwards, the captain started to feel remorse for that grievous act. The captain told the girl to keep their affair secret and say nothing about it to the Caliph. When the Caliph saw the girl, he too became strongly obsessed with her beauty. But his manliness was no match to that of the captain. It happened that at the moment of his first encounter with the girl, the Caliph heard some noise made by a tiny mouse. The Caliph thought that it might be a snake. At that thought his potency evaporated. When the girl saw that the Caliph's became impotent by the noise made but a tiny mouse, she could not restrain her amazement and started to laugh. As her laughter was not ceasing, the Caliph became enraged and fierce. He drew his sword from its sheath and said, 'Tell me the cause of your laughter! From this laughter a suspicion has come into my heart. Tell the truth, you cannot charm me anymore with your sweet talk'. The girl got scared and related what had happened between her and the captain. The Caliph came to himself, 'I took the girl by force from the king of Mosul. So, she was soon taken by force from me too. My treacherous deeds made a traitor of him who was my trusted friend and servant. This is no time to inflict punishment and revenge. I prepared this disaster with my own hands. If I wreak vengeance on the captain and the girl, that trespass also will come on my head'. So he said to the girl, 'I will unite you with the captain. But do not relate to anyone this story which I have heard from you. Otherwise the captain may be ashamed to face me. Yet he has done one bad deed and a hundred thousand good services'. The Caliph summoned the captain to his presence. He made an excuse to him, saying, 'I have become disinterested in this slave-girl, because the mother of my children is nursing envy and jealousy. She is feeling great bitterness on account of this girl. Since I wish to give this girl to a worthily person, it is most fitting that I should give her to you. For you did hazard your life for the sake of obtaining her. It would not be fair to give her to anyone but you'. He handed her over to him and married them. He showed true manliness by pardoning the captain's fault and uniting him with the girl.

Rumi concludes the story with the following comment, 'If the Caliph was deficient in the masculinity of asses, yet he possessed true manliness. It is true manliness and the nature of a fully developed man to abandon anger, lust, and greed. Let the masculinity of the ass be lacking in his nature. Recognising this abandonment of sensuality is the kernel of manliness, and indulgence in sensuality is like the husk'. (Book V, 3830-4034)

The episode of the Caliph and the portrait of the slave-girl resembles the last scene of Shakespeare's "Two Gentlemen of Verona". In this scene Shakespeare further elaborated on the nature of true "manliness" and its effect on those around. In that scene Valentine handed over his beloved Silvia to his friend Proteus. Valentine gave away his beloved, apparently out of friendship, without even asking for her consent. It is the effect of Valentine's gesture on Proteus that is important in Shakespeare's presentation of the process. It is this effect that constitutes Shakespeare's sequel to Rumi's story.

The overall goal of the process is to form a spiritual union. This union may be realized by the assimilation of the available evolutionary impulse. This is symbolically represented by a marriage. In the case of "Two Gentlemen of Verona", it is represented by the marriage of two couples, i.e., Valentine with Silvia and Proteus with Julia[101]. This is why Valentine cannot marry Silvia when Proteus is still oblivious to Julia's beauty. Both Silvia and Valentine understand the situation; they cannot be united as long as Proteus' perception is veiled and he does not recognize Julia's inner beauty. Proteus, like the captain in Rumi's story, is still

---

[101] "Implementation" (Shakespeare for the Seeker, Volume 3, Chapter 6.7)

driven by his inner idol, i.e., sensual attraction to Sylvia, his friend's beloved. Proteus' attempt to rape Silvia is a symbolic indication of his destructive tendency. This tendency prevents the completion of the process. In the following comment Silvia indicates the challenge they are all faced with:

> "Had I been seized by a hungry lion,
> I would have been a breakfast to the beast,
> Rather than have false Proteus rescue me."
> (Two Gentlemen of Verona, V.4)

Silvia alludes to the fact that an unfulfilled spiritual potentiality ("false Proteus") reduces man to its ordinary beastly state of "a hungry lion". Proteus' sensual attraction to Silvia does not allow him to see the evolutionary essence that is contained in Julia. Proteus' spiritual reformation can only be completed through an artfully delivered rebuke. It is up to Valentine to instigate it. When Valentine sees Proteus's attempt to rape Silvia, he delivers the rebuke:

> "Who should be trusted, when one's own right hand
> Is perjured to the bosom? Proteus,
> I am sorry I must never trust thee more,
> But count the world a stranger for thy sake."

Proteus' response to the rebuke is immediate:

> "My shame and guilt confounds me.
> Forgive me, Valentine: if hearty sorrow
> Be a sufficient ransom for offence,
> I tender 't here; I do as truly suffer
> As e'er I did commit."

At this moment Proteus' inner state is instantly changed. Then Valentine prepares the ground for the second rebuke. Its aim is the formation of the spiritual union:

"Then I am paid;
And once again I do receive thee honest.
Who by repentance is not satisfied
Is nor of heaven nor earth, for these are pleased.
By penitence the Eternal's wrath's appeased:
And, that my love may appear plain and free,
All that was mine in Silvia I give thee."
(Two Gentlemen of Verona, V.4)

The last two lines of this quote are the most significant in the entire play. However, their meaning is difficult to comprehend if one tries to analyse them from an ordinary or conventional point of view. It is only when analysed in the context of the above-described process that the last scene can be understood. Namely, this scene illustrates the moment when the aspect represented by Valentine has been completely purified ("that my love may appear plain and free"). Silvia represents the impulse of the unitive energy of love that is designated for him. Now, Valentine is able to assimilate it. Moreover, because of his spiritual purity, Valentine is capable of delivering a constructive impact to Proteus. This is the meaning of his words: "All that was mine in Silvia I give thee". Of course Silvia does not protest against Valentine's gesture, because "the more I give to thee, the more I have". It is then that Julia swoons. When Julia recovers, she removes her disguise and delivers the final rebuke to Proteus:

"O Proteus, let this habit make thee blush!
Be thou ashamed that I have took upon me
Such an immodest raiment, if shame live
In a disguise of love:
It is the lesser blot, modesty finds,
Women to change their shapes than men their minds."

At this moment Proteus' blinding veil is removed. Now he is able to see the true beauty in Julia:

> "O heaven! were man
> But constant, he were perfect. That one error
> Fills him with faults; makes him run through all the sins:
> Inconstancy falls off ere it begins.
> What is in Silvia's face, but I may spy
> More fresh in Julia's with a constant eye?"

Julia's beauty is of the same nature as Silvia's, but is targeted, or coloured, for Proteus. And only now Proteus is able to recognize it. This is why Proteus perceives it as "more fresh". Proteus' constructive response to the rebuke allows for the formation of the union:

> "One feast, one house, one mutual happiness."
> (Two Gentlemen of Verona, V.4)

This quote is the last line of the play. It constitutes the final scene of Shakespeare's Italian evolutionary branch. The projection of the Italian branch onto the ordinary world was marked by the Italian Renaissance. Shakespeare's Italian plays are a precise record of how this new civilization cell within the European society was designed and implemented.

5.14 The Jewel of Mahmud

"Proper conduct" is a technical term describing a formula leading to the unveiling of inner states. In its nature, proper conduct is developmentally constructive. Proper conduct, however, has nothing to do with artificial and socially acceptable rules of etiquette. Etiquette is based on a blind imitation of current fashions; it is of an automatic and reactive manner. Such behaviour is part of the civilizing of people, but is spiritually sterile. Rumi illustrates the difference between these two modes of behaviour in the story of King Mahmud's jewel.

One day King Mahmud hastened to the court where all the courtiers were assembled. He showed them a beautiful pearl. He put the pearl in the hand of the Vizier. 'How about this pearl?' he asked, 'what is it worth?' The Vizier replied, 'It is worth more than a hundred ass-loads of gold'. The king said, 'Break it!' 'How can I break it?' replied the Vizier, 'I am a well-wisher to your treasury and riches. How should I deem it allowable that a priceless pearl like this should go to waste?' 'Well said!' exclaimed the King and he presented him with a robe of honour. The King took the pearl from him. For a while he engaged the courtiers in conversation concerning new events and old mysteries. Afterwards he put the pearl into the hand of a chamberlain, saying, 'What would be its worth to a purchaser?' The chamberlain replied, 'It is worth half a kingdom. May God preserve it from destruction!' 'Break it', demanded the King. 'How can I be an enemy to the King's treasure-house?' answered the chamberlain. The King praised the chamberlain's intelligence, gave him a robe of honour and increased his salary. After a short time, the King handed the pearl to the Minister of Justice. The King said the same to all the other courtiers. All the fifty or sixty courtiers, one by one, gave the same answer in imitation of the Vizier. The King bestowed a costly robe of honour on every one of them. Finally the jewel came into the hands of Ayaz, the favourite slave of the King. 'Now, Ayaz, will not you say how much a pearl of this splendour and excellence is worth?' Ayaz replied, 'More than I am able to say'. The King said, 'Now break it immediately into small fragments'. It happened that Ayaz had two stones in his sleeve. He quickly reduced the pearl to dust, for that seemed to him the proper thing to do. When Ayaz broke that choice pearl, thereupon from the courtiers arose a hundred clamours and outcries, 'What recklessness is this! By God, whoever has broken this luminous pearl deserves punishment'. And yet the whole assembly of courtiers in their ignorance and blindness had broken the pearl of the King's command. Ayaz replied, 'O renowned princes, is the King's command more precious or the pearl? In your eyes, is the command of the sovereign or this pearl superior? Devoid of the spiritual pearl is the soul that prefers a coloured stone and puts my King behind'. The King made a sign to the executioner, as though to say, 'Remove these vile wretches from my seat of honour. How are these vile wretches worthy of my seat of honour, when they break my command for the sake of a stone? For the sake of a coloured stone my command is held contemptible and cheap by evil-doers like these'. But Ayaz interceded for the courtiers, saying, 'It is better to forgive'. (Book V, 4035-4238)

Shakespeare goes a step further into the process by showing how an ordinary person may arrive at such a spiritual state as that demonstrated by Ayaz. In his play entitled "The Taming of the Shrew", Shakespeare used the term "taming" to denote the process that leads to learning proper conduct. Katharina, the main character of the play, is widely reputed to be a shrewish, foul-tempered and sharp-tongued woman. Petruchio, a brash man from Verona, is the teaching master:

"Ay, mistress, and Petruchio is the master;
That teacheth tricks eleven and twenty long,
To tame a shrew and charm her chattering tongue."
(The Taming of the Shrew, IV.2)

Petruchio is able to recognize Katharina's inner state, which is hidden from the others. He decides to teach her. Petruchio has seemingly strange ways of imposing his teaching on her. For example, when they arrive at his house, he declares he will "kill her with kindness" by pretending that he cannot allow her to eat his inferior food or sleep in his inferior bed:

> "This is a way to kill a wife with kindness;
> And thus I'll curb her mad and headstrong humour.
> He that knows better how to tame a shrew,
> Now let him speak: 'tis charity to show."
> (The Taming of the Shrew, IV.1)

Because Petruchio couches his attempt to tame Katharina with "perfect love", it is impossible for her to confront him with outright anger:

> "And that which spites me more than all these wants,
> He does it under name of perfect love;
> As who should say, if I should sleep or eat,
> 'Twere deadly sickness or else present death."
> (The Taming of the Shrew, IV.3)

As a result, she is gradually awakened from her "sleep":

> "In her chamber, making a sermon of continency to her;
> And rails, and swears, and rates, that she, poor soul,
> Knows not which way to stand, to look, to speak,
> And sits as one new-risen from a dream."
> (The Taming of the Shrew, IV.1)

Tired, hungry, and weary, Katharina at last relents and starts to adapt to the correct conduct. This is illustrated by Katharina's answer to Petruchio when he insists that the sun is really the moon:

> "Then, God be bless'd, it is the blessed sun:
> But sun it is not, when you say it is not;
> And the moon changes even as your mind.
> What you will have it named, even that it is;
> And so it shall be so for Katharina."
> (The Taming of the Shrew, IV.5)

Her answer is a sign of her obedience. Her answer, in its nature, corresponds to Ayaz' proper conduct. When Katharina realizes that it is beneficial for her to be fully obedient, Petruchio is able to remove her inner barrier of shrewishness. Thus, Katharina's obedience brings her to a position where she is discovering something that is beyond the ordinary. Katharina's change shows that she has developed an understanding that does not correspond to a tamed shrew, but rather to a person who arrived at a higher stage of being[102]. One cannot arrive at such a stage by following social etiquette. Katharina has arrived at her current understanding by a spiritual method.

Following the spiritual path demands various capacities. Among these is the use of intelligence and also obedience. Obedience is as important as intelligence and common sense. The vast majority of humanity, however, considers that to obey is less important than to think of a way out of a situation. But it is in fact known that none of these things is more important than the others. It is the nature of a particular situation that dictates the correct approach.

---

[102] "Taming school" (Shakespeare for the Seeker, Volume 3, Chapter 6.5)

Book 6. Subtle Faculties

The "Mathnawi" consists of six volumes: Book 6 is the last one. The spiritual journey is usually described as consisting of seven stages. Therefore, the lack of a seventh book is somehow surprising. It seems that a concluding book is missing. In his introduction to Book 6, Rumi alludes to this fact:

> "The six Books of the Mathnawi are a Lamp in the darkness of imagination, perplexity, fantasies, doubt and suspicion. This Lamp cannot be perceived by the animal sense. The state of animality is the lowest of the low, since the animals have been created to keep in good order the outward form of the lower world. Around the animals' senses and manifest faculties has been drawn a circle beyond which they cannot pass. The limited measure of their actions and the confined range of their speculation are manifested in the same manner in the orbits to which every star is restrained." (Book VI, Introduction)

Rumi indicates that his description of the evolutionary process is limited to six volumes. As long as the readers need words and letters, the Seventh Book will remain invisible to them. It will remain invisible because it cannot be perceived through the physical senses: the last and the final book can only be perceived through the use of the subtle faculties.

On several occasions Rumi refers to the five subtle faculties. However, he neither describes nor specifies them. We may presume that, at that time, this information was not needed in that particular environment. The discrimination between the five subtle faculties was not a part of the spiritual technology implemented in that place at that time. The methodology was focussed on earlier stages of the process. Only once a certain progress was achieved, more advance steps of the process could be disclosed.

It seems that such a progress was achieved in 16th century Western Europe. This is why Shakespeare was able to provide further details on the activation and the nature of the five subtle faculties. Shakespeare used the colours yellow, red, white, black, and green to indicate symbolically the five subtle faculties. The yellow and the red faculties are associated with the inner layers of the spiritual heart; the white and the black faculties belong to the spiritual intellect. The green, i.e., the fifth faculty is formed as the result of fusing together the other four faculties. Such fusing or uniting corresponds to the transmutation of the inner being and the forming of a new man[103]. The presence of the unitive energy of love is needed to complete such a transmutation. This is why the colour green is considered to be the colour of true lovers.

Shakespeare uses young men to represent the inner faculties in their latent forms. Young women represent the corresponding evolutionary energies that are needed for the activation of the latent layers. In this symbolic representation, marriage marks the activation of a specific inner layer of the heart or the intellect. An exchange between Don Adriano and his servant Moth, in "Love's Labour's Lost", refers to the five faculties. Moth refers to the various modes of evolutionary energies and the relationship between them as women of various complexions:

> Don Adriano:
>
> "Who was Samson's love, my dear Moth?"
>
> Moth:
>
> "A woman, master."

---

[103] "Technical background" (Shakespeare for the Seeker, Volume 2, Chapter 5.3)

Don Adriano:

"Of what complexion?"

Moth:

"Of all the four, or the three, or the two, or one of the four."

Don Adriano:

"Tell me precisely of what complexion."

Moth:

"Of the sea-water green, sir."

Don Adriano:

"Is that one of the four complexions?"

Moth:

"As I have read, sir; and the best of them too."

Don Adriano:

"Green indeed is the colour of lovers."
(Love's Labour's Lost, I.2)

As a result of exposure to an evolutionary impulse "of all the four, or the three, or the two, or one of the four" subtle faculties may be activated. When all the four subtle faculties are present, there is a possibility for their union, which leads to the appearance of "the best of them", i.e., the "green ... the colour of lovers".

The subtle faculties enhance the ordinary senses. In this way each subtle faculty may become a visionary for the physical senses, i.e., it may provide insights into the invisible world. Without speaking and without conveying metaphorical meaning, a subtle faculty allows man to experience Truth. Truth, which is immediate and intuitive, cannot be expressed by conventional art, poetry or imagination. Duke Theseus in Shakespeare's "A Midsummer Night's Dream" alludes to these limitations in the following way:

"The lunatic, the lover and the poet
Are of imagination all compact:
One sees more devils than vast hell can hold,
That is, the madman: the lover, all as frantic,
Sees Helen's beauty in a brow of Egypt:
The poet's eye, in fine frenzy rolling,
Doth glance from heaven to earth, from earth to heaven;
And as imagination bodies forth
The forms of things unknown, the poet's pen
Turns them to shapes and gives to airy nothing
A local habitation and a name.
Such tricks hath strong imagination."
(A Midsummer Night's Dream, V.1)

Theseus points out that poetical and artistic presentations driven by overactive imaginations, fantasies and emotions may have a confusing effect on the audience. He says that there are some events and forces that are entirely misunderstood by the ignorant and untrained. Such events and forces are outside of the ordinary understanding of a lunatic, a lover, or a poet[104].

Rumi adds a comment on the nature of the subtle faculties. He says that the five subtle faculties are linked with one another. They are entangled because all of them grow from a common root. The activation of one of the subtle faculties helps to develop the other inner faculties of that particular being, because they are entangled.

Shakespeare illustrated the working of such a spiritual entanglement in "The Comedy of Errors". Antipholi, i.e., the twin brothers who appear in the play, represent two aspects of the intellect faculty. The twins are entangled. This means that they are intertwined with each other even though they may be at different locations, in different environments, or placed in different time

---

[104] "The lunatic, the poet, and the poet" (Shakespeare for the Seeker, Volume 4, Chapter 8.3)

dimensions. At the beginning of the play they are in their dormant state. They look alike and are not recognizable. Then, during a sea storm, they are split up and separated. After they are split up, each of the twins goes through a different set of experiences. One brother goes to Syracuse; the other ends up in Ephesus. The Syracusian twin goes through the purification process; the Ephesian brother is exposed to reforming experiences. They are placed in two different time dimensions. These two time dimensions are indicated by the periods of their traveling. Before his arrival in Ephesus, the Syracusian brother has traveled on the sea for "seven short years". The "seven short years" on the sea correspond to his brother's seven days in Ephesus. It was during "this week" that the Ephesian brother started to feel distraught and troubled. This change was noticed by his wife:

> "This week he hath been heavy, sour, sad,
> And much different from the man he was."
> (The Comedy of Errors, V.1)

In accordance with the entanglement principle, the Ephesian brother was affected by the experiences of his twin brother. The "seven short years" on the sea were needed to complete the purification process. The seven days ("this week") in Ephesus allowed for an accelerated reformation of the Ephesian twin. At the end of the play, the twins are united. In this way a new advanced being is formed. In accordance with Shakespeare's presentation, the newly formed being provided a link that was needed to activate the process in Bohemia. It was this link that was used to project evolutionary energies to initiate the Reformation in Central Europe[105].

---

[105] "Conclusion" (Shakespeare for the Seeker, Volume 2, Chapter 4.4)

6.1 The Hindu Slave who loved his Master's Daughter

As long as a person is driven by ordinary senses he, or she, will not be able to recognize the operation of the cosmic matrix which indicates the most constructive course of action. An ordinary person is usually distracted by the pleasures of this world. Shakespeare used Cupid to represent distracting sensual and passionate affections. Cupid's role is defined in the masque presented to Timon in "Timon of Athens". Cupid brings the Amazons who represent the five physical senses. Here is Cupid introducing the Amazons[106]:

> "Hail to thee, worthy Timon, and to all
> That of his bounties taste! The five best senses
> Acknowledge thee their patron; and come freely
> To gratulate thy plenteous bosom: th' ear,
> Taste, touch and smell, pleased from thy tale rise;
> They only now come but to feast thine eyes."
> (Timon of Athens, I.2)

The Amazons are under Cupid's control. Cupid's role is to trigger "maculate", i.e., ordinary sensual and emotional love. This is why in Shakespeare's plays Cupid is the cause of interferences in the process. For example, Berowne in "Love's Labour's Lost" refers to Cupid as "king of codpieces"[107]. Here is Berowne complaining about Cupid's meddling into his affairs:

> "This whimpled, whining, purblind, wayward boy;
> This senior-junior, giant-dwarf, Dan Cupid;
> Regent of love-rhymes, lord of folded arms,
> The anointed sovereign of sighs and groans,
> Liege of all loiterers and malcontents,

---

[106] "First exposure" (Shakespeare for the Seeker, Volume 2, Chapter 4.3)
[107] "The Fair Youth, the Dark Lady, and Cupid" (Shakespeare for the Seeker, Volume 2, Chapter 5.3)

Dread prince of plackets, king of codpieces,
Sole imperator and great general
Of trotting 'paritors"
(Love's Labour's Lost, III.1)

Cupid's role is diminished at the moment when the inner faculties
are purified. It is only in such a purified state that a person
becomes immune to Cupid's arrows. For example, disarming Cupid
is illustrated in Shakespeare's last two Sonnets. A description of
how "the general of hot desire" was disarmed is given in Sonnet
154:

"The little Love-god lying once asleep
Laid by his side his heart-inflaming brand,
Whilst many nymphs that vow'd chaste life to keep
Came tripping by; but in her maiden hand
The fairest votary took up that fire
Which many legions of true hearts had warm'd;
And so the general of hot desire
Was sleeping by a virgin hand disarm'd."
(Sonnet 154, 1-8)

Rumi states that sensual and emotional pleasures seem to be very
delightful when viewed from a distance, i.e., before they are tasted.
But when approached, they turn out to be just a mirage. Every
human being is affected by such self-delusion at every stage of his
or her life. Rumi illustrates this form of self-delusion in the
following story.

A certain man had a Hindu slave, whom he had brought
up along with his children, one of whom was a daughter.
When the time came for giving the girl in marriage, many
suitors presented themselves and offered large dowries.
At last her father selected one who was by no means the
richest or noblest of the number, but pious and well-
mannered. The women of the family would have

preferred one of the richer youths, but the father insisted on having his own way, and the marriage was settled according to his wishes. As soon as the Hindu slave heard of this he fell sick. The mistress of the family discovered that he was in love with her daughter and aspired to marry her. She was much annoyed. She consulted her husband as to what was best to be done. He said, 'Keep the affair quiet, and I will cure the slave of his desire'. He directed his wife to flatter the slave with the hope that his wish would be granted, and the girl given to him in marriage. He then celebrated a mock marriage between the slave and the girl. At night he substituted the girl with a boy dressed in female attire. As the result of this bed-trick, the bridegroom spent the night with another boy. The next morning he openly complained to the girl in the front of her parents, saying, 'By day your face is the face of fresh young ladies; but at night your penis is more repulsive than that of an ugly ass'. (Book VI, 249-434)

An instance of the bed-trick, similar to that described by Rumi, can be found in Western literature as early as the Book of Genesis. It was described as Laban's bed-trick. In this story Laban promised his younger daughter Rachel to Jacob in return for seven years' service. On Jacob's wedding night, however, Laban substituted his older daughter, Leah, for her younger sister, Rachel. Afterwards, Laban offered to give Rachel to Jacob in second marriage in return for another seven years of work. Jacob accepted the offer and married Rachel after the week-long celebration of his marriage to Leah. The sequence of Jacob's marriages represents a sequential exposure to two evolutionary impulses. Namely, Leah represents an impulse that was released earlier (reforming); while Rachel symbolizes a later, or higher (purifying) impulse of the evolutionary spectrum. Therefore, Jacob could be exposed to the purifying impulse through his marriage to Rachel but only after he was "reformed" while being married to Leah.

Shakespeare has used the bed-trick to illustrate the implementation of a more advanced evolutionary methodology. In this advanced approach the exposure to the higher impulse is greatly accelerated. The implementation of this advanced methodology is described in "All's Well That Ends Well".

In "All's Well That Ends Well" Helena directs the entire process. At the same time, she is the carrier of an impulse of unitive energy[108]. Bertram is the intended recipient of this impulse. This impulse, however, is too subtle for the current state of Bertram. Therefore, an impulse of less subtle energy is needed to assist the process. Such an impulse was not available in 13th century France. However, this impulse was available within 16th century Florence. It is represented by Diana Capilet. This is why Helena and Bertram have to travel from 13th century France into 16th century Italy. When Bertram meets Diana, he immediately falls in love with her. It is then that Helena executes the bed-trick by inviting Bertram to Diana's bedchamber. In the darkness, Helena takes Diana's place and Bertram has sex with Helena. In this way, Bertram is exposed to a "modulated" impact of unitive energy. Here is how Helena explains the rationale of the bed-trick:

> "Why then to-night
> Let us assay our plot; which, if it speed,
> Is wicked meaning in a lawful deed
> And lawful meaning in a lawful act,
> Where both not sin, and yet a sinful fact."
> (All's Well That Ends Well, III.7)

The above-quote about "wicked meaning in a lawful deed" underlines a significant feature of a genuine developmental process. Namely, what matters is the spiritually constructive act that cannot be judged by the simplistic and moralistic rules of what is "infidelity" and what is "religion," or what is "right" and what is

---

108 "Modulation of beauty" (Shakespeare for the Seeker, Volume 2, Chapter 5.1)

"wrong". This was underlined by Rumi in the following lines: "the Man of God is beyond infidelity and religion; to the Man of God right and wrong are alike".

By exposing Bertram to an impact of unitive energy (in the bed-trick), it was possible to accelerate his inner reformation. The advanced methodology implemented by Helena helped to achieve optimal evolutionary gains that were needed in that place and at that time. As in Rumi's story, Shakespeare used the bed-trick to illustrate how a seemingly sinful act was needed to execute a lawful action.

6.2 The Fowler and the Bird

It is not destiny which leads people into difficulties, but their own errors and vices. Namely, ignorance and greed are especially potent at the time of excessive wants. The evolutionary path is full of trouble and challenges for the reason that it is not a path for any one whose inner nature is weak. On this road men's souls are tried by many traps, just like a sieve used for sifting bran. In the following story Rumi explains the working of such traps.

> A fowler went out to catch birds. He disguised himself by wrapping his head up in leaves and grass, so as to avoid frightening the birds away from his snare. A clever bird came near him and suspected that there was something wrong. But he foolishly lingered near and began to question the fowler as to his business. The fowler said he was a hermit who had retired from the world and dressed himself in weeds for the health of his soul. The bird said he was surprised to see a Moslem practicing a solitary life as any form of monasticism was forbidden by Islam. The

fowler replied, 'Anyone, whose intelligence is infirm, is in reality like a clod and rock. Being in his company is like being among clay and stones. One whose only desire is for bread resembles an ass. Anyone who lives with such worldly people is a monk. It is the companionship with such people that is the essence of monasticism'. Hearing that, the bird said to him, 'Well, then, the spiritual war is waged at the time when a brigand like this is on the road. The valiant man enters on the unsafe road for the purpose of protecting, helping and fighting. The innate quality of manhood only becomes apparent at the time when the traveler meets his enemies. This is why at the time of Jesus the right thing was retirement to cave and mountain; but since the appearance of Mohamed the right thing is war against one's inner enemy'. The fowler said, 'Yes; if one has strength and righteous guidance to make a mighty attack on evil and mischief. But when there is no strength, it is better to abstain from confronting such dangerous enemy'. The fowler argued his way and the bird defended his way: their debate on this subject was prolonged by the vehemence with which they argued. The bird then asked what the grains of wheat scattered on the trap were. The fowler replied that they were the property of an orphan, which had been deposited with him because people deemed him to be trustworthy. The bird then asked permission to eat some, as he was very hungry. The fowler, with much pretended reluctance, allowed him to do so. The moment the bird touched the grain, the trap closed upon him and he found himself a prisoner. The bird then abused the fowler for his trickery, but the fowler said he had only himself to blame for his greediness in eating the food which belonged to an orphan. (Book VI, 435-642)

Shakespeare's Hamlet goes through a very similar experience as the bird in the fowler's story. Earlier in the play Hamlet encounters the Ghost of his father who tells him that he had been murdered by Claudius, Hamlet's uncle. When a troupe of traveling actors arrives in Elsinore, Hamlet seizes upon an idea to use the actors to test his uncle's guilt. He would have the players perform a scene closely resembling his father's murder. So, if Claudius was guilty, he would surely react. Hamlet calls the players' performance "The Mouse-trap", for he hopes to catch the villain. However, he does not realize that the players have arrived in Elsinore with their own message for him. The players' message is designed in such a way as to warn Hamlet that he should be cautious of the Ghost's purpose. Namely, the players' performance consists of two sequential episodes[109]. The episodes are presented in reverse order, i.e., the first is the later one. The players' performance starts with a dumb show. The dumb show illustrates Hamlet's adaptation of the Ghost's report, i.e., the murder of Hamlet's father. The second episode that follows the dumb show illustrates the story of Gonzago, i.e., events that took place prior to the murder of Hamlet's father. (These events are a sequel to "Measure for Measure", a play that takes place in Vienna.) In this second episode Hamlet's father is represented by Lucianus. At that time Gonzago was the Duke of Vienna:

> "This play is the image of a murder done in Vienna:
> Gonzago is the duke's name; his wife, Baptista."
> (Hamlet, III.2)

Gonzago is presented as a sick and elderly man. He is liberal and considerate, and in this respect, very different, even opposite to the character of Hamlet's father. In this second episode Lucianus murders Gonzago. In this way, the players intends to inform Hamlet about his father's ascent to the throne. Namely, Hamlet's father killed the previous ruler in order to get the crown. Hamlet,

---

[109] "Elsinore" (Shakespeare for the Seeker, Volume 4, Chapter 7.3)

however, driven by his crude hunger for the revenge of his father's death, abruptly interrupts Lucianus' performance:

> "Begin, murderer;
> pox, leave thy damnable faces, and begin. Come:
> 'the croaking raven doth bellow for revenge'."
> (Hamlet, III.2)

And he delivers his own concluding line:

> "you shall see anon how the murderer
> gets the love of Gonzago's wife."
> (Hamlet, III.2)

But this line does not belong to this particular episode. This line belongs to the murder in the first episode of the players' performance. Hamlet's interruption does not allow the players to finish the second episode. The players are not able to deliver their message. As a result, Hamlet falls into his own mouse-trap.

6.3 The Drunken Turkish Emir and the Minstrel

Rumi uses the drinking of wine as a symbolic means to spiritual purification which leads to the activation and uniting of the subtle faculties. When friends drink wine they become intoxicated. Through this intoxication their inner faculties are purified. It is such wine which is bubbling in the barrels about the mysteries. Anyone who has rid himself of worldly desires may be transformed by drinking wine. For others, this wine is just a form of intoxication of the ordinary senses. Therefore, one of the cupbearers fetches spiritual wine, while the other serves ordinary wine that intoxicates the physical senses. The net result is that ordinary wine veils Truth from men's eyes. In order to lift themselves to higher states, those ignorant drinkers would need to choose the other form of drunkenness. This is the same thing as saying that they would need to pass from ignorance to the highest knowledge or from negation of the mysteries to their understanding.

So is it with music. One minstrel leads his listeners to an intoxication of their senses. The other minstrel guides them to the spiritual tavern. In this context, the cupbearer and the minstrel are partners. A witless traveler is like a ball in the sway of a polo-game, being caught between consecutive strikes of the polo-bat, i.e., his worldly desires. Rumi illustrates this in the story of the Turkish noble and the minstrel.

> A Turkish noble awoke from his drunken sleep, and called his minstrel to enliven him. The minstrel was a spiritual man. He proceeded to improve the occasion by singing a song:
>
> 'I know not whether Thou art a moon or an idol,
> I know not what Thou desirest of me.
> I know not what service I shall pay Thee,
> whether I shall keep silence or address Thee in words.
> It is marvellous that Thou art not separate from me,
> and yet where am I, and where Thou, I know not.
> I know not how Thou art drawing me:
> Thou drawest me now into Thy bosom, now into blood.'
>
> In this fashion he was repeating endlessly one phrase, 'I know not, I know not'. At one point the Turk leaped up and fetched an iron mace to smite the minstrel's head with it. But an officer seized the mace, saying, 'Nay; it is wrong to kill the minstrel at this moment'. The Turk replied, 'This endless and countless repetition of his has pounded my nerves. So I will pound his head'. And he

addressed the minstrel, 'If I ask you when you came or
what you have eaten for breakfast, and you answer only
by negations, your answer is a waste of my time. Say what
you mean by all these negations'. The minstrel replied,
'My meaning is a concealed one. Until you deny all else,
the meaning evades you. I am denying everything in order
that you may perceive the means of attaining to
affirmation. I play the tune of negation; when you die to
your desires, death will disclose the mystery. You have
suffered much agony, but you are still in the veil. Dying to
self was the fundamental principle of your drunkenness,
but you have not fulfilled it. Your agony is not finished till
you die; you cannot reach the roof without climbing the
ladder. You are wielding the mace against yourself. O
base man, this reaction is the reflection of yourself in the
mirror of my signing 'I know not'. You have seen the
reflection of yourself in the mirror of my action and have
risen in fury to fight with yourself. Like the lion who went
down into the well, for he fancied that the reflection of
himself was his opponent. Beyond any doubt, *not to be* is
the opposite of *to be*. This is in order that by means of the
one opposite you may gain a little knowledge of the other
opposite. At this time there is no means of making truth
known except by denying the opposite. O you who
possess sincerity, if you want that Reality unveiled, choose
death and tear off the veil. Not such a death that you will
go into a grave, but a death consisting of inner
transformation, so that you will be able to see a Light'.
(Book VI, 643-887)

Shakespeare's Hamlet is able to experience such a death, but only
for a very brief moment (see Chapter 5.9). During that moment he
is able to experience the state "to be". Only then Hamlet is able to
perceive the meaning of everything he has experienced, i.e., the
story of his father and the players' performance, the role of the

Ghost; the function of Ophelia, Claudius' guilt, Gertrude's behaviour, the interview with the gravedigger, and the arrival of Fortinbras. All of these formed one consistent chain of events leading him to the final scene. Because of his awakened state of "to be" he is able to convey his understanding with a single sentence:

> "I do prophesy the election lights on Fortinbras."
> (Hamlet, V.2)

Hamlet is not only able to perceive the Truth: during this brief moment of "to be" he is able to discharge the remaining fraction of his evolutionary function by expressing his support for Fortinbras' election as the next ruler of Denmark[110]:

> "He has my dying voice;
> So tell him, with the occurrents, more and less,
> Which have solicited. The rest is silence."
> (Hamlet, V.2)

Hamlet's last words tell everything. Nothing else needs to be added. Therefore, "The rest is silence".

6.4 The Purchase of Bilal

Man does not live very long and he can control very little of his circumstances. The things which happen to him may have far more effect on his life than the things which he causes to happen. In order to be more effective, therefore, he has to learn how to dominate his environment. He may do it by being able to stand aside from it, when necessary, and in this way allowing it to have only the minimum effect on him; or by meshing with it, when

---

[110] "The fencing match" (Shakespeare for the Seeker, Volume 4, Chapter 7.3)

indicated. Following the ordinary reason or intellect is not sufficient enough to recognize these various moments of action and inaction. Man needs to develop inner senses that will act as a guiding beacon. This is symbolically illustrated in the following story by a surprising remedy from Abu Bakr:

> Bilal was an Abyssinian slave belonging to a rich man of Mecca. Bilal had incurred his master's displeasure for having embraced the teaching of Mohamed. For this offence his master tortured him by exposing him to the heat of the midday sun and beating him with thorns. But notwithstanding his anguish, Bilal would not recant his faith and uttered only the cry, 'The One! The One!' At this moment Abu Bakr, one of the companions of Mohamed, happened to pass by and he heard Bilal's cries. He was so struck by Bilal's steadiness, that he resolved to help him. He went to Bilal in private and advised him, saying, 'Keep thy belief hidden from your master. God knows all secrets; therefore conceal your feeling'. Bilal answered, 'I repent my error, O prince'. Early the next day, Abu Bakr was in that area and he again heard cries of "The One! The One!" followed by the sound of blows inflicted by the whip of thorns. He became angry and admonished Bilal once more. Bilal again promised to comply. He complied for same time, till he could not hold back any longer and started loudly proclaiming his feeling, saying, 'Love is the All-Subduer, and I am subdued by Love; by Love's bitterness I have been made sweet as sugar'. Afterwards Abu Bakr related to Mohamed the troubles of Bilal. Abu Bakr noticed that Mohamed was pleased hearing the story. Mohamed asked him, 'Now, what is the remedy?' Abu Bakr answered that he was going to buy the slave at whatever price from the owner. Mohamed said that he will pay half of the cost, 'Be my agent, buy a half share in him on my account, and receive

the payment from me'. After much haggling and many attempts at cheating on the owner's part, Abu Bakr succeeded in doing so. When the purchase was made, the owner started to mock and jeer at Abu Bakr, saying, 'Your eagerness allowed me to get ten times more from you than this wasteful slave is worth'. Abu Bakr answered him, 'O simpleton, like a silly boy you have given away a pearl in exchange for a walnut. For in my opinion he is worth the two worlds. I am regarding his soul, you his colour. He is red gold that has been made like black iron on account of the enviousness of this abode of fools. The eye that sees these seven bodily colours cannot perceive the soul because of this veil. If you had haggled in the sale more excessively than you did, I would have given the whole of my property and riches. And if you had then increased your price, I would have borrowed a bag full of gold in my eagerness to purchase him. You gave him up easily because you got him cheaply. You did not recognize the pearl; you did not split this oyster's shell'. When Mohamed saw Abu Bakr, he said to him, 'Give me a share in Bilal'. But Abu Bakr answered that he had already set him free. Mohamed reproached him saying, 'Why, I told you to make me partner in your generosity. I asked you to buy him in partnership with me. Why have you bought him for yourself alone?' Abu Bakr replied, 'Bilal and I are two slaves of yours. I set him free so you may keep me as your slave and loyal friend. I want no freedom'. (Book VI, 888-1292)

Shakespeare used even the more startling behaviour of Othello to illustrate the limitations of ordinary perception. Iago is the villain of the play and Othello is supposedly his victim. But Shakespeare played a trick: it is not Othello but the audience watching the play that is the prime victim of Iago's scheming[111]. For the last 400 years or so, Iago has managed to lead the audience in the same way he did with Roderigo, i.e.:

> "And will as tenderly be led by the nose
> As asses are." (Othello, I.3)

At the end of the play, Shakespeare delegated Othello to provide the audience with a hint. The hint is embedded in Othello's last words. First of all, Othello asks the audience to record his actions precisely without exaggerating or toning them down:

> "Soft you; a word or two before you go.
> I have done the state some service, and they know't.
> No more of that. I pray you, in your letters,
> When you shall these unlucky deeds relate,
> Speak of me as I am; nothing extenuate,
> Nor set down aught in malice." (Othello, V.2)

Then Othello delivers his two-fold message. The first part of the message is addressed to ordinary men. The ordinary man sees things piecemeal and cannot distinguish the hidden trend in events because his mind is fixed on conditioned patterns; he follows linear thinking that relies on intellectual speculations, socially imposed terms of reference and emotional reactions. Othello presents himself as a member of this particular section of the audience:

> "then must you speak
> Of one that loved not wisely but too well;
> Of one not easily jealous, but being wrought
> Perplex'd in the extreme; of one whose hand,
> Like the base Indian, threw a pearl away
> Richer than all his tribe." (Othello, V.2)

---

[111] "Conclusion" (Shakespeare for the Seeker, Volume 3, Chapter 6.2)

Othello lists typical excuses for doing things wrong, e.g., that one was not wise enough and allowed himself to be tricked and manipulated. Such an interpretation of Othello's actions corresponds to a fool who, like the rich owner of Bilal in Rumi's story, throws away a "pearl", because he is incapable of recognizing its value. Such a conditioned thinking pattern has to be broken down before hidden trends in the events can be recognized.

In the second part of his message, Othello addresses those who are capable of breaking away from their ordinary thinking patterns. Othello gives a piece of advice that may help them perceive the hidden trend in his actions:

> "Set you down this;
> And say besides, that in Aleppo once,
> Where a malignant and a turban'd Turk
> Beat a Venetian and traduced the state,
> I took by the throat the circumcised dog,
> And smote him, thus."
> *(Othello stabs himself)*

Othello confirms that he was freed from selfish influences. Othello calls his selfish tendencies "a malignant and a turban'd Turk" that he killed in Aleppo. It was then that Othello "died before dying" and in this way completed his own spiritual journey. This took place many "years" before his arrival in Venice. In other words, Othello's actions were not driven by his earthly desires, such as jealousy. Othello's actions were in response to the evolutionary needs of this particular time, place, and people. When projected onto the ordinary world, Othello's actions revitalized the evolutionary seed that led to the birth of the Italian Renaissance.

6.5 The Sick Man

When one has developed one's subtle faculties, everything that one does is constructive because one follows the greater design. Therefore whatever this person does, he is not responsible for it. The responsibility lies within the design, not with the trustee of the design. The incurable man in the following story is an illustration of the operation of the design. The ascetic and the Judge are examples of the various tendencies that are characteristic of the intermediate stages of the journey.

> A sick man went to a physician for advice. The physician felt his pulse and perceived that no treatment would cure him. Therefore he told him to go away and do whatever he had a fancy for. He said, 'In this way malady may quit your body. Do not withhold anything that your inclination craves, lest your self-restraint and abstinence turn into illnesses'. The sick man blessed the physician for his prescription. At once he went for a walk on the bank of the river. On the river-bank he saw an ascetic who was washing his hands and face. Like a crazy man, the sick man felt a strong desire to give him a slap. Saying to himself, 'The physician told me it would make me ill if I would not let my desire have its way'. At once he carried his wish into effect. The ascetic jumped up and was about to return the blow. But when he saw the weakly and infirm condition of his assailant, he restrained himself. He disregarded his present anger, and thought about the future. In this way the non-existent future became to him more real than the present moment: 'If I give him a blow with my fist, he will crumble like dead, and then the king will punish me'. The ascetic, therefore, did not retaliate on his weak assailant. Instead, he brought him before the Judge and said, 'Mount this scoundrel on an ass and parade him through the streets. Or punish him with

blows of the whip, according as your judgment may deem fitting'. On learning the facts of the case the Judge said, 'This old man is sick to death. I am a judge of the living. How may I judge the corpse that belongs to the grave?' And he addressed the ascetic, 'Do not concern yourself with anger and hatred against a dead man. Beware, do not wage war on one who is dead'. The ascetic was dissatisfied with this view of the case. He again pressed the Judge to do him justice. He said, 'Then do you think it is right for him to slap me without my taking retaliation and without his paying for it?' On this the Judge asked the sick man how much money he had. The man said that he had six dirhams. The Judge let him off with a fine of three dirhams because he thought that the defendant was weak, poor, and infirm and would need three dirhams for his food. The moment the sentence was pronounced, the sick man went up to the Judge, struck him a blow on the back, and cried out, 'Now take the other three dirhams and let me go!' The Judge was incensed. 'Hey', cried the ascetic, 'Your decision was just. Now I have no doubt about it because it has brought you a slap on the nape'. The ascetic then pointed out to the Judge that his ill-timed leniency to the man had brought this blow upon himself. The Judge answered that, for his part, he recognized every blow and misfortune that might befall him as Divinely ordained, and sent for his good: 'Whatever blow may come to you from Heaven, always expect to receive a gift of honour after it; for He is not the King to slap you and then not give you a crown and a throne on which to recline'. He added that his judgment in the matter of the sick man had not been dictated by impulse, but by inspiration. The ascetic asked him how evils and misfortunes could proceed from the Divine fountain of goodness. The Judge replied that what seems good and evil to us has no absolute existence, but is merely as the

foam on the surface of the vast ocean. Moreover, every misfortune occurring to the wise in this life will be amply compensated for in the life to come. The ascetic asked why this world should not be so arranged that only good should be experienced in it. The Judge replied by telling him the anecdote of the Turk and the tailor. The Turk, who typifies a careless pleasure-seeker, was so intent on listening to the jokes and amusing stories of the tailor, typifying attachments to worldly pleasures, that he allowed himself to be robbed of the silk which was to furnish him with vesture for eternity. The ascetic again retorted that he did not see why the world would not get on better without evil in it. The Judge replied that there would be no possibilities of being virtuous if there were no temptations to be vicious. He said, 'Knowledge and wisdom exist for the purpose of distinguishing between the right and the wrong paths. If all paths were right, knowledge and wisdom would be void of meaning'.
(Book VI, 1293-1907)

The entire canon of Shakespeare's plays is an illustration of the operation of the Greater Design. In other words, the plays illustrate the evolutionary process. Sometimes the Greater Design requires approaches that lead to a happy ending; at other times the required approach ends in seemingly tragic events, like the slapping in the story of the sick man. This is why the process may be illustrated by both comedies and tragedies. It would be superficial, however, to separate and group the plays as comedies and tragedies. Such classification and categorization of Shakespeare's plays diminishes their original intent[112]. Shakespeare pointed this out in "Hamlet" by making fun of such categorizations in the following remark delivered by Polonius:

---

[112] "Introduction" (Shakespeare for the Seeker, Volume 4, Chapter 7.3)

> "The best actors in the world, either for tragedy,
> comedy, history, pastoral, pastoral-comical,
> historical-pastoral, tragical-historical, tragical-
> comical-historical-pastoral, scene individable, or
> poem unlimited." (Hamlet, II.2)

Such a categorization applies only to the plays' emotional or artificial interpretation. The evolutionary process includes many experiences, which sometimes may seem comical, sometimes may be perceived as tragic. Nevertheless, all these experiences have to be encountered and are unavoidable. Each of these experiences is a preparation for other ones; in all cases they lead to a constructive outcome. For example, Shakespeare's "The Tempest" is the projection of the outcome of the Italian plays onto the New World. Some of the previous episodes of the Italian evolutionary branch are presented in "Othello" and "Romeo and Juliet"[113]. These seemingly tragic episodes were needed to arrive at the advanced stage of the process that is illustrated in "The Tempest". The episode in which Ferdinand and Miranda are playing chess alludes to the gains achieved within the Italian branch of the modern evolutionary cycle:

> Miranda:
>
> "Sweet lord, you play me false."
>
> Ferdinand:
>
> "No, my dear'st love,
> I would not for the world."
>
> Miranda:
>
> "Yes, for a score of kingdoms you should wrangle,
> And I would call it, fair play."
> (The Tempest, V.1)

---

[113] "New being of Naples" (Shakespeare for the Seeker, Volume 4, Chapter 8.1)

Miranda does not have to go through the difficult experiences that Desdemona in "Othello" and Juliet in "Romeo and Juliet" were faced with. Yet, Miranda is worried that Ferdinand does not play a fair game because he is too gentle with her ("Sweet lord, you play me false"). When Ferdinand protests, Miranda demonstrates her spiritual maturity by expressing her readiness to accept whatever is needed to achieve their goal ("Yes, for a score of kingdoms you should wrangle, and I would call it, fair play").

Miranda does not have to go through such challenging experiences, because she has already arrived at her destination, i.e., at the Island which corresponds to Desdemona's Mauritania and Juliet's Mantua. This sequel of Desdemona's, Juliet's, and Miranda's experiences is in accordance with the Judge's pronouncement, "every misfortune occurring to the wise in this life will be amply compensated for in the life to come".

6.6 The Fakir and the Hidden Treasure

Everyone seeks relief from fear, and in consequence of this a whole world is set in order. Fear, therefore, is the pillar of this world. Because of fear everyone has devoted himself to work. All fearful people are afraid of losing goods and of suffering evil. In this way, fear is the architect and means for the improvement of the world. But they are not afraid or frightened of themselves. In reality, the ruler over them all is that One who is near. He is not perceived by the physical senses. He is perceived in a certain hiding-place within the inner being. The sense to which that One is manifested is not a sense of this world. This inner sense is called the organ of superior perception. Rumi illustrates this in the following story.

An inner voice directed a poor youth to go to the house of a certain scribe and take a certain scroll that he would find there. The voice also told him to read the scroll in privacy and not disclose the information to anyone. He did so, and on reading the writing he found that it contained directions for finding a hidden treasure. The directions were as follows: 'Go outside the city to the dome which covers the tomb of the martyr; turn your back to the tomb and your face towards Mecca. Place an arrow in your bow, and let it loose. When you have shot the arrow from the bow, dig up for the treasure in the place where the arrow falls'. Thereupon the youth fetched a strong bow and let fly an arrow into the air. Then he brought a pick-axe and dug up the spot where his arrow had fallen. But both he and the pick-axe were worn out in vain efforts; there were no traces of the hidden treasure. Every day in like fashion he was shooting arrows, but never found the treasure. Since he made this his daily routine, a rumour arose in the city and among the people. The rumour reached the ear of the king. It was reported to him that the poor fakir had found a treasure-scroll. When the youth heard that it had come to the knowledge of the king, he saw no remedy but resignation. So, before he would suffer torture on the rack by order of the king, he laid the note of the treasure before him, saying, 'Ever since I found this scroll, I have seen no treasure but only troubles. Not even a single mite of treasure has been discovered, but I have suffered much. During a whole month I have been in bitter distress. Maybe your fortune will disclose to you this mine of riches'.

For six long months and more the king shot arrows and dug pits where the arrows fell. Wherever an archer was to be found, the king gave him arrows to shoot and searched for the treasure in every direction. The result was nothing but vexation and grief. At last the king became sick at heart and weary. He gave back the scroll to the fakir, saying, 'Take this scroll which has no value for me; you are the fittest owner of it, since you have no work. If you cannot find it, you will never weary of seeking. And if you find it, I grant you the right of possession'.

When the king handed over to that grief-stricken man the treasure-scroll, he became secure from rivals and fears. He devoted himself to meditations and prayers. One day, when he was deeply in his meditation, a voice came to him, saying, 'You were directed to fix an arrow on your bow, but not to draw your bow with all your might, as you have been doing. You should shoot as gently as possible, that the arrow may fall close to you. Because of your vanity, you were shooting proudly. Remember, the farther one shoots, the farther away and more separated is he from a treasure like this. This is why the philosophers kill themselves with thinking because their backs are turned towards the treasure'.

In this way the poor fakir was transformed into a finder. He should not, therefore, be regarded as a seeker of treasure for he is the treasure himself. (Book VI, 1908-2375)

Shakespeare's guide also told him that the treasure was hidden within himself. At one point, the guide insisted that it was the right time for him to make efforts toward his inner development. Otherwise, the poet would rob the world of this treasure. Shakespeare described the guide's appeal in Sonnet 3:

> "Look in thy glass and tell the face thou viewest,
> Now is the time that face should form another,
> Whose fresh repair if now thou not renewest,
> Thou dost beguile the world, unbless some mother.
> For where is she so fair whose uneared womb
> Disdains the tillage of thy husbandry?

Or who is he so fond will be the tomb,
Of his self-love to stop posterity?
Thou art thy mother's glass and she in thee
Calls back the lovely April of her prime,
So thou through windows of thine age shalt see,
Despite of wrinkles, this thy golden time.
    But if thou live, remembered not to be,
    Die single and thine Image dies with thee."
(Sonnet 3)

In this Sonnet, the guide tells the poet that by remaining idle, he will prevent Nature from fulfilling her desire for growth[114]. So, who would be so stupid as to allow his own self-indulgence to cut him off from immortality? The poet, like the poor fakir in Rumi's story, is Nature's greatest treasure. And it is his duty to preserve it and make good use of it. Within his lifetime, and despite his aging, he is capable of fulfilling his evolutionary purpose. But, warns the guide, if the poet fails to arrive at the state of "to be", his potentiality will die with him ("but if thou live, remembered not to be, die single and thine Image dies with thee").

6.7 The Three Travelers

The Divine secret is not available to those who seek to infer and deduce its nature and quality from the lofty abstractions and sophistication of philosophy. Lofty intellectual speculation does not lead to knowledge. Divine guidance is revealed as an immediate intuition to those who seek it with sincerity and obedience.

---

[114] "Shakespeare's Sonnets or How heavy do I journey on the way" (Sonnet 3)

Three men were traveling together on a journey. When these three fellow-travelers arrived at a certain caravanserai, a man of fortune brought them some sweetmeat as a gift. Two of the travelers had already eaten their evening meals when the sweetmeats arrived. Therefore they said, 'We have eaten our fill; let us practice self-restrain and refrain from food. Let's put it away tonight and eat it tomorrow'. The third one was starving because he had been fasting all day. He suggested that the sweetmeats be eaten that night. To this the other two refused to consent, alleging that the man wanted to eat the whole of the sweetmeats himself. Then the third man proposed to divide the sweetmeats into three portions, so that each might eat his own portion when he pleased. But the proposal was objected to by a dogmatic elaboration of the others. The third man therefore agreed, and lay down to sleep in the endurance of pangs of hunger. Next morning, when they awoke, it was agreed between them that each should relate his dreams. And that the sweetmeats would be awarded to him whose dream was the best. The first man said that he had dreamed that Moses had carried him to the top of Mount Sinai, and shown him marvellous visions of the glory of heaven and the angels. The second man said he had dreamed that Jesus had carried him up to the fourth heaven and shown him all the glories of the heavens. Finally the third one said that Mohamed had appeared to him in person. After commending him for his piety in keeping fast so strictly on the previous night, Mohamed said, 'The first of your companions has gone with Moses to the top of Mount Sinai; and the other has been carried by Jesus to the zenith of the fourth heaven. So, they have attained to their proper eminence and because of their talents have mingled with the angels. But you have been left behind and have suffered. Arise therefore and, at least, eat up the sweetmeats'. The third man said that he had done as he was told. The other two men were at first annoyed with him for stealing their portions of the sweetmeats. But on his pointing out that he had no option but to obey the command, they admitted that he had done right thing. They realized that his dream was the best as he had been awake, while they were asleep. (Book VI, 2376-3013)

As demonstrated by the experiences of the third traveler, Divine intervention is manifested in such a way that it helps to deal with worldly matters. Dealing correctly with worldly matters allows man to gain insights into the invisible worlds. Pericles' experiences described by Shakespeare in "Pericles, Prince of Tyre" illustrate further this particular aspect of the evolutionary process. At one point during his descending journey from Pentapolis, Pericles ended up in Mytilene. It was there that he was reunited with Marina, his lost daughter. During his reunion with Marina, Pericles heard "the music of the spheres":

"The music of the spheres! List, my Marina."

"Most heavenly music!
It nips me unto listening, and thick slumber
Hangs upon mine eyes: let me rest."
(Pericles, Prince of Tyre, V.1)

Shakespeare uses the "most heavenly music" to indicate the manifestation of Divine intervention[115]. Immediately after hearing "the music of the spheres" Pericles falls asleep. It is then that the goddess Diana appears to him in his dream. As in the case of the third traveller in Rumi's story, Pericles is commanded to perform a certain task. He is commanded to go to Diana's temple in Ephesus and there reveal his story:

---

[115] "Reactivation of creative energy" (Shakespeare for the Seeker, Volume 2, Chapter 4.1)

"Before the people all,
Reveal how thou at sea didst lose thy wife:
To mourn thy crosses, with thy daughter's, call
And give them repetition to the life."
(Pericles, Prince of Tyre, V.1)

When Pericles wakes up, he goes to Ephesus. In the front of the temple he tells his story to those who have gathered. It is then and there that Pericles is reunited with Thaisa, his wife.

Pericles' story, revealed in Ephesus, contained the description of techniques of spiritual technology as well as descriptions of various spiritual states of the human mind. In this way, Pericles' experiences were passed over to those who were present at Diana's temple in Ephesus. As always, such an account was given in a symbolic form that contained an outward and an inner meaning.

The process leading to the activation of such perception, as illustrated by Pericles and the third traveler in Rumi's story, is quite sophisticated. The entire "Mathnawi" was dedicated to a gradual disclosure of some elements of the methodology of the activation of inner perception. Shakespeare further expanded the description of the methodology of activation of the subtle faculties. This advanced methodology is based on the so-called "stop technique". The stop technique allows one to split the inner faculties and then to diagnose them separately. Afterwards each of the inner faculties is treated accordingly. There are three forms of the stop technique. These three forms are known as "the number stop", "the time stop", and "the heart stop". Shakespeare gave quite a precise description of this technique in "The Tempest". Prospero, the main character of the play, implemented all three forms while working on the survivors of the wrecked ship.

The survivors represent the being of Naples. The various aspects of the intellect faculty are represented by King Alonso and his courtiers, i.e., Sebastian, Antonio, Gonzalo, Adrian, and Francisco.

The heart faculty is represented by Ferdinand, Alonso's son. Alonso's servants, Trinculo and Stephano, are aspects of the self faculty. The being of Naples is capable of activating its inner heart. This may be achieved through the marriage of Ferdinand and Miranda, Prospero's daughter. However, the presence of severely corrupted aspects of the intellect and the self faculties would interfere with the activation process. First, therefore, it is necessary to neutralize the corrupted aspects. Prospero's task is to prepare and then implement this particular stage of the process. Prospero applies the stop technique to complete his task.

In accordance with "the number stop" technique, the inner being may be divided into parts. Each part is related to one of the manifest faculties. Such a division enables each faculty to be subjected to specific experiences, which aim at balancing the entire being. A properly developed inner being should form a certain balance that is analogous to a musical or colour harmony. This is why after their arrival on the Island, Prospero separates the Neapolitans into three groups. Each group represents one of the manifest faculties. Then each of these faculties is exposed to specific experiences[116].

The number stop techniques applied to the self faculty allow one to align correctly with respect to the intellect faculty. Stephano, the drunkard and Trinculo, the jester are separated from the others and put together with Caliban. This encourages them to show off their most destructive behaviours. Caliban represents a degenerated aspect inherited from the past. Caliban's role is that of a whisperer. He encourages Stephano to kill Prospero and make himself the king of the Island:

> "Why, as I told thee, 'tis a custom with him,
> I' th' afternoon to sleep: there thou mayst brain him,
> Having first seized his books, or with a log

---

[116] "Process" (Shakespeare for the Seeker, Volume 4, Chapter 8.1)

Batter his skull, or paunch him with a stake,
Or cut his wezand with thy knife."
(The Tempest, III.2)

Stephano happily follows Caliban's whispering. All of this is in preparation for the rebuke in the final scene, where Prospero will set upon them spirits in the shape of hunting dogs. In this way, Stephano and his companions will discover what their correct function within the being of Naples is. Here is Caliban's conclusion from that experience:

"Ay, that I will; and I'll be wise hereafter
And seek for grace. What a thrice-double ass
Was I, to take this drunkard for a god
And worship this dull fool!"
(The Tempest, V.1)

In parallel, the aspects of the intellect faculty are subjected to "the time stop" technique. "The "time stop" requires stopping conditional thinking to allow the consciousness to receive the guiding impulse that is needed in a given situation. The guiding impulse is symbolically presented as "some heavenly music". Prospero implements the time stop with the help of Ariel. Ariel appears and plays solemn music that puts all but Alonso, Sebastian and Antonio to sleep. A moment later, Alonso also falls asleep. The most corrupted aspects, i.e., Sebastian and Antonio, are immune to the music:

Sebastian:

"What a strange drowsiness possesses them!"

Antonio:

"It is the quality o' the climate."

Sebastian:

"Why
Doth it not then our eyelids sink? I find not
Myself disposed to sleep."

Antonio:

"Nor I; my spirits are nimble.
They fell together all, as by consent;
They dropp'd, as by a thunder-stroke."
(The Tempest, II.1)

As soon as the leading aspect of the intellect is put in a state of "time stop", the corrupted aspects appear in their greater prominence. This is illustrated by Sebastian's and Antonio's attempt to kill their sleeping companions. In other words, "the time stop" technique allows, among other things, one to identify and sort out the most destructive aspects of the intellect. In the next step of the process these destructive aspects are exposed to a reforming rebuke.

"The heart stop" technique allows one to arrive at a state where love is perceived as the supreme priority, i.e., over emotional attachments such as sorrow, fury, or passion. Prospero applies the heart stop technique to Ferdinand, who represents Naples' heart faculty. Again, he sends Ariel to guide Ferdinand with music. The following comment by Ferdinand is a precise account of the working of "the heart stop" technique:

"Sitting on a bank,
Weeping again the king my father's wreck,
This music crept by me upon the waters,
Allaying both their fury and my passion
With its sweet air: thence I have follow'd it,
Or it hath drawn me rather. But 'tis gone.
No, it begins again."
(The Tempest, I.2)

Ferdinand follows the music and ends up meeting Miranda. Miranda and Ferdinand are immediately smitten with each other.

As a result of the experiences to which they were exposed, the three faculties have been partially reformed and purified. At the end of the play they are all reunited to form a new being of Naples. This being is "equipped" with a newly activated inner heart. Although the corrupted self and intellect faculties were partially neutralized, the most destructive aspects were not removed. Sebastian and Antonio represent those destructive aspects that were not affected by Prospero's treatment. This means that the new being of Naples was improved but only partially.

The advanced methodology described by Shakespeare is quite challenging because depending on the initial make-up of a person, a different sequence of activation should be applied. Shakespeare presented such challenges in the Sonnets. For example, in Sonnet 46 he describes an experience that he was faced with. At that time the inner layers of his heart and intellect were activated but only partially. The poet describes such an imbalanced inner state to a war between these two inner faculties, which fight between themselves for their right to the guide. He refers to the subtle faculty of the heart as "the dear heart". The subtle faculty of the intellect is described as "mine eye". The poet says that his eye does not allow his inner heart to keep the guide's image. The poet's inner heart, on the other hand, disputes whether the eye has the right to the guide's image. The inner heart pleads that the image is stored in him, i.e., a place beyond the eye's reach. But the defending eye denies that claim, and argues that the image is stored in him:

> "Mine eye and heart are at a mortal war,
> How to divide the conquest of thy sight,
> Mine eye, my heart their picture's sight would bar,
> My heart, mine eye the freedom of that right,

My heart doth plead that thou in him dost lie,
(A closet never pierced with crystal eyes)
But the defendant doth that plea deny,
And says in him thy fair appearance lies.
To side this title is impannelled
A quest of thoughts, all tenants to the heart,
And by their verdict is determined
The clear eye's moiety, and the dear heart's part.
　　As thus, mine eye's due is thine outward part,
　　And my heart's right, thine inward love of heart."
　(Sonnet 46)

To decide whose claim is right, the poet has set-up a panel of jurors ("all tenants to the heart"). The jurors have declared that the poet's eye has the right to admire the guide's beautiful form, while the inner heart has the duty to immerse itself in the guide's love[117].

It took Shakespeare 154 Sonnets to illustrate the various challenges of the activation of higher states of mind.

6.8 The Man who received a Pension

As indicated in the introduction to Chapter 3.18, there are two attractions placed in the nature of man. Therefore, two forms of external agencies are needed to bring these attractions into operation. The external agency which activates the attraction to higher forms of living is often called an angel. It is this agency that provides man with extraordinary forms of protection, safety, and guidance. The following story describes the operation of such a constructive agency.

---

[117] "Shakespeare's Sonnets or How heavy do I journey on the way" (Sonnet 46)

A certain dervish who was in debt came to Tabriz. His debt amounted to nine thousand pieces of gold. It happened that the Prefect of Tabriz was well known as a very generous man. This dervish came to Tabriz in hope of the Prefect's generosity. He had come previously many times to the Prefect's door and he was never turned away without being given some money. Relying upon this generous patron, the poor man ran into debt, for he was confident he would receive his donations. When the poor dervish arrived at the Prefect's house, the people told him that the generous man had passed away. They said, 'The day before yesterday he left this world; each man and woman in this city is grieving the departure of this angelic soul'. The poor man shrieked and fell senseless; one would think that he too had given up his life and followed on the heels of his friend. When he came to his senses, he said, 'O Maker, I am a wrongdoer: I was setting my hopes on Thy creatures. Though the Prefect had shown great generosity, yet that was never a match for Thy bounty'. In the meantime, the Prefect's bailiff endeavoured to raise funds for the poor man, because he was distressed by his grief. He appealed to the citizens to aid him, but only succeeded in collecting a very small sum. The bailiff took then the poor man and went with him to visit the grave of the generous Prefect. When the debtor arrived at the tomb of his benefactor, he began to weep bitterly and broke into loud lamentation. Afterwards, the bailiff invited him to his house and handed over to him the purse of a hundred dinars, which had been collected from the citizens of Tabriz. On that night the bailiff dreamed that he saw the blessed Prefect seated on a high-seat in the heavenly palace. The Prefect announced, 'Now hear about the bounty which I have reserved for my guest. I foresaw that he would arrive. I had heard about his debt, so I packed some jewels for him; two or three of these jewels should be enough to pay for his debt. I did this so that the heart of my guest is not torn with anxiety. Death, however, did not allow me to hand these jewels over to him. He owes nine thousand pieces of gold. Let him discharge his debt with some of these jewels. There will be a great many of them left over. Let him spend the surplus. All the jewels are stored in a vessel on which his name is written. I have buried it in a vault. None but kings can know the value of that treasure. Take care, then, that the purchasers do not cheat him in the sale'. Thus the dead Prefect proved a more efficient benefactor than the citizens of Tabriz who were still living. (Book VI, 3014-3583)

The story of Helena from Shakespeare' play "All's Well That Ends Well" may help to unfold the inner meaning of this story. Helena, the ward of the Countess of Rousillon, is the orphaned daughter of a respected physician (see Chapter 6.1). Helena's father left her a prescription to cure a certain malignant disease. When hearing that the King of France was affected by this particular disease, Helena went to Paris. She offered to cure his illness:

"On's bed of death
Many receipts he gave me: chiefly one.
Which, as the dearest issue of his practise,
And of his old experience the oily darling,
He bade me store up, as a triple eye,
Safer than mine own two, more dear; I have so;
And hearing your high majesty is touch'd
With that malignant cause wherein the honour
Of my dear father's gift stands chief in power,
I come to tender it and my appliance
With all bound humbleness."
(All's Well That Ends Well, II.1)

Helena is a spiritual guide. Through an invisible link with her father, i.e., the previous guide, she was able to perceive the currently operating cosmic matrix. She was able to see what was needed to advance the process. Bertram was a man who would greatly benefit from Helena's presence if he could recognize her beauty. At the beginning of the play, however, Bertram was completely unaware of Helena's function. Therefore, he was not able to recognize the "treasure" that was designated for him. But Helena was able to bring him back to the treasure[118].

Now we may recognize that in Rumi's story, the bailiff is the guide. Through an invisible link with the Prefect, i.e., the previous guide, he knows what needs to be done. Therefore, he was able to guide the debtor to his treasure.

6.9 The King and his Three Sons

The story of the king and his three sons outlines the developmental methodology that was implemented at the time of Rumi. This particular methodology was based on a sequential approach, i.e., reformation was the first step that was then followed by purification. Only a correctly reformed inner being could be exposed to the process of purification. The story of the three sons illustrates various difficulties of the evolutionary process when the developmental methodology is not correctly implemented. The experiences of the first son illustrate the limitations of the approach based on spiritual reformation but without purification. The second son goes through the process of spiritual purification but not through the reformation. The story implies that only the

---

[118] "Developmental mismatch" (Shakespeare for the Seeker, Volume 2, Chapter 5.1)

third son was capable of experiencing the stage of union, i.e., when the purified inner faculties were fused together to form the inner organ of supreme perception.

A certain king had three sons. One day he called his sons before him and commanded them to travel through his realm, and to inspect the behaviour of the governors and the state of the administration. He strictly charged them not to go near a particular castle which he called 'the robber of reason'. He told them, 'Keep far away from that castle adorned with pictures'. But the three princes disobeyed their father. Before going anywhere else, they proceeded to visit the forbidden castle. If their father had not warned them against that castle, they would never have known about its existence. Therefore, they would never have desired to go there. For it was not well-known; it was exceedingly remote and far away from the other fortresses and the highways. In spite of the orders of the king, they advanced to the fortress, which was a destroyer of self-restraint and a robber of rationality. Being driven by disobedience they approached the tree of the forbidden fruit. They entered into the beautiful fortress. The fortress had five gates to the land and five gates to the sea. Five of those gates, like the physical senses, were facing towards the material world; the other five were leading towards the higher worlds. The castle was full of pictures, images, and forms. Amongst them was the portrait of a beautiful damsel. The image of the damsel made such a deep impression on the three princes that they all became distracted with desire for her. They began to make inquiries, asking, 'Who in the world is she of whom this is the portrait?' After much inquiry, a Sheikh, endowed with insight, disclosed the mystery. The Sheikh told them, 'This is the portrait of the Princess of China. She is kept by the king in a secret bower in a secret palace.

Neither man nor woman is admitted to her presence.
Only those who were prepared to yield up their lives for
the king would be able to gain access to his daughter. This
is in accordance with the formula: you must die before
you die'. The eldest prince convened his brothers and
insisted on undertaking the journey to the secret palace,
risking its perils. The princes agreed to set out for China
towards the object of their desire. They left their kingdom
and they took the way to the hidden beloved. After
enduring many toils and misfortunes, the three princes at
last arrived in the metropolis of China. The eldest prince
decided to present himself before the king, as he could
wait no longer. His brothers tried to dissuade him from
risking his life, pointing out that he acted on blind
impulse and vain conceit. They argued that without
proper preparation and guidance he would surely go
astray. But the eldest brother refused to be dissuaded
from his purpose, saying he could no longer hide his
passion for his beloved. He added that he was convinced
that he would obtain his desire in some way or other. The
eldest brother then rushed into the presence of the king
and kissed his feet. The king, like a good shepherd, was
well aware of his troubles and cravings. He knew that the
prince had abjured earthly rank and dignity through love
for his daughter. The only reason why the prince had
arrived unprepared was that he had lacked the 'inner eye',
or the inner senses, which discern spiritual qualities. But
his eye had now been opened by the king's grace, so he
was able to escape from the bondage of worldly
attachments. Yet, his life sped away. The waiting
consumed him exceedingly and his soul could not endure
it. For a long time he suffered this agony. Before he
attained his desire, his life reached its end. When the
eldest prince died, the second brother came to the court
to attend his funeral. At that time the youngest brother

got sick and could not come. The king observed the second prince. He took pity on him and entreated him kindly. He instilled into him spiritual knowledge of the qualities hidden beneath phenomenal objects, and conveyed to him a deep perception of spiritual truths. When the second prince was thus nourished by the spiritual food given him by the king, he began to be puffed up with self-conceit. He forgot what he owed the king and rebelled against him. He felt self-sufficiency within himself, and from self-sufficiency emerged a feeling of insolent pride. He was saying to himself, 'Am I not both a king and a king's son? How have I let this king take control of me?' The king was hurt by the prince's ingratitude. He said, 'O base ill-mannered fellow! Was this what my bounty deserved? I have become for you a ladder to heaven, and you have become a bow and arrow in combat with me'. When the prince found himself cast off by the king, he came to himself. He repented and humbled himself with deep remorse. The king then pardoned him. But his doom had already been decreed and he was slain by the king he had injured. The prince acknowledged the king's goodness with his last breath.

And what about the youngest brother?

The youngest brother was the laziest of the three. This is why he succeeded where his brothers had failed. He won the prize completely, i.e., the form as well as the essence. Because it is said that the wise are the laziest folk in the two worlds: they get their harvest without ploughing. They have made laziness their prop and rely upon it since God is working for them. The ignorant ones, on the other hand, do not see God's working and therefore never rest from toil from morning to evening. (Book VI, 3584-4916)

The castle called "the robber of reason" symbolically represents the lower inspirational state. The journey towards the castle corresponds to the initiation, i.e., the first stage of the path. It was there that the princes met their guide. The guide instructed them on how they could reach China, i.e., the intermediate state. The palace of the king of China is the higher state. Within the palace was a secret bower. Only there the union with the princess could take place. Rumi, however, did not give any details about the final stage of the third prince's journey. He clearly stated though, that the youngest brother won his prize completely. But Rumi did not disclose the details of the third prince's arrival at the union with the Princess of China.

Some commentators assume that there should be a last, i.e., the seventh book of the "Mathnawi" in which the concluding episode of the third prince story is fully described. Such an assumption is incorrect. By not finishing the last story, Rumi introduced the second gap in his presentation of the "Mathnawi". In other words, the "Mathnawi" consists of seven books, but the last book is presented in a different form. The seventh book is contained within the previous six books; but it remains invisible to the ordinary intellect. Rumi indicated in the introduction to Book 6, that as long as the readers need more words and letters to perceive his message, Book 7 would remain invisible to them:

> "If there are a hundred spiritual books, yet they are but one chapter." (Book VI, 3667)

The purpose of the second gap is the same as the first one, which was inserted between Book 1 and Book 2. This gap is needed so the readers would pause to absorb the content presented in the previous books. Because it is necessary to absorb and digest the previously disclosed information first, before man can be brought onto the next stage of the teaching. Otherwise, man would be overwhelmed by such an exposure and would not benefit from it.

In other words, the second gap is needed so the readers may "stop" and digest the previously disclosed content.

Rumi, however, left a hint that indicated how to proceed in order to find out more about the third prince's adventures. The hint is contained in the following quote:

> "We had previously told of the sickness of the slave-girl and the story of the physicians and also their lack of understanding." (Book VI, 3672)

This quote makes a reference to the ignorant physicians in the story of the King and the Slave-girl. For those readers who need more words and letters, the first story of the first book is the continuation of the third prince's adventures. The king in that story, like the third prince, followed the prescriptions described in the "Mathnawi". He started to practice spiritual "laziness". Instead of searching for the Princess of China, he engaged in meditation. During his meditation he encountered a beautiful maiden. Because he was still driven by ordinary attractions, he was not able to sustain her presence. Therefore, he prayed for help. His prayers were answered: the Sheikh reappeared. The king recognized the Sheikh, because he had met him before in the forbidden castle. The Sheikh helped him to remove the veil of worldly attachments. Then the king could eventually win the prize completely, i.e., the form as well as the essence. But he could win the prize only when he managed to die before dying. The various experiences leading to "dying before dying" are described in the remaining stories of the "Mathnawi".

In this way, Rumi pointed out the leading characteristic of his contemporaries. The evolutionary state of Rumi's contemporaries corresponded to that of the king in the first story. Despite being exposed to the unitive energy of love, Rumi's contemporaries were incapable of absorbing it effectively. They were not ready yet to benefit from it. Their inner heart remained veiled. The veil would be removed sometimes in the future.

The veil could be removed by following Rumi's teaching contained in the "Mathnawi". Rumi's teaching, however, can be discerned only by reading and re-reading all six books. Because in order to learn, one may have to read the books many times. And one also has to read them in a specific environment and give them the kind of attention which will enable him to learn. Only a guide is capable of creating such an environment.

A very similar message was attached to Shakespeare's 1623 First Folio, i.e., the first printed collection of his plays. The instruction was provided in the introduction to the First Folio. The message said:[119]

> "Read him, therefore, and again, and again. And if then you do not like him, surely you are in some manifest danger, not to understand him. And so we leave you to other of his Friends, whom if you need, can be your guides: if you need them not, you can lead yourself, and others. And such Readers we wish him."

The instruction applies to Shakespeare's plays as well as to Rumi's poetry. Just like in the case of Rumi's "Mathnawi", only by reading and re-reading the plays is it possible to discern gradually their inner content. However, the instruction implies that having "Friends" as guides is needed to unlock the meaning of Shakespeare's plays.

---

[119] "The First Folio of Shakespeare" (The Norton Facsimile, W.W. Norton and Company, New York-London, 1996)

Evolutionary Sequel

Rumi illustrated the evolutionary state of 13th century man as a triad consisting of an aspirant to higher knowledge (the lover), an impulse of evolutionary energy (his beloved), and a guide. It was a fertile triad: the lovers could be united. Rumi pointed out, however, that his contemporaries were not quite ready yet for such an experience.

In this context it is interesting to compare Rumi's evolutionary triad to that of the Troubadours, whose songs and poems appeared in 11th century southern France. The triad of the Troubadours was encoded in the various forms of "ménage à trois". It consisted of a king, a queen, and a young lover. The lover was an aspirant to higher knowledge. The power figure of the king represented the guiding principle. The evolutionary impulse to which the lover was drawn was represented by the queen. The queen was the lover's ideal mistress whom he worshiped from afar. But the lady of the Troubadours was unattainable, for she was not a maid but a married woman. The triad of the Troubadours represented a certain evolutionary potentiality, but it was a sterile triad. At that time this particular potentiality was beyond the reach of 11th century man. Such a situation lasted till the time of Rumi, i.e., the beginning of the 13th century. As indicated by Rumi, during his time the "lady" became available. This means that the unitive energy of love was made available to 13th century man.

According to Shakespeare's presentation, the next phase of the evolutionary process was activated at the end of the 13th century. At that time the spiritual guides could use a more sophisticated evolutionary impact. The impact allowed for splitting the inner layers of the mind into a set of four subtle faculties: the lover and his beloved were replaced by four couples of lovers. Symbolically, this may be illustrated as the formation of an inner octagon. In other words, the evolutionary template was transformed from a fertile triangle into an octagon. At that time "the most remote temple" took a shape of the octagon. This is why within Shakespeare's French, English, Italian, and Bohemian plays there is a gradual progression towards a situation with four married couples. The four married couples are like an X-ray image of the inner structure of the human soul.

The splitting permitted a more precise diagnosis of man's evolutionary state. Therefore, a more effective developmental methodology could be implemented. It was then that the "stop technique" was introduced. As illustrated by Shakespeare in "The Tempest", this advanced methodology could be customized in accordance with the natural tendencies of a disciple. It allowed for the prescription of a more effective spiritual therapy.

When activated, the inner octagonal structure allows the formation of an organ of inner perception. In this way, as expressed by Chorus in Shakespeare's "Henry V", it was possible within such a structure to overcome the limitations of time and space and, for example, to bring to the 17th century theatre the troops that had fought in the famous battle at Agincourt in 15th century France:

> "Can this cockpit hold
> The vasty fields of France? or may we cram
> Within this wooden O the very casques
> That did affright the air at Agincourt?"
> (King Henry V, I, Prologue)

The "O" in this quote stands for an "octagon". The octagon indicates a state of "perfect balance" of the inner faculties. Shakespeare's plays illustrate efforts which aimed at achieving such an octagonal inner structure. The formation of the inner octagon was the purpose of the evolutionary process at that time. This purpose was also reflected in the external form of Shakespeare's Globe Theatre. The Globe was a wooden building in the shape of an octagon ("this wooden O").

Shakespeare concluded his plays in a similar way to Rumi's books, i.e., by pointing out the leading characteristics of his contemporaries. The spiritual characteristics of a specific fraction of 16th century Western European society are summarized in "A Midsummer Night's Dream". "A Midsummer Night's Dream" is the concluding play of Shakespearean canon.

Shakespeare's presentation starts with the ancient Hellenic civilization. An episode belonging to the Hellenic civilization is described in "Troilus and Cressida". This episode illustrates the evolutionary chaos caused by an event that occurred in antiquity. "Troilus and Cressida" is the starting point for all episodes illustrated in Shakespeare's plays.

The Celtic and the Roman cycles, which are illustrated in Shakespeare's Celtic and Roman plays, were intended to fix the evolutionary impasse. These attempts, however, did not fulfil their evolutionary potential. The fiascos of the Celtic and the Roman evolutionary cycles are symbolically presented in "Macbeth" and "Titus Andronicus". Instead, the modern European civilization was formed through the Bohemian, the English, the French, and the Italian branches of the modern evolutionary cycle. All four of these branches were activated as the result of Pericles' mission described in "Pericles, Prince of Tyre". We may look at these branches as four different evolutionary impulses to which Western Europe was simultaneously subjected. In accordance with the stop technique, two of these impulses were directed at the reformation and purification of the intellect (i.e., the path of the intellect); the other two impulses were aimed at the activation of the spiritual heart (i.e., the path of the heart).

The Bohemian branch was activated at the time of Pericles' arrival in Mytilene, i.e., at the time when the Roman cycle was terminated. As illustrated in "Timon of Athens", the Mytilene's episode was projected onto 4th century Athens. In this way Shakespeare marked Athens as a seed of modern Europe. At that time the evolutionary seed was represented by the "gold" that Timon buried in the forest near Athens. Timon's seed, however, had to be replanted. As described in "The Comedy of Errors", it was replanted onto the western coast of the Balkan Peninsula. Its germination was delayed till the 13th century, the time of "The Winter's Tale". A partially patched-up octagonal union was formed within the Bohemian branch at the time of "Measure for Measure". The Bohemian union provided a seed for the European Reformation that was initiated in Central Europe. Later on, this union completely collapsed at the time of "Hamlet". In the ordinary world, the collapse was manifested as the fiasco of the Reformation.

The English and the French branches sprouted out from a root, which was planted in Moorish Spain. The French branch was activated in the early 12th century, i.e., when Pericles returned to Pentapolis. At that time the Celtic cycle was terminated. The first European fertile triad, i.e., corresponding to that described by Rumi, was formed within the French branch at the time of "All's Well That Ends Well". An octagonal union was activated within the same branch at the time of "As You Like It". This union was used in an attempt at the revitalization of the Iberian Peninsula after the Reconquest of Moorish Spain. As illustrated in "Love's Labour's Lost", the attempt was unsuccessful. Afterwards, the union was transferred into the English branch. The English branch concluded with the formation of a repository of supracognitive energy at the time of "Henry VIII". In the ordinary world this repository was manifested as the birth of the English Renaissance.

The Italian branch sprouted from the Bohemian branch in the 13th century at the time of "The Winter's Tale". It culminated with the union of the heart at the conclusion of "Two Gentlemen of Verona" in 16th century Milan. The Italian union led to the Italian Renaissance. Afterwards, the Italian union was used as a springboard for a new evolutionary cell transplanted into the New World at the time of "The Tempest".

The outcome of all four modern branches is summarized in "A Midsummer Night's Dream". The outcome represents the evolutionary state of Western Europe at the end of the 16th century. "A Midsummer Night's Dream" is the 16th century equivalent to Rumi's story "The King and the Slave-girl".

Athens in "A Midsummer Night's Dream" encompasses the European experiences of the most recent as well as the previous evolutionary cycles. This being consists of the faculties that have been developed within the four modern developmental branches. The leading aspects of Athens are represented by Theseus, Lysander and Demetrius. Theseus represents Athens' intellect; Lysander and Demetrius are two aspects of its heart. These aspects were developed within the Italian evolutionary branch. They are the 16th century equivalent to the king and the slave-girl in Rumi's first story. Because of the availability of the advanced developmental methodology, Shakespeare was able to provide a more detailed description of this being's inner structure.

Theseus' state is quite advanced. Theseus is presented as the conqueror of Hippolyta, Queen of the Amazons. According to Shakespeare's presentation, the Amazons represented ordinary senses. By conquering Hippolyta, Theseus overcame his earthy attachments. As the result, he gained access to a higher inspirational state that is represented by the fairyland. King Oberon and Queen Titania are super corporeal aspects of that state. Yet, this state is not perfect. Its imperfection is marked by Titania's disobedience. Titania symbolically represents an evolutionary deficiency that modern man inherited from antiquity. It is the same sort of deficiency which was represented by the Queen of Sheba at the time of King Solomon. Titania's deficiency is marked by the fact that she is prone to the effect of Oberon's magic juice. The juice is equivalent to Cupid's arrows. The effect of the juice is similar to the impact of the goldsmith on the slave-girl in Rumi's story. Shakespeare explained in the Sonnets that only maculated aspects are affected by the magic juice or Cupid's arrows; spiritually purified beings are immune to its effect[120]. Titania's quarrel with Oberon is projected down onto the ordinary state and it affects Athens. This is why Theseus, like the king in Rumi's story, has to ask for help. Theseus' request is answered. Nick Bottom, a stage-struck weaver, is a cosmic physician. This particular guiding aspect was developed within the English and the Bohemian branches. Nick Bottom is able to travel to the fairyland to fix the situation there.

The young lovers Demetrius and Lysander represent two aspects of the heart faculty. Like the slave-girl, they are still driven by their sensual desires. Their adventures in the forest clearly demonstrate that they are not purified from their developmental deficiencies. This is illustrated by their vulnerability to the effect of Oberon's magic juice. Lysander's love for Hermia was easily nullified by the juice. Similarly, Demetrius' inconstancy was not removed; it was patched up with the magic juice. Lysander's and Demetrius' experiences in the forest were needed so they could be temporarily mended to form an octagonal union. The union consisted of four couples, i.e., Theseus and Hippolyta, Oberon and Titania, Demetrius and Helena, and Lysander and Hermia. It is a patched up union that is formed at the end of the play.

The union formed in Athens was the representation of the spiritual state of Shakespeare's contemporaries, i.e., a certain fraction of 16th century Western European society. Like Rumi's contemporaries, the Europeans were exposed to unitive energy of love, but they

---

[120] "Shakespeare's Sonnets or How heavy do I journey on the way" (Sonnet 154)

were still unable to absorb it effectively. For whatever reasons, it was not possible to fulfill that evolutionary potentiality. This time, however, the advanced methodology enabled the bringing to light of a more detailed diagnosis of man's inner state. Therefore, a more effective therapy could be administered. The inner state was temporarily patched up, so a certain fraction of European society could briefly experience a taste of the higher world. Since that time, Shakespeare's plays and his Sonnets have served as part of the administered medicine.

"Pyramus and Thisby", i.e., the play-within-the play inserted into "A Midsummer Night's Dream", was a test for Lysander and Demetrius. Lysander and Demetrius symbolically represent that fraction of 16th century Western European society, which was directly exposed to Shakespeare's impact. The structure and the content of "Pyramus and Thisby" are quite complex. By using a few symbols and a few seemingly confused words, this play-within-the play summarizes the evolutionary history of Western civilization. This is why Philostrate introduced "Pyramus and Thisby" as "tedious" and "brief"[121]. At the same time, "Pyramus and Thisby" contained an explanation of Lysander's and Demetrius' adventures in the forest. However, Lysander and Demetrius completely missed the message that was prepared for them. They were incapable of grasping the meaning of the play. They scorned and ridiculed the performance of "Pyramus and Thisby". Such a reaction marked their arrogance and ignorance.

Yet, Theseus announced that the performance was "very notably discharged", that is, it fulfilled its purpose:

> "... for your play needs no
> excuse. Never excuse; for when the players are all
> dead, there needs none to be blamed. Marry, if he
> that writ it had played Pyramus and hanged himself

---

[121] "Pyramus and Thisby" (Shakespeare for the Seeker, Volume 4, Chapter 8.3)

> in Thisbe's garter, it would have been a fine
> tragedy: and so it is, truly; and very notably
> discharged."
> (A Midsummer Night's Dream, V.1)

If the play was addressed to the young lovers and it was not understood by them, why did Theseus say that the performance served its purpose? Obviously, the evolutionary potential available to the 16th century man was not fulfilled.

Shakespeare provided another hint that helps us to understand Theseus' comment. The hint is delivered by Nick Bottom. At the end of their performance Bottom offers to deliver the epilogue:

> "Will it please you to see the
> epilogue, or to hear a Bergomask dance between two
> of our company?"
> (A Midsummer Night's Dream, V.1)

Theseus replies that there is no need for an epilogue, but asks for a Bergomask dance. The dance took its name from Bergomask, a fool, or a clown, a native of Bergamo, a small Italian town situated in Lombardy in the foothill of the Alps. Harlequin, a "patched fool" from the Italian commedia dell'arte, is purported to be a Bergomask. The commedia dell'arte formed in Italy in the mid-16th century was a kind of theatre characterized by masked characters and improvised performances. The actors' performance was customized in such a way as to induce a specific impact on the audience.

The performance of "Pyramus and Thisby" served the same purpose, i.e., to induce a specific effect on the audience. Spiritual teaching is like an organic process. This means that its initial impact upon humanity may be taking place without any conscious understanding on the part of the audience. And it takes a long time before the audience is able to digest the administered medicine. In other words, it was going to take a long time before the effect of "Pyramus and Thisby" would have its full therapeutic effect.

It is in this context that the performance of "Pyramus and Thisby" constitutes the epilogue to the entire corpus of Shakespeare's plays. It tells us that 16th century man was exposed to unitive energy. However, similarly to Rumi's contemporaries, 16th century Western European man was incapable of sustaining it. Therefore, some patching-up was required to give man a diluted taste of such an experience. This fuller experience of unitive energy had to be delayed until some future time.

Let's recall that the main features of this being were Lysander and Demetrius, i.e., inconstant aspects of the heart faculty, and Theseus, i.e., a highly developed but partially maculated aspect of the intellect faculty. This inconstant spiritual heart has been manifested as a passive and recessive feminine element. It has been suggested that this element has probably been defective in the entire history of European society. The projection of a highly developed intellect onto the ordinary state has been manifested in two ways. On the one hand, such ideas as the relativity of time and space, the evolution of higher states of mind and their relation to the cosmic structure have gradually percolated into the consciousness of ordinary men. Later on, these ideas in their simplified and fragmented forms emerged among ordinary men as Darwin's hypothesis of evolution, Jung's hypothesis of archetypes, and Einstein's theory of relativity. Then there was an outburst of scientific discoveries that took place in the 19th and 20th centuries. On the other hand, the intellect, which is partially maculated and not balanced by a properly developed heart faculty, has also been manifested in its atrophic form. In this form it shows up as the futile sophistry and excessive intellectuality that are so prevalent in our contemporary society. Thousands of books, commentaries, and papers dedicated to various fragmented interpretations of

Shakespeare's phenomenon and Shakespeare' plays are an unmistakable testimony of such intellectual atrophy.

By now we may realize that Shakespeare's plays, including their most recent movie and theatre productions, have been a continuation of the teaching that was introduced by Rumi in the 13th century and augmented by Shakespeare in the 16th century. Shakespeare's writings were designed to provide the evolutionary impact that was needed at that time in order to keep European society on the course of its evolutionary growth. For the last 400 years this impulse was preserved through the theatre and movie productions of his plays. These productions have been like numerous coatings, painted over and over again, until such time when the audience would be ripe for their fuller assimilation.

CONCLUSION

The fact that only now, i.e., after 400 years or so, we are able to perceive Shakespeare's message indicates that a significant adjustment has recently taken place. It seems that preparations for this latest evolutionary adjustment were initiated in the 1960s. It was then that certain hints about Rumi's and Shakespeare's writings were released to the general public. Without these hints it would still be impossible to recognize the design on which Shakespeare's plays are based. This would indicate that our contemporary society has arrived at a critical stage when the human mind has reached the capacity to process higher evolutionary energies and, for the first time, man has earned an entitlement to an active participation in the evolutionary process. It would mean that the inner content of Rumi's poetry and Shakespeare's writings have been absorbed, at least partially, by contemporary audiences.

References

"Teaching of Rumi – The Masnavi", Abridged & Translated by E.H. Whinfield (The Octagon Press, 1979)

"The Mathnawi of Jalaluddin Rumi", Books I and II, Edited and Translated by Reynold A. Nicholson (The E.J.W. Gibb Memorial Trust, 1982)

"The Mathnawi of Jalaluddin Rumi", Books III and IV, Edited and Translated by Reynold A. Nicholson (The E.J.W. Gibb Memorial Trust, 1982)

"The Mathnawi of Jalaluddin Rumi", Books V and VI, Edited and Translated by Reynold A. Nicholson (The E.J.W. Gibb Memorial Trust, 1982)

"Shakespeare for the Seeker", Volume 1, W. Jamroz (Troubadour Publications, 2012)

"Shakespeare for the Seeker", Volume 2, W. Jamroz (Troubadour Publications, 2013)

"Shakespeare for the Seeker", Volume 3, W. Jamroz (Troubadour Publications, 2013)

"Shakespeare for the Seeker", Volume 4, W. Jamroz (Troubadour Publications, 2013)

"Shakespeare's Sonnets or How heavy do I journey on the way", W. Jamroz (Troubadour Publications, 2014)

www.ingramcontent.com/pod-product-compliance
Lightning Source LLC
Chambersburg PA
CBHW060245100426
42742CB00011B/1641